SELF, PERSON, WORLD

PSYCHOSOCIAL ISSUES

General Editor
Eric A. Plaut, M.D.

Advisory Board
Richard D. Chessick, M.D.
Solomon Cytrynbaum, Ph.D.
Kenneth I. Howard, Ph.D.
Alan A. Lipton, M.D., M.P.H.
Thomas F. A. Plaut, Ph.D., M.P.H.

The
Interplay of
Conscious and
Unconscious
in Human Life

SELF, PERSON, WORLD

Donald McIntosh

Northwestern University Press

Evanston, Illinois

Northwestern University Press

Evanston, Illinois 60208-4210

Copyright © 1995 by Northwestern University Press

All rights reserved. Published 1995

Printed in the United States of America

ISBN 0-8101-1233-7 cloth

ISBN 0-8101-1217-5 paper

Library of Congress Cataloging-in-Publication Data

McIntosh, Donald, 1924–

Self, person, world : the interplay of conscious and

unconscious in human life / Donald McIntosh.

p. cm. — (Psychosocial issues)

Includes bibliographical references and index.

ISBN 0-8101-1233-7 (cloth : alk. paper). —

ISBN 0-8101-1217-5 (paper : alk. paper)

1. Self. 2. Identity (Psychology) 3. Self—Social aspects.

4. Identity (Psychology)—Social aspects. I. Title. II. Series.

BF 697.M225 1995

155.2—dc20   94-47481

CIP

The paper used in this publication meets the minimum requirements

of the American National Standard for Information Sciences—

Permanence of Paper for Printed Library Materials,

ANSI Z39.48-1984.

CONTENTS

PREFACE

This work was initially intended to be an examination of the nature of the human self and its identity, undertaken because in my view a satisfactory account of these has not yet come forth. As work progressed, however, it became increasingly clear to me that selfhood and identity cannot be understood except in the context of a detailed developmental treatment of the person who has this self, and that an adequate treatment of person, self, and identity require in turn an examination of their interrelations with other people and finally of the social matrix in which they are embedded and of which they partake. I see no alternative; in this area it is simply impossible to understand the part except in the context of the whole. The result is a book whose subject matter is nothing less than the human condition.

An inquiry this broad requires an equally broad approach, and I have here attempted to employ and integrate concepts, modes of analysis, and conclusions drawn from such diverse and often rigidly separated fields as philosophy, psychology (both psychoanalytic and cognitive), sociology, and the study of religion. What is presented below is not only a theory, but also a vision, of what it is to be a human being living in the world.

The central theme throughout is the interplay of conscious and unconscious thought in human life. The importance of the unconscious in the life of the individual is of course by now widely recognized both within and without the Freudian fold. The treatment of this theme in the present work is, however, special in three respects.

First, Freud thought of the unconscious as a largely unknown and almost unknowable realm. He held that unconscious thought can become conscious only by being translated into words, a process which necessarily introduces radical changes. By now this point is widely accepted, but it does not follow that the unconscious is unknowable. Obviously it is not open to direct introspective awareness. However, a large body of work in recent decades in the fields of cognitive and developmental psychology has supplied us with a wealth of information about unconscious thought, and by now the main outlines of its nature and the characteristic modes of its operation are known. I shall draw extensively on this work in the second and third chapters.

Second, this work lays heavy stress on the constant interaction between conscious and unconscious thought. This interaction is also an interpenetration. In part, unconscious thought lies hidden underneath consciousness, but it also unobtrusively enters into and shapes much of everyday conscious life.

Third, the unconscious is pictured as foundational and pervasive in the life, not only of the individual, but of society as well. In this connection, the idea of the 'collective unconscious' will be introduced, in a formulation, however, which is quite different from that of Jung.

——— II

Since the approach taken in this work is an unusual one, combining hermeneutical and nonhermeneutical perspectives often thought of as antithetical, it may help to orient the reader if I describe briefly some of the route by which I arrived at this approach, and compare it to some other and better-known contemporary views. Well over two decades ago (1969) I completed the first volume of what was projected as a three-volume systematic theory of human society. This work was quite general and abstract in character. My plan was to use it as the basis for more concrete substantive analysis in subsequent volumes. As my work proceeded, however, I became increasingly dissatisfied with its results. Try as I might, I found myself unable to use the general theory of the first volume to get at the substantive topics I wished to tackle. Eventually I abandoned the whole project and set about rethinking matters from the ground up.

My studies took me into three areas: the methodology of the human sciences, a reassessment of Weber and Freud (who had already been influential in the 1969 work), and a program of reading in recent continental philosophical and social thought, from Brentano through Foucault and Derrida—a literature with which I was relatively unfamiliar.

In a piecemeal process of gradual crystallization, I reached a number of conclusions which in retrospect may be summarized as follows. My previous approach had been on the right track in adopting what is often called the 'intentional stance', in which human thought and action is understood in terms of its meaning for the actor. Weber and Freud both exemplify this method. I had also been on the right track in using motivation as the central explanatory idea. Once again, Weber and Freud are exemplars.

My previous approach had, however, suffered from the use of several strategies drawn from the natural sciences which are inappropriate to the human sciences. First, I had implicitly been treating motivation as causing action in a sense which is essentially a loose version of the idea as found in the natural sciences. This is in fact the predominant usage in contemporary Anglo-American philosophy of mind (e.g., Davidson 1982), but I was persuaded otherwise by thinkers such as Charles Taylor (1964, 1971, 1980), C. Von Wright

(1971), and Peter Winch (1958, 1964), as well as my restudy of Weber and Freud. For reasons explained in chapter 1, I concluded that a motive can be said to cause an action only in a sense quite different from the inductive and in principle nomological meaning of the term associated with the natural sciences, even the relatively loose usage often found in contemporary treatments.

It followed that I had been on the wrong track in attempting to work out an inductive general theory, in the form of a set of general lawlike propositions, under which the particular case could be subsumed. Explanation must take a different form in the human than in the natural sciences. The proper approach, I concluded, needed to be interpretive and not predictive. On the model of such figures as Aristotle and Weber, a general theory should take the form of a set of logically interconnected concepts and distinctions which are brought to bear on whatever subject matter is at hand. The approach to these subjects needed to be historical or developmental in character. All of these are of course well-known views.

Finally, I had underestimated the importance of the fact that all inquiry proceeds from and is influenced by the perspective of the inquirer. This indeed is true both in the natural and the human sciences, but it assumes a special significance in the human sciences, because not only the inquirer, but also the objects of inquiry, possess a perspective. One is therefore dealing not only with the play, but also the *inter*play of perspectives. This point, which has been made by Winch (1958, 1964) and worked out in detail by Gadamer (1965), creates difficult philosophical problems, which for me were resolved by my study of the work of Edmund Husserl.

In connection with my restudy of the work of Freud and Weber, I became dissatisfied with the standard interpretive approaches to both, and resolved to come to terms with them on my own, which I eventually did—in the case of Freud only after a rather long journey. As a result, the use made of these thinkers in this work is quite different than in the previous book.

There is scarcely a page below on which the mark of Freud's thought will not be apparent. It is, however, more than a half century since Freud died, and not even the thought of a genius is wholly immune to the ravages of time. By now it is clear that there are a number of areas where his conclusions were in error, and others where they seem one-sided or of doubtful validity. I have therefore departed from Freud's views whenever this seemed warranted by the evidence or the logic of the argument. The most telling evidence in this respect has come from some major developments in the field of cognitive and developmental psychology over the past two decades. I have drawn heavily on this work, which has confirmed some of Freud's ideas and overturned others.

On several important topics the interpretation of Freud's thought is my own. These matters are discussed in the text, and here it will be sufficient to mention that his theories do not, in my opinion, constitute what Ricoeur has called a "mixed discourse," but rather are consistently psychological (intentionalistic) throughout, without any adulterating physicalist elements, as he himself repeatedly claimed.

The influence of Max Weber will be most evident in chapter 6, which follows his accounts of the evolution of traditional social-political systems, and chapter 7, which draws on his treatment of religion and its relation to magic. But his influence has been wider than this, because I have employed what I take to be his method of ideal-typical analysis throughout the book. This method has been the subject of a good deal of debate, not only as to its validity, but also on what exactly it consists of. I have set forth my own understanding of this method and its rationale elsewhere (1977b), and have put it into practice without any further defense here.

In my study of continental thought, by far the most influential figure turned out to be Edmund Husserl. While I am by no means an adherent of his philosophical position as a whole, nor an expert on his thought, my study of his work has enabled me to find a philosophical ground on which to stand and from which I feel able to proceed.

Husserl's main interest and work was in the field of transcendental philosophy, an area into which I shall not venture, but his approach to the understanding of human life, as well as his views on the proper method of the human sciences, have influenced me greatly. On the former question, what impressed me most is his refusal to accept the distinction between the natural and the human as basic or ultimate. In this he departed decisively from the tradition which runs as a leitmotif in Western culture, from the Book of Genesis, through such figures as Augustine and Kant, down to contemporary thinkers like Habermas and Gadamer. This tradition sees the natural and the human as radically opposed, and seeks to subordinate the former to the latter. I shall return to this theme later.

In addition to Husserl, a number of other thinkers of a phenomenological or hermeneutical bent have also been influential, especially Gadamer. While hermeneutical analysis is capable of providing deep insight into the human condition, however, it has important limitations, which are most evident when it comes to explanatory accounts, especially of chains or courses of human events. Habermas has argued, in my view persuasively, that the hermeneutical method cannot successfully be used as the sole basis of an explanatory human science. As a result he has rejected this approach and looked to a structural-functional systems theory for an explanatory strategy.

Husserl also saw the limitations of an exclusively phenomenological (and, we may add, hermeneutical) method in the human sciences, but drew a different conclusion. Although empirical explanatory human science can and should make important use of phenomenological analysis, he held, it needs to be conducted primarily in the natural attitude. It is important to note the sense in which 'empirical' and 'natural attitude' are used here. By the 'natural attitude' Husserl is referring, in this context, not to a physicalist approach, but to the ordinary commonsense orientation to the world taken by the average person. By 'empirical' he means primarily the facts of the subjective world of experience and its objects, although the distinction between these and the facts of the objective world is by no means as sharp from the point of view of the natural attitude as it is for either a physicalist or a phenomenological perspective.

In this work, I shall follow Husserl's advice, and adopt the natural attitude as the main orientation, despite extensive use of phenomenological and hermeneutical modes of analysis. In doing so, I shall not abandon the intentional stance; rather, I shall work within this stance, but mainly in the natural attitude. These matters will be explained at some length in the first chapter.

Husserl's thought is widely regarded as suffering from an excessive subjectivism, and as foundering on the problematic of subject and object. The first criticism is, I believe, unjustified, but the second has more substance. An attempt to overcome this problem is to be found in the work of Heidegger and his followers. In this work a different route is taken, as I hope will become clear as the argument advances.

─── III

The central theme of the role of the unconscious in human life will be presented developmentally, with respect to both the individual person and societal institutions. In both cases, but especially for the latter, the attempt is not to present a detailed and accurate description of actual historical processes, which in practice are highly variable. Instead, the purpose of these accounts, which are often schematic and simplified, is to draw a picture of the essential features of complex wholes by building them up in stages.

After an introductory chapter, in which the main concepts and methods of analysis will be presented, the following two chapters will take up the nature of unconscious mental activity and its relation to the evolving self. Chapter 2 will focus on the innate and hence universal characteristics of unconscious thought, with the influence of society noted, but not heavily stressed. In chapter 3, the social dimension will come to the fore, in an examination of the impact of the acquisition of language and the 'Me' of the initial socially defined self on the already established unconscious life and unconscious self of the child.

In these chapters the distinction between the person and the self plays a pivotal role. This distinction, which I believe to be original to this work, employs the method of analysis described earlier. The self is defined in phenomenological terms as one's own person, as experienced by oneself, while the person is the individual understood in the natural attitude from a third-person perspective.

Chapter 4 examines the origins and nature of conscious thought, especially the decisive role played by syntactically organized language, and traces how as a result of this process the 'lifeworld' of everyday conscious awareness comes to be divided into an inner world of subjective experience and an outer world of (supposedly) objective objects and events. Chapter 5 introduces the conscious self (the 'I') as it evolves out of the interaction of the conscious socially defined lifeworld with the 'underworld' of unconscious awareness, and describes the struggle to shape a coherent and stable identity for the 'I' out of the crosscurrents of this interaction. Chapter 6 examines how people are linked together by ties of identification, and how these ties act as the largely unconscious foundations of social wholes which, as they evolve, feed back and reshape these foundations. In chapter 7, the world of the sacred is introduced, as central to the lifeworld and its social organization, even in our secularized age. The world of the sacred is rooted in turn in the underworld of unconscious awareness, which now emerges as a social, not an individual formation, which is both a foundation and in part a product of the lifeworld. In the final summary chapter, the developmental approach is left behind, and self and society, lifeworld and underworld, are presented as a complex interactive nexus.

In order to communicate better with the nonspecialist, I have avoided technical terms throughout, dispensed with footnotes, and used in-text citations sparingly. At the end of each chapter there is a section listing and in some cases discussing the sources drawn on. I do not pretend to expertise in all of the many areas touched on in this book, and I hope that specialists will not be too harsh in their assessment of my attempts to incorporate work done in their fields into the overall perspective adopted here. Wherever possible I have attempted to ground my conclusion in empirical work, or at least in views which are widely accepted in the relevant discipline. In a work of this scope, however, such support is unavailable at many points, and here for the sake of presenting a completely worked out theory I have not hesitated to fill in the gaps in a speculative way. In the sections on sources I have indicated in main outline where I have drawn on the work of others and where I have struck out on my own.

While a good deal of the analysis in the later chapters is broadly sociological, it must be emphasized that what is presented is an account of the human condition, not of the nature of human society. The latter project would require a treatment of the structural level of social action and social organization, as well as of the role played by the material conditions of life. It is not that these questions are unimportant; it is just that I am after something else.

——— I V

Finally, it may perhaps help orient the reader to compare the approach taken here with some well-known contemporary perspectives. First and foremost this work challenges what has been called the 'linguistic turn' that has characterized much philosophical and social thought in recent decades. The central thesis of this point of view has been stated in an especially sweeping way by Gadamer:

> The phenomenon of understanding, then, shows the universality of human linguisticality as a limitless medium that carries *everything* within it—not only the "culture" that has been handed down to us through language, but absolutely everything—because everything (in the world and out of it) is included in the realm of "understandings" and understandability in which we move. (1976, 25)

Nothing could be further from the truth. Quite simply, the facts are otherwise. By now there is overwhelming evidence that most human thought is unconscious, and that much of this is nonlinguistic in character. Lacan has argued that the unconscious is structured like a language, but the structure of unconscious thought has been well established, and it differs radically from the structure of linguistically articulated thought. The evidence for all this is reviewed in the early chapters.

Moreover, despite the great importance of language in human life, the role of the unconscious is more fundamental. In one of its major aspects, this book is an attempt to set the record straight on this basic issue.

The ground covered in this work is much the same as that treated by Jürgen Habermas in chapter 5 (volume 2) of his *Theory of Communicative Action* (1981b). I have elsewhere (1994) presented a detailed critique of Habermas's account, and will here be content with a brief treatment of the most important differences.

The main difficulty in Habermas's position seems to me to lie in the radical division he makes between the natural and the human. In a conception derived from Kant, Habermas sees nature as the arena of deterministic forces that govern everything except the human spirit, which alone is able to rise above the heteronomic thrall of nature into the autonomy of the truly human, in which reason, not nature, holds sway. Habermas clings stubbornly to this outmoded conception of nature, which has not only been subjected to a thorough deconstruction by Husserl, Heidegger, and Merleau-Ponty, but has by and large been abandoned by mainstream philosophy of science as well.

Having made the linguistic turn, Habermas finds language at the heart of what is human. As a consequence, the unconscious, which is nonlinguistic, lies within the realm of "inner nature." Unconscious motives have a causal power which is lacking in conscious, especially reflective, thought. By depriving it of its linguistic character, repression distorts conscious motivation "into a demonic force of nature" (1967, 186). Habermas's outlook on the human condition is distinctly Manichaean.

In this work, the natural does not stand in contrast to the human, but rather to the cultural. A stone and a bathtub are both physical objects, but the former is a natural and the latter a cultural object. The natural world is the realm of animals, plants, mountains, streams, snowstorms, the stars, not, primarily, as they are for specialists such as physicists or botanists, but for us as human beings who live in this world. The most important constituent of culture is of course language. If the cultural realm is abstracted out of human life, people are reduced to a state which is natural in the above sense. They do not have language, but they remain fully human, although their lives are conducted within a much narrower compass. In contrast to Habermas, natural and human are not at all here regarded as sharply separate, much less antithetical realms. On the contrary, as will be seen in detail throughout this work, the natural infuses pervasively into the cultural, and the cultural in turn picks up and incorporates into itself much that is natural—with the major and unfortunate exception of the predominant worldview of Western civilization, which sees and has seen itself as wholly exterior to nature in either sense.

A second difficulty in Habermas's position, which springs from the first, is his identification of intentionality (conceptually shaped awareness) with consciousness, and (since consciousness is linguistic in character) with language. In fact he *derives* intentionality from language. He ignores, and in effect denies the existence of, coherent unconscious (nonlinguistic) intentionality. In this he is not alone. By now, however, it is clear that this position is untenable, for a wealth of empirical studies, some of which are discussed below, have shown that prelinguistic infantile thought is fully and coherently intentional in character, and, as I shall argue, this early mode of thinking remains active through life, underlying and infusing conscious linguistically articulated thought.

Volume 1 of Habermas's *Theory of Communicative Action* contains a lengthy and on the whole effective critique of the 'philosophy of consciousness', which takes the fact and character of human consciousness as its starting point. Habermas argues that the philosophy of consciousness founders on the problematic of subject and object. But, as will be argued below, the most important characteristic of unconscious (nonlinguistic) intentionality is the fusion of subject and object. Consciousness arises precisely via a differentiation of the two, induced by language. When one starts with unconscious intentionality, as is done here, the difficulties pointed out by Habermas do not arise.

Furthermore, the fact of unconscious intentionality establishes a vital link between humans and the rest of the animal kingdom. Animals are not, as Habermas thinks, automatons operating under the iron regime of a stimulus-response model. Instead, they exhibit well-developed intentional processes, which utilize levels of conceptualization less sophisticated than, but of the same kind as, unconscious human intentionality.

The logic of Habermas's argument forces him into an extreme version of the linguistic turn. If intentionality is derived from language, since language is the central constituent of society, it follows that the human self is a social construct. In Habermas, the oversocialization of the self, and of human nature in general, which is endemic in contemporary interpretive sociology, reaches its zenith. Once again, however, the facts are otherwise. As will be shown below, infants develop a distinct and coherently articulated personality and self-hood well before the advent of language and consciousness. What Habermas's account misses entirely is the ongoing interaction of the socially defined self (the 'Me') with the preexisting unconscious core self, out of which the 'I' of the mature conscious self progressively emerges. Correlatively, he ignores the polarity and constant mutual shaping of the lifeworld, the world which is opened to and by conscious linguistic awareness, and what I have called the 'underworld' opened to and by unconscious awareness. In sum, as the materials presented below will show, Habermas's account presents us with a radically truncated version of the human condition.

Hans-Georg Gadamer's *Truth and Method* has had a considerable impact on this work, especially the later chapters. In particular it has influenced my attempt to present interpretation as a process that is essentially the same, and plays much the same role, in the social sciences, psychoanalysis, and the mythic understanding of the world. My account, however, places much greater stress on the idea of motivation as playing the key explanatory role in all three forms of interpretation.

There are more important points of difference. As mentioned earlier, Gadamer wholeheartedly embraces the linguistic turn, against which this book, in one of its aspects, is a reaction. For Gadamer the lifeworld constituted by language encompasses everything. In this book the lifeworld is juxtaposed with the unconscious and nonlinguistic realm I have called the underworld. The two, understood as an interpenetrating and interactive whole, are included in the 'world' referred to in the title of this work.

Perhaps an even more fundamental difference concerns Gadamer's concept of 'habitat' (*Umwelt*, literally "surrounding world"). This term carries a different meaning than is usually associated with 'environment'. We are dealing here with nature, not in Habermas's sense, but in a meaning much closer to the one described above: the natural as opposed to the cultural. Gadamer holds that for animals other than humans, nature is an environment in which they are embedded and to which they are subject. For humans, however, nature is transformed into habitat by the alchemy of language, and hence becomes a part of the lifeworld, a part, however, which plays a subordinate role, as the term '*Um*welt' suggests.

Man's relationship to the world is characterized by freedom from habitat. This freedom includes the linguistic constitution of the world. Both belong together. . . . Animals can leave their habitat and move over the whole earth without severing their environmental dependence. For man, however, to rise above the habitat means to rise to "world" itself, to true environment. This does not mean that he leaves his habitat, but that he has another attitude towards it, a free, distanced attitude, which is always realized in language. (Gadamer 1965, 402–3)

It is significant that Gadamer traces this attitude back to the Book of Genesis:

Wherever language and men exist, there is not only a freedom from the pressure of the world, but this freedom from the habitat is also freedom in relation to the names that we give things, as stated in the profound account in Genesis, according to which Adam received from God the authority to name creatures. (1965, 402)

As is well known, and as will be argued in chapter 3, psychologically speaking, the power to name is the power to control. God gave Adam suzerainty over nature, which he may freely subordinate to his own purposes. Gadamer's endorsement of the account in Genesis shows that he has not entirely freed himself from the technical-instrumental orientation which he and Heidegger saw as the root ailment of the West. He rejects this orientation in the relation of one human to another, but not in the relation of humanity to nature.

But, as will be argued in chapter 7, nature always has a meaning for us, a meaning which is experienced as 'wholly other' in origin. The understanding of nature is an act of mythic interpretation which requires, as always when we understand the other, what Gadamer calls a 'fusion of horizons'. In the process, not only does nature become humanized (as habitat), but also, we as humans become naturalized. Gadamer sees the first but not the second phase. (Those who are under the illusion that we, as Moderns, have shed the impulse to understand the world in mythic terms, need only examine the calculations and speculations of contemporary cosmology.) Gadamer's *Umwelt* is in fact a full-fledged region of the world. By 'world' I mean to include not only lifeworld and underworld, but also nature.

Throughout the preparation of this work I have been sustained and edified above all by the generous help of two persons: my wife, Susan, and my long-time friend Eric Plaut, M.D. Both have loyally read and constructively commented on each and every of the many drafts this book has undergone. I am especially grateful to Susan for her unfailing but not uncritical encouragement, and the good humor with which she has put up with my mood swings as the work progressed, or failed to progress; and to Eric, not only for technical advice on psychoanalytic issues, but also for his repeated, often exasperating, but always correct insistence that yet another revision was needed.

The comments of the anonomyous reader for Northwestern University Press were helpful, especially the suggestion that the work needed to be put better into the context both of the thought of such contemporary figures as Habermas and Gadamer, and of my own previous efforts. My thanks also to Stanley Rothman for some good advice on the final two chapters.

————————— Note on Sources

I wish to make it clear that I am not claiming the mantle of exclusive truth for what is presented below. On the basis of any set of facts an indefinite number of tenable theories is always possible. My only hope is that mine is one of these. I am, however, claiming that, on the basis of the facts presented, theories such as those of Habermas and Gadamer, which operate with an extreme form of the linguistic turn, and/or which make a radical distinction between the natural and the human, are untenable.

As discussed in the section on sources at the end of chapter 8, I have by no means abandoned the whole of my 1969 work. The overall approach of this book, however, is quite different.

For the evolution of my views on Freud, see 1970, 1979, 1986a, 1986b, 1993. My interpretation of Weber is presented in 1970, 1977b, 1983. The article on Weber's ideal types (1977b) was written before I had become acquainted with the work of Husserl. I would now add that the Weberian ideal type bears a striking resemblance to the Husserelian 'eidos': the pure concept that exists independently of anyone's awareness of it, and which can be instantiated in and by human mental activity, typically in a more or less incomplete or garbled way. For a recent treatment of this theme, see Hanna 1993. Habermas's critique of the hermeneutic method in human science is found in 1967, 143–70 and 1981b, 119–52.

Husserl's mature views on the method of the human sciences are most fully developed in his *Phenomenological Psychology* (1925). There are also extensive discussions in the *Crisis* (1954), although there his preoccupation with refuting the naturalistic (physicalist) approach overshadows his rather sketchy treatment of what he regards as the correct method.

The position taken here on Husserl's views on the relation of phenomenology to the human sciences is not the usual one (but see Drummond 1988). It is widely held that Husserl thought that the human sciences should adopt a fully phenomenological method, and a number of his followers have followed such a course (e.g., Schutz and Luckmann 1973). (For a critique of Schutz's approach, see Michaud 1987–88, as well as Habermas, 1981b.) Indeed such an interpretation would, I think, be correct for his earlier work, such as 1910–11 and 1913. But Husserl's repeatedly stated later view is that a purely phenomenological psychology leads inexorably to transcendental phenomenology. It follows that in order to remain an empirical discipline that deals with matters of fact, the science of psychology must be conducted primarily in the natural attitude.

1 PERSPECTIVES

This introductory chapter will be devoted to a description of
the analytic framework employed in this book and a preliminary
treatment of the three concepts which make up its title: person, self,
and world.

Perhaps the most basic premise from which this work proceeds
is that all human engagement with the world, whether it takes the
form of action, thought, perception, belief, feeling, or whatever,
is perspectival in character. We cannot take a stance toward the
world without standing *somewhere*, and how the world looks depends
heavily on where we are standing. Throughout the range of human
societies and human history one finds many different perspectives

used, and many more are possible. On examining some of these it becomes clear that what is true or valid or 'objectively there' from the point of view of one perspective may not be so from another. To put this point another way, it is a fallacy to talk of anything as existing or possessing certain traits in itself. The in itself always turns out to be a 'for someone'. This insight, which already had been advanced by Nietzsche (1886), was developed in detail in the first two decades of this century by Edmund Husserl and his pupil Martin Heidegger, whence it has spread to much of contemporary philosophy, social and political thought, and literary criticism.

As must already be evident, the tenet of the perspectival character of all engagement with the world has strongly relativistic implications, against which both Husserl and Heidegger struggled, but which have been embraced by many of those influenced by them, including figures whose thought takes a phenomenological, hermeneutical, deconstructionist, or postmodern character. Although this issue will receive a preliminary discussion in this chapter, my full answer will emerge only in the final chapters, where I shall take a stand against the extreme relativism found in (or implied by) many of these writings, in favor of what might be called a limited or moderate relativism.

The Lifeworld and the Natural Attitude

The terms 'lifeworld' and 'natural attitude', which were originated by Husserl, have achieved wide usage among philosophers and social theorists. There has been some variation in the meanings assigned these terms, but I shall stick to the way in which Husserl formulated them.

Take a blade of grass in the field. If the basic tenet is granted that we cannot speak of this blade as existing in itself but only for someone it would seem that we have here not one blade of grass but many. There is the blade of grass as it exists for the botanist, the golfer, the greenskeeper, the picnicker, the poet, the physicist, and so on. Each of these perspectives has its own method by which valid conclusions can be determined, even, perhaps, in the case of the poet. By using these methods, each of these persons can arrive at objective truth about the blade of grass. For example, by gathering and evaluating evidence, the botanist can draw conclusions about how the blade carries out photosynthesis. When these methods are properly used, the conclusions arrived at will be objectively valid, not in the sense of being final and incontrovertible truths, but rather in the sense, first, that if others working in the field gather and evaluate the same kind of evidence, they will come to the same conclusions, and second, that it is highly probable (but not certain) that these conclusions will provide a reliable basis for further work. The conclusions will be objectively true not only for botanists, but also for anyone else who wants to look at the blade of grass from a botanical point of view.

So also for the greenskeeper, who will be able to describe the blade of grass in terms of a set of conclusions which will be objectively true for anyone who wishes to design, maintain, or use a golf course. We have here, perhaps, a blade of Bermuda grass, which grows so many millimeters a day, is best suited to sandy soil, should be mowed to a certain length, and so on. For the physicist, in turn, the blade has a certain atomic structure, and so on. Each person approaches the blade of grass from a different perspective, and so the facts, while they admit of objectivity within their own framework, are different for each, as is the nature of a blade of grass for each. How then can I speak, as I have, of a single blade of grass which can be seen from many different perspectives, and so implicitly transcends all of them? Since I have ruled out the blade of grass in itself, we seem to have not one blade of grass but many, with nothing behind them to hold them together. The point I am making is illustrated by the three blind persons who on feeling different parts of an elephant, came up with widely differing accounts of what they had encountered. If everything is perspectival, and if each of us has a different perspective on the world, why does the world not dissolve into a variegated multiplicity of worlds?

An answer emerges if we assume further that the viewers of the blade of grass belong to the same social order, that they speak the same language and are members of an intersubjective community, which may be tight and uniform or loose and diverse, but which provides a general frame of reference and understanding that everyone in the culture more or less shares. This language and frame of reference provide a relatively clear account of what it is to be a blade of grass. We can expect that all of our viewers accept this account, very likely without noticing that they do so, any more than they notice the air they breathe. The entire contents of the everyday world in which we live are defined in the same way. This socially and linguistically defined world common to the members of a community of understanding is what Husserl called their "lifeworld."

The lifeworld blade of grass is the blade of grass taken from the perspective of the natural attitude: the naive unreflective attitude that we take in our everyday dealings with the everyday world. From the perspective of this attitude the world in which we live is stable, secure, familiar, and unproblematic; it is given as independent of our own particularity, as objective, the same for everyone. We are born into this world and we leave it behind us when we die.

The blade of grass as it is for the botanist, the greenskeeper, and so on, are all specialized versions of the lifeworld blade of grass, which is their common point of departure and common ground. There is a basic experience of a blade of grass which is the same for all, and which hence provides a common denominator that all share. This is what makes it possible for them to recognize that they are all dealing with the same blade of grass, and to bring their different versions to terms with each other. This may be a difficult task for perspectives that specialize and abstract from the lifeworld in radically different directions, as with the physicist and the poet, but at least in principle the common grounding of the different blades of grass in the lifeworld makes it possible to understand them as different versions of the same thing, which is not a Kantian "noumenon" that lies behind them all but rather the ordinary blade of grass we all know.

The twin concepts of the natural attitude and the lifeworld act greatly to mitigate the relativistic specter opened up by the doctrine of the perspectival nature of all awareness, for within that overall framework matters of fact always in principle admit of objective determination by the process of gathering 'good enough' evidence.

This point may be illustrated by reference to the film *Rashomon*, in which a significant event is portrayed three times, each time from the perspective of a different person. Each version is drastically different from the others, and the audience is left wondering what 'really' happened and, on reflection, whether there is in fact any objective reality that transcends the different perspectives from which people approach the world.

We can attempt an answer by imagining a court of inquiry looking into the incident, sifting the evidence, and establishing what really happened. Every society has rules of evidence by which such conclusions can be drawn, and judicial systems utilize specialized versions of these. Most such systems even have procedures by which the subjective mental states of the participants, their intentions, states of mind, and perceptions, can be assessed by a careful scrutiny of the way these persons have behaved. On the assumption that the persons involved belonged to the same lifeworld, and so shared much the same views on the rules of evidence, we can imagine that the conclusions reached by the board of inquiry would be valid for them as well.

The real force of the film, therefore, is to call the validity or even the very existence of the lifeworld into question, and once that is done the problem of relativity returns. As I mentioned before, this issue will be addressed later. Meanwhile, I shall take the lifeworld in the natural attitude as the unproblematic objectively existing real world in which I and my readers live, and which we all take for granted at least most of the time.

The Intentional Stance

The intentional stance is a special perspective in which the mental life of the person is understood and described on its own terms without attempting to reduce that life to something else. In other words, it takes such terms as 'idea', 'belief', and 'desire' seriously, as real entities or processes, not as fictional, metaphorical, or unreal. The term 'intentionality' is a technical term in philosophy and psychology which designates a concept introduced (in the Modern era) by Brentano, (1874), and extensively developed by Husserl. The fundamental insight is that the defining characteristic of a broad spectrum (though not all) of mental activity is that it is 'of' or 'about' something. Such mental activity is 'intentional' not necessarily in the sense of a resolution to do something, but in the broader sense of 'intending' an object. If I am thinking of a tree, for example, my thoughts consist of a stream or process of mental activity which is about something (the tree), and my thinking is therefore intentional in character. Correspondingly, the tree is the 'intentional object' of my thoughts. On the other hand, if I have a vague mood, e.g., of sadness, without being sad about anything in particular, the mood is not intentional, at least on the conscious level. Perception, belief, desire, and such emotions as love, hate, and fear are all intentional activities, because they typically have objects which are perceived, believed, desired, loved, hated, or feared.

It needs to be emphasized that an intentional object is not generally something mental. If I think of a tree, the tree I am thinking of is not in my head; it is something physically existing in the field. As I shall argue, even an imaginary tree is not something mental; it is a physically existing object, which, however, is not real but imaginary – i.e., it is the object of my imagination, not my perception. There are, however, intentional objects that are mental states; for example if I think about my fear of flying, the object of my thought, my fear, is a mental state.

Although an intentional object is not in general something mental, its character is nonetheless intimately connected with the intentionality of which it is the object. When I look at the tree, for example, I see it from a certain perspective, and in a certain way. Intentional objects therefore appear to be at once independent of and shaped by the intentionality of which they are the object. I shall treat this apparent contradiction later.

The most fundamental property of intentionality is 'awareness', used here in the ordinary meaning of the term. Awareness occurs in various modes. For example, if I perceive the tree, I am aware of it in the mode of perception. If I desire a glass of water, I am aware of a (perhaps imaginary) glass of water in the mode of desire, and so on. It is also important to note that an intentional object need not be a thing (i.e., a physical object); it can be an action (e.g., desire to take a walk), an event (e.g., hope that it will stop raining), or intentional activity itself (e.g., I become aware that the child is afraid of the tiger).

Not only human thought, but also human action is intentional not only in the narrow sense of being deliberate, but also in the broader sense just described. Human action is generally understood to consist of overt behavior (i.e., physical activity) that is motivated by a complex of desires and beliefs. To put this point another way, action always has a meaning for the actor, and this meaning consists of a complex of intentional states. Husserl broadened the concept of action to include any mental activity that has an intentional character. Freud also saw mental activity as action in this broad sense, not only because he described thought as a kind of trial action, but also more fundamentally because he saw all thought as motivated. I will here understand the term 'action' and 'act' in this broad sense of including both motivated behavior and motivated mental activity. From the intentional stance all action, whether overt or purely mental, is understood and explained in terms of its meaning for the actor, i.e., its intentionality.

Husserl took the most basic mode of intentionality to be perception, but I will follow Freud instead in assigning this role to desire. Human action is best explained by describing its motivation, and the decisive element in the motivation of an act is its impelling desire or desires. Normally, however, such desires make up only a part of the intentionality of an act, which typically also contains a complex of beliefs and assumptions that must be taken into account if a full understanding is to be achieved.

The motivation is often thought of as causing the act, but it is a mistake to see this as the same kind of causation that is used in the physical sciences, in which an event is explained as caused by another event. The most important reason is that the motive is not exterior to the act, but an intrinsic part of it. An act consists of motivated behavior, and it is the motivation that gives it its meaning. To put this another way, the motive is the act looked at from the point of view of its meaning for the actor. To describe the motive is therefore to *interpret* the meaning of the act. Motivational explanation is interpretive, not inductive.

In this work I shall adopt the intentional stance almost exclusively, and for a good deal of the time shall do so without abandoning the natural attitude. To adopt the intentional stance in the natural attitude is to engage in what philosophers of mind call 'folk psychology', for this is the normal everyday way in which people understand and explain human action. The natural attitude takes for granted that human life has a physical and a mental side, which are in constant interaction. The intentional stance focuses mainly on the mental side, but not exclusively so, for it is held that to understand and explain the mental life of the individual, it is often necessary to take the physical circumstances into account, and correlatively, the physical activities of the individual are regularly described and explained in relation to the person's mental activity. In particular, physical activity is explained by citing its motivational basis: the desires, emotions, and beliefs from which the activity springs and which it expresses.

The folk psychology employed here will, however, take an extended and specialized form. The main extensions will be, first, that not only overt behavior but also thought itself will be understood and explained in motivational terms, and second, that much use will be made of the idea of *unconscious* thought and motivation. The specialization will consist in the liberal use of both Freudian and contemporary cognitive psychology, both of which also take the intentional stance. (It is important to distinguish here between cognitive psychology and the related field of cognitive science, where the approach to intentionality is typically reductive.)

The Physical Stance and Materialism

The physical stance departs from the natural attitude by looking at the world exclusively in physical terms. The approach is perhaps most at home when it comes to inanimate nature, but it is entirely appropriate to extend this stance to living things, including humans. There is nothing unreasonable or illegitimate about treating mental activity in purely physical terms, as activity of the brain, or more broadly of the central nervous system. What cannot be justified is the further step beyond physicalism to materialism. Here we have a kind of imperialism of the physical stance, which claims for it a privileged epistemological standing. The physicalist perspective is turned into a metaphysical truth. The world, it is claimed, is nothing but matter in motion. Reductive materialism holds that mental states are nothing more than 'ghosts', i.e., fictions or at best 'epiphenomena'. Nonreductive materialism sees mental states as special kinds of physical states which as a practical matter need to be treated differently from the other kinds.

Both forms of materialism represent what might be called the self-forgetfulness of physicalism. What is forgotten is that the 'reality' which materialism takes as basic is actually derivative, a specialized, abstracted, and one-sided version of the lifeworld perspective, where people are treated as both physically and mentally active. As Husserl and Heidegger have shown in detail, if one analyzes the procedural and evidential foundations of the physical sciences, it becomes clear that these are not independent of the lifeworld, but instead derive from and rest on it. It is not the case that the lifeworld is in reality nothing but matter in motion; on the contrary the world of the physical scientist is nothing but an abstracted and specialized version of the lifeworld. It is therefore an error to claim a privileged epistemological or metaphysical standing for physicalism. It is only one of the many valid ways of looking at the world.

The Phenomenological and Hermeneutical Stances

In common with physicalism, phenomenology departs from the natural attitude of the lifeworld, but in the opposite direction. Husserl took this stance into a transcendental realm beyond all empirical inquiry and all questions of empirical fact, but most phenomenological analysis in both philosophy and the human sciences has adopted a less radical approach, and operated essentially in what Husserl termed the "psychological-phenomenological reduction." I will follow this lead by using "phenomenology" in this more restricted sense. In these terms, phenomenology describes and analyzes the contents and objects of awareness simply as they are given in and to awareness, without regard to whether they are given accurately or inaccurately, or in the correct ontological mode (real or imaginary; possible, probable or certain, etc.). Since there has been a good deal of confusion and misunderstanding in this area, in may be helpful to make this point via an example.

Riding across the plain, Don Quixote and Sancho Panza encounter an object, which they see differently. Whereas the Don sees the object as an enemy knight, Sancho sees it as a windmill. The natural attitude is typically oriented toward the ontological standing of the objects of awareness. In this case, we must make it clear that the object is really a windmill, and that the Don is in error when he takes it for a knight. So we say something like, "Sancho saw

9

the windmill," implying that his perception was correct, and that the windmill was really there. On the other hand, we do not say, "The Don saw the knight," but rather "He thought he saw a knight," or some such qualification, implying that it possibly or probably was really something else. In the natural attitude we almost invariably pass some sort of judgment about the ontological standing of the intentional object: whether it is real, imaginary, illusory, fictitious, pretended, and so on.

In the phenomenological attitude such judgment is suspended. Quixote saw a knight and Panza saw a windmill, and that is that. Note that we are still in the empirical realm, but a restricted area of it. We are stating that *as a psychological fact*, i.e., in terms of their own experience, Panza saw a windmill and Quixote saw a knight. We refrain, however, from asking the further empirical question, "Who was correct: What was really there on the plain?" The advantage of this apparently paradoxical perspective is that it enables us to get at some important aspects of human intentionality that are normally obscured or ignored from the perspective of the natural attitude. This holds true for both philosophy and the human sciences.

In common with physicalism, the phenomenological stance has its own form of imperialism, which is called *idealism*. What gives rise to this view is the fact that the intentional object, purely as intended, is brought into being and shaped by the subject's mental activity in much the way that a statue is brought into being and shaped by the sculptor. To employ a commonly used term, the object is 'constituted' by the subject. When this perspective is carried through, as it is in Husserl's *Cartesian Meditations* (1929), the whole universe emerges as constituted by an all-creating transcendental ego. Such a way of looking at things is entirely feasible, as is the correlative project of physicalism, when it sees the entire universe as nothing but matter in motion. What is unwarranted, as in the case of materialism, is the conclusion that this is the *only* truly viable way to look at things, i.e., that idealism is *the* correct metaphysical position.

Hermeneutics is a special version of the phenomenological stance, as just described. The main founders of this approach are Heidegger and Gadamer, and especially in the case of the latter, it is marked by three additional characteristics. First is the emphasis on language, and since language is a social product, on the extent to which human intentionality is socially shaped. Second is the emphasis on the historical embeddedness of human intentionality. Hermeneutical analysis is typically historical or developmental in character. Third is its emphasis on interpretation as involving a fusion of horizons between the subject of the interpretation and the interpreter. The interpretation is the result of an encounter between two perspectives, and typically results in an enlargement and revision of the perspective of the interpreter.

Like the physicalist stance, the phenomenological stance presents us with a highly abstracted, one-sided view of the world. Both stances have distinct advantages. The physicalist stance, in its Modern mathematized form, has led to an explosion of knowledge about physical processes, and as a consequence a quantum leap in our ability to control, or at least influence, events in the natural world (although many have come to question how much of an advantage this really is). Its disadvantage is that it is unable to deal with human (and for that matter, animal) awareness, except in a way that ignores the living presence which is the essence of experience.

In its own turn, the phenomenological or hermeneutical approach can lead to deep insights into the ways in which the world we live in is shaped by the awareness we bring to it. Above all, it does away with the pernicious dualism of subject and object that has plagued Modern thought since Descartes. What it cannot deal with is the ways in which the events of the world are shaped by processes that lie outside of the awareness of those who take part in them. To do this we must go back into the natural attitude and even at times into the physicalist stance.

Weber and Freud as Exemplars

Weber's well-known method of *verstehen* is essentially phenomenological in character, for it attempts to describe and explain human action in terms of its meaning to the actors, without passing judgment on whether their understanding of their situation and their motivations are realistic or unrealistic, moral or immoral. But Weber was also well aware that the results of human action frequently depart widely from what was intended by the actors. One cannot understand or explain the actual course of events by confining oneself to the meanings which these events have for the actors. One must also take into account the realistic consequences of human actions, even (or especially) when the actors themselves do not do so. So Weber's historical analyses switch back and forth, from a treatment of the meaning that action has for the actors, to an examination of the actual consequences of these actions, and then to how these consequences are understood and dealt with by the actors. In other words, his analysis switches back and forth between the phenomenological and the natural attitudes.

Freudian psychoanalysis proceeds in a closely similar fashion. Analytic therapy starts and ends in the natural attitude: the patient has difficulties in dealing with the world, and if successful the treatment ends with an improved relationship with the world. The therapy itself, however, has pronounced phenomenological elements. Suppose for example that a patient reports having been seduced or sexually molested by a parent. What is explored in the analytic sessions, first and foremost, is the meaning of the event for the patient; the question of whether or not the event actually occurred is temporarily set aside (as Husserl would say, bracketed). The initial analytic focus is not on the accuracy or inaccuracy of the memory, but on the motivational complex that has produced it and surrounds it. This phase of analysis consists of an exploration of the content and dynamics of mental acts without asking if what these acts represent or assert is realistic or unrealistic, true or false, proper or improper. However, the question concerning whether the seduction, like Quixote's hostile knight, is a fantasy in the guise of reality or something which really happened cannot be ignored indefinitely, for this question is usually crucial to the course that therapy takes. Often it is precisely the motivational analysis that reveals the truth of the matter.

The phenomenological phase of psychoanalysis just described is not the only one. As the analysis proceeds, the insights that have been achieved about the motivations of the patient are increasingly placed in the context of the actual events of the patient's present and past life, which are examined and assessed in terms of the realistic consequences of the actions that have been the result of these motivations. In short, the conduct of psychoanalysis switches back and forth between the natural and the phenomenological attitudes. Most psychoanalytic case studies follow the same method.

The Person and the Self

The material covered so far has laid the groundwork for an explanation of the meaning that will be assigned here to the two central concepts of person and self. By a person (in the plural persons or people) I mean to convey the ordinary commonsense idea of a living human being, who thinks, feels, desires, and acts, and who is thought about, felt, desired, and acted on. In other words, a person is a human being taken in the natural attitude of the lifeworld perspective, with the stress on the intentional rather than the physical side. While the idea of a person will undergo a good deal of development, this basic perspective will be maintained throughout. In contrast, the perspective from which the human self is approached will be primarily phenomenological. A discussion of the problems and difficulties traditionally associated with the concept of the self will make clear why this approach has been adopted.

The term 'self' has been used in a number of senses. Sometimes it is roughly synonymous with 'person' as just defined, as for example in Jacobson's *The Self and the Object World* (1964). More often the meaning is narrowed down to the person as subject. This is one of the several senses in which Freud used *das Ich*. Perhaps most often nowadays the term carries the idea of the person seen reflexively, i.e., from the perspective of that very person, and this is the approach that will be adopted here. To say that the self is one's own person seen reflexively, however, is not so much to define the term as to set the problem: Who is this reflexively seen person?

At first glance it would seem that to define the self as the reflexive first person does not establish anything more than a minor distinction between person and self. This will become clear if my discussion of the blade of grass is recalled. Taking up the same argument for this case, obviously a given person will be seen differently by different people. There is the person as she is for her mother, father, sister, son, boss, subordinate, and so on. All of these people see her somewhat differently. The way she sees herself is yet another version. But with respect to all these versions, the argument goes, there is the basic common denominator of the lifeworld concept of a person shared by all, which provides the point of departure and remains a standard of reference for all the individual variations, including the reflexive variation.

But the comparison with the blade of grass does not hold, because how we experience our own person is so radically different from how we experience others, right across the board. Merleau-Ponty (1945) has developed this point in great detail. It is true that in childhood we learn to some extent to think of ourselves as a person like other persons, but, as we shall see, this awareness is at best limited and partial. There remain fundamental differences between my own person as everyone else sees me, and my own person as I see myself, i.e., my self.

Not only is the reflexive perspective radically different from all others, but also there is only *one* person who can assume this perspective with respect to any given person. This raises knotty problems of objectivity. While there are differing views on what exactly constitutes objectivity, two criteria are generally accepted. First, there must be pragmatically warranted standards and procedures by which the correctness or incorrectness of a judgment can be tested, and second, this inquiry must proceed within a community that shares these standards. In part 'objective' means 'the same for everyone'. For example, suppose greenskeeper X forms the conclusion that Bermuda grass makes a better putting surface on sandy soil than Zoysia grass. There are (I presume) generally accepted procedures whereby such a conclusion can be tested, and we can imagine our hypothetical inquirer presenting a paper at a greenskeeper's convention, describing how these procedures were followed and the conclusion verified. Other greenskeepers, and perhaps golfers, can now check this conclusion by repeating the described procedures, and perhaps utilizing other accepted procedures as well. This is the kind of context in which objective knowledge about grass can be attained from a greenskeeping perspective. Such a context is lacking, or at least gravely attenuated, when it comes to the reflexive stance toward one's own person.

These considerations help explain the notorious unreliability of self-assessment. Dennett (1988) has gone so far as to call the self a 'fictitious person', i.e., an imaginary person whom we have invented. Note that Dennett is here taking the intentional stance in the natural attitude. From this point of view, the *real* person is the lifeworld person (the person as he or she is for everybody else), whereas the self (the person as he or she is for that person alone) shares with Quixote's hostile knight the property of being a purely imaginary person, far different from the real (lifeworld) person. This argument, however, states the case too strongly. In most cases the self, from the natural attitude, is actually a mixture of fact and fancy, the product of a combination of accurate and inaccurate assessment. The self is partly fictional, partly real.

From the point of view of someone wishing to undertake a psychological analysis of the human self, the natural attitude just described is an impediment; the ontological stance and its native distinctions simply get in the way. When we look at the emotional relations that people have toward their own persons, for example self-love and self-hatred, it is clear that the person toward whom these emotions are directed is not the actual lifeworld person, but the person they believe themselves to be. It is the person *we take ourselves to be* whom we love or hate. The fact that some aspects of this loved or hated person are imaginary, illusory, or fictitious is irrelevant in this context. The psychic processes are exactly the same for both cases, real and fictitious, and it will simply sidetrack the inquiry to attempt at this stage to sort them out. This is why the psychoanalyst initially takes a phenomenological stance toward the thoughts of the patient. The same procedure will be followed here. Although eventually I will move to a consideration of the human self from the natural attitude, for the most part my approach will be phenomenological. Specifically, the self is defined as one's own person from the reflexive perspective, without regard to whether the self-assessment is accurate or inaccurate from the point of view of the natural attitude. The self is therefore not at all to be equated with the person. There is instead a complex interrelationship between them which, as we shall see, plays a central role in their evolution.

Since there is so much confusion and misunderstanding on the subject, a point made earlier needs here to be repeated and reinforced. Not only is the self not to be equated with the lifeworld person, but also it should not be equated with a self-image or self-representation as is so often done, not only in popular thought, but also in the literature of cognitive psychology and psychoanalysis. When I think about myself, have feelings about myself, look at myself, what I am thinking about, having feelings about, and perceiving is not an image or representation of anything, but quite simply a *person*, my own person seen from my own perspective, as distinct from the lifeworld perspective.

Suppose, to make this point metaphorically, that I am looking at a portrait of Winston Churchill, and say, "That is a formidable person." Here I am talking not about the representation of Churchill which is hanging on the wall, but about the person who is there represented. I am looking 'through' the painting (in the two senses of 'past the painting' and 'by means of the painting') at Churchill the person. Alternatively, I could say, "That is a formidable painting." Here the representation of Churchill, not Churchill himself, is the object of my attention. Not only physical representations but also, as I pointed out earlier, mental representations or ideas can become objects of intentional states, but more usually they are not themselves objects of awareness but instead serve as a part of the intentional activity by which we become aware of and relate to the world.

Riding across the plain, Don Quixote and Sancho Panza undergo perceptual activity, and as a part of this form mental representations, respectively, of a hostile knight and a windmill. These representations are, so to speak, in their heads; they are mental activities or perhaps mental structures. But the hostile knight himself, what the Don's mental representation is of or about, is no more in his head than the windmill is in Sancho's. They are both physically existing objects, whether one takes the natural or the phenomenological attitude. The difference, in the natural attitude, is that the Don is mistaken; what he sees as a knight is actually a windmill.

I belabor this point because the confusion between an intentional state and its object, especially where the object is imaginary or illusory, is an especially stubborn remnant of long-discredited ideas deriving from Descartes. Those who are still unreconstructed are referred to Richard Rorty's *Philosophy and the Mirror of Nature* (1979), where the argument is presented in extenso.

This confusion is closely related to two other confusions mentioned earlier, which are widespread in the literature of psychoanalysis, cognitive psychology, and even philosophy. The first is between the self and the person. It is quite common to find the 'self' as the object of awareness sliding over into the 'self' as the person who has this awareness (e.g., Jacobson 1964; Kohut 1971). This by no means destroys the value of such works, but at times it lends a distinctly muddy or confused quality to the discussions. The same holds for the frequent confusion between the self and the self-image or self-representation (e.g., Kernberg 1982). Obviously we become aware of ourselves via concepts, images, mental representations, or something of the kind. But the self is no more a representation or image than is the Washington Monument. It is not the ontological standing of the self, but the perspective from which it is seen, that marks it off from the person.

Consciousness and Unconsciousness

It is by now generally recognized in the human sciences that much if not most mental activity is unconscious, and in this book I will have a lot to say about unconscious processes. My principal debt in this area will be to Freud. Freud's theory of the unconscious and its relation to consciousness is quite complex and, moreover, has been widely misunderstood. A preliminary discussion of this topic is therefore needed.

In recent years the concept of unconscious thought has spread beyond the field of psychoanalysis, and it is now widely used in cognitive psychology and allied fields. In cognitive psychology the term is often used in connection with processes that play a role in the formation of conscious awareness, but which are not themselves conscious. Such processes are not intentional (i.e., they do not have objects) but are rather components or aspects of processes that culminate in intentional states. I will not here treat of such processes, and as a result the word 'unconscious' will not be used in this sense.

Leaving aside the case just mentioned, unconsciousness always has an intentional character, i.e., it is a mode of awareness and the awareness is always of or about something. In other words, we can be aware of the world and of ourselves in two ways, consciously and unconsciously. The fact that unconsciousness is a form of awareness must be kept firmly in mind in the discussions that follow this chapter. It is quite common in the literature, especially in philosophy, to equate consciousness with awareness in general, and once this is done the idea of unconscious thought becomes unintelligible. Freud distinguished between the topographic and the dynamic unconscious. While the dynamic unconscious played a greater role in his writings, especially after 1920, the concept of the topographic unconscious is the more basic, and that is the sense that will most often be employed here.

The main division in the topographic theory is between the unconscious and the conscious-preconscious. The defining property of unconscious awareness is its nonlinguistic character. An unconscious thought enters conscious-preconscious awareness, Freud said, by being "put into words." The nonlinguistic presentation and its linguistic translation, taken together, constitute the conscious-preconscious presentation. Freud saw unconscious thought as concrete and visual ("thinking in pictures"), in contrast to the more conceptual and basically auditory character of the conscious-preconscious system. As we shall see, recent work in the psychology of language acquisition requires that the matter be put somewhat differently, but Freud's basic insight, that the essential difference between conscious and unconscious thought turns on whether or not the thought has a linguistic character, is right on target.

Recent work in cognitive psychology, both animal and human, has greatly clarified the matter. What distinguishes awareness in general, both conscious and unconscious, is its conceptual nature. We become aware of objects and events by conceptualizing them. The key point is that the cognitive level achieved by such conceptualization cannot be accounted for on the traditional behaviorist stimulus-response model. Awareness is, as Husserl put it, 'transcendent': it goes beyond what can be constructed solely out of sensory registration. Such awareness is by no means unique to humans, and is exhibited by many animal species, including birds and even insects. Awareness seems to be a product of evolution, absent in the most primitive species, appearing to an increasing degree as we go up the evolutionary ladder.

Conscious thought always has a reflexive element, which derives from the fact that it is linguistic in the sense of being syntactically organized. Throughout this work, I will use 'linguistic' in this sense.

The presyntactic stage of language use, before words come to be organized into sentences, will be called the 'lexical' stage. In these terms, it is the linguistic, not the lexical stage that marks the true dividing line between humans and other animals. While a number of animal species can be taught to understand and use words, only humans can organize words into sentences, and think on the syntactic level. Even this must be qualified, for children who have not been exposed to language by the age of twelve or so appear to be unable ever to progress significantly beyond the lexical level.

Linguistically organized thought is not always conscious, but the structure of language makes possible the reflexivity on which consciousness depends. Consciousness consists of awareness plus awareness of that awareness, or, to be more precise, awareness which has such a reflexive element. The qualification 'reflexive element' is needed because consciousness is not always purely reflexive, and the reflexive element is not always at the center of attention. Husserl's distinction between the foreground and the background of awareness is useful here. All awareness takes place within a broad context of intentionality of which we are not sharply aware, but which serves unobtrusively to shape and define what is at the center of attention. In these terms, the reflexive quality of consciousness is always present, but often only in the background of awareness.

In the light of these considerations, Freud's typology of awareness seems to need only a slight revision. Unconscious thought is nonlinguistic, but may have a lexical character. The conscious-preconscious is characterized by linguistic (syntactic) organization. Thought that has a linguistic but not a reflexive character is preconscious, and requires a further psychic action (Freud's "attention cathexis") which is reflexive in character (i.e., in which an awareness of awareness is introduced) to become conscious.

The topographic unconscious just described needs to be distinguished from Freud's dynamic unconscious, which consists of intentionality that has been repressed: awareness that is prevented from entering or returning to consciousness. There are two forms of repression: a deep form, where a thought is divested of its linguistic (but not necessarily its lexical) character, and hence becomes both topographically and dynamically unconscious; and a shallower form, where reflexive awareness is warded off, but the linguistic form is retained. This presents us with the anomaly of awareness that is dynamically unconscious but topographically preconscious, and it turns out that much preconscious thought is unconscious in this sense. It was partly to avoid this terminological problem that Freud introduced his 'structural' theory of id, ego, and superego. The structural theory, however, did not replace the topographic, but rather overlaid it. The topographic theory remained basic to Freud's thought throughout, as it will be in this book.

In these terms, the unconscious self is one's own person as the object of one's own unconscious awareness. The unconscious self may contain, for example, a 'bad me' of which the conscious person is wholly unaware. Corresponding to the unconscious self there is an unconscious world, the world of which the person is unconsciously aware. For example, the unconscious world of a person may contain a 'bad mother' of which that person is aware only unconsciously. Since lifeworld modes of awareness are linguistically shaped, such awareness is inherently conscious-preconscious, though parts of it may be repressed. The relation of the unconscious world to the lifeworld is a theme which will come up for discussion repeatedly in this work.

Finally, a word is needed about the term and concept 'identity', which was popularized by the writings of Erikson, and which has since been the subject of much discussion and debate. Here, the term will be defined simply as the stable character of the self – as a relatively clear-cut set of traits formed into a relatively coherent and enduring whole, which people attribute to themselves, and which therefore forms the center or core of their selfhood. The search for identity is the search for such a self; an identity crisis arises when a person is no longer sure who he or she is, and a national identity is an identity that the members of a nationality see as common to them all and as deriving from their membership. This definitional strategy, which I think hews fairly closely to one of the commonly accepted meanings of the word, has the advantage of transferring issues concerning identity over to issues concerning the self, where I think they are much more readily dealt with.

This completes my outline of the main perspectives and concepts that will be employed in this book. In the chapters that immediately follow, the main focus of attention will be on the person and the self. Neither of these is monolithic; rather both are made up of layers, which are established successively, with each new layer growing out of, interacting with, but not replacing, what is already there. My account of the self must therefore take a developmental form. A continuing theme will be the interaction of self and person during this evolution. Initially the concept of 'world' will be dealt with in terms of the division between the unconscious underworld and the conscious lifeworld, and the evolution of the person and the self will be described in relation to these two worlds. In the later chapters the focus will shift from the individual to society as a network of interconnected individuals, and the theme of the interaction of society with the lifeworld in which its members live will move to the fore.

Sources

Husserl and phenomenology. The main indebtedness for this chapter is of course to Husserl, 1913, 1925, 1929, and especially 1954. The exact standing of the Husserlian intentional object has been the subject of much debate (e.g., Sokolowski 1984; Føllesdal 1990, Hanna 1993). On my reading of Husserl, I think he distinguishes three objects: first the actual object, or object simpliciter, which is the object from the point of view of the natural attitude (the windmill); second, the empirically existing intentional object as experiential fact with real immanent existence or Dasein (the knight); third the abstract ('irreal') object or noema, defined by the 'eidos' (essence) of a knight, which is not something psychological, but which is instantiated in a relatively vague and incomplete way (as intentional object) via Quixote's intentionality.

The relativistic implications of the work of Husserl and Heidegger are discussed in Carr 1987, and Watson 1988. For Husserl's attitude toward natural science, see Sofer 1990. The similarity between Husserl's psychological-phenomenological reduction and the interpretive phase of the psychoanalytic method is pointed out by Ricoeur (1970, 377). The relation of Weber's approach to phenomenology is dealt with in Natanson 1963.

The two phases of therapeutic process in psychoanalysis (interpretation and working through) are emphasized in Strachey 1934, which is generally regarded as the standard treatment.

I have labeled the Weberian and Freudian approaches as, in part, phenomenological rather than hermeneutical, because both thinkers lack any significant emphasis on the role of the perspective of the interpreter in the interpretive process, which Gadamer stresses strongly. I regard this as a weakness in both. The orthodox Freudian view is that of the incognito analyst, who insofar as possible presents a blank screen onto which patients can project their fantasies. But this is an unrealistic and even grandiose view of the analyst's role. Patient and analyst are bound to interact on the unconscious level. As some recent treatments (e.g., Natterson 1991) have emphasized, it is better not to try to avoid unconscious interaction, but to become aware of it and utilize it in the therapeutic process. Here the phenomenological phase of psychoanalysis begins to move toward hermeneutics.

For treatments of the intentional stance which remain wholly within the natural (as against the phenomenological) attitude, see Dennett 1987, and Searle 1983.

The nature of the self. There is of course a huge literature on the self and such related concepts as person, subject, identity, and the I. Most voluminous, perhaps, is the stream concerned with the problematic of the subject, stretching from Descartes 1642, to Foucault 1986, and Ricoeur 1990. Another stream, in linguistic philosophy, stems from Wittgenstein 1960 (1933–35). Recent works in this genre include Parfit 1986, and Rosenberg 1986. The literature in cognitive psychology, which is almost entirely isolated from the above two streams, has its main origin in Mead 1934. I will draw extensively on this literature in the following chapters. Works that attempt to cut across these divisions include Holland 1978, Tugendhat 1986, Habermas 1981b, and Ricoeur 1990. The psychoanalytic literature that revolves around Freud's multiple uses of *das Ich* is another isolated stream. Kohut's work, (e.g., 1971) strikes me as marking more of a departure on the clinical than the theoretical level.

The concept of the self and the distinction between the person and the self used in this work were arrived at by reflecting on the

Freudian texts in the light of Husserl's thought. Freud's use of the 'I' to designate the conscious self (one of the main senses of his protean *das Ich*) corresponds exactly to Husserl's 'the empirical I' (*das empirische Ich*). My previous treatment of these themes (McIntosh 1986b) marks a transitional phase to the stance presented in this chapter.

Conscious and unconscious awareness. The section on consciousness and unconsciousness is an attempt to integrate the findings and conclusions of the works cited in the next paragraph into Freud's topographic theory, which was developed mainly in 1900 (especially chap. 7), 1915a, and 1915b. There is very little in Freud's mature works on conscious, as distinct from conscious-preconscious, thought. He once wrote that he had written a paper on consciousness, but if so he destroyed it or it has been lost. For a discussion and defense of the interpretation taken here, see McIntosh 1986a.

Cairns 1972 discusses the various senses in which Husserl used 'consciousness' (*Bewusstsein*). Non-Freudian approaches to unconscious awareness can be found in Marcel 1983a and 1983b, Lewicki 1986, and Winson 1985. For animal awareness and cognition, see Carruthers 1989; Gallup and Suarez 1986; Gould and Marler 1987; Griffin 1984; Seidenberg 1986; Terrace 1985; Walker 1983; Roitblat, Bever, and Terrace 1984; and Weiskrantz 1985 and 1988. Weiskrantz 1985 contains no less than five articles on concept formation in pigeons! So much for Skinner. The reflexive and/or linguistic character of conscious as against unconscious thought is stressed in Armstrong 1981, Flavell 1988, Garfield 1989, Haldane 1988, Johnson-Laird 1988, and Marcel 1988.

2 THE PRELINGUISTIC SELF

The infant human being is born with a distinct though rudimentary personality, which quickly begins its long development. Selfhood begins to emerge about two months later. The promptness with which personality appears and the speed with which it develops were not generally recognized prior to the recent introduction of a number of sophisticated techniques for observing and drawing conclusions about the life of the very young. By now there is a substantial body of evidence that decisively overthrows or heavily modifies many of the traditional views of infancy and, consequently, of human nature in general. Several of these traditional views merit brief discussion.

The first outmoded view is the so-called tabula rasa theory, which sees humans as products of their environment. While we are born with certain basic desires and capacities, these are so generalized and amorphous, it is held, that they do no more than establish limits to what experience can shape us into, much as the nature of clay imposes certain limits on the sculptor.

A major variant of this view is behaviorism, which once dominated academic psychology in the United States. While its influence there has largely vanished, it is still a widely held view among social scientists and social workers who received their education during the period of this dominance – and who thus unwittingly and ironically confirm the now discredited theory. More sophisticated and so relatively less vulnerable forms of behaviorism have been advanced by some philosophers, for example, by Wittgenstein, Ryle, and currently Dennett.

Another view that emphasizes the importance of environment has its main origins in Europe, in the thought of such figures as Heidegger, Saussure, and Gadamer. Here two themes intertwine: first, the pervasive influence of culture and especially language; and second, the historical embeddedness of all human life. Language, and through language history, combine decisively to shape all human action, and the meaning that it has for the actors. The deconstructionism of Derrida and his followers is an offshoot of this perspective, as is, more ambiguously, the dark vision of Foucault. Less extreme but equally relativistic versions are to be found in the thought of such figures as Rorty, Charles Taylor, and Lyotard. Although this tradition rests on very different philosophical grounds, and takes a very different character than the views of Locke and the behaviorists, it shares with them the tendency to deny the importance of innate factors in what is distinctively human.

As the evidence cited below will show, the decisive weakness of these different versions of the tabula rasa theory is that the slate is not at all blank. It contains much that is genetically inscribed, including major developmental patterns and important ways in which experience is created and shaped. The vicissitudes of experience produce a wide variation in the way these innate factors work their way into the life of the person, but they do not change their basic character.

A second traditional view of human nature that will be rejected here could be termed biological determinism. This view, which in the United States had been more or less inundated by behaviorism, is currently making something of a comeback. It holds that the character and content of human thoughts, emotions, and desires, and therefore of human actions, are genetically preprogrammed. Especially notable has been the vigorous counterattack on the cultural determinists that has been launched under the banner of sociobiology, arguing that the character of human culture itself is biologically determined and just as subject to the march of evolution as the physical structure of the human skeleton.

The trouble with biological determinism is that it is not deterministic. Even if all its arguments are granted (and some of them are highly questionable), they are insufficient by themselves to account for the huge variety that one finds in the life of both individuals and cultures. True, one can always reason from these variations back to biology, because obviously every manifestation of the human must have a genetic basis; but this basis does not determine, but only enables, what happens.

In the face of the debate between the biological and the cultural determinists it has become almost the conventional wisdom to assert that it is not a matter of either/or and that both factors play a major role. But this middle ground is just as reductionist as the two extremes. The one side reduces what is human to society, the other to biology, while the middle ground reduces it to a combination of the two. On the contrary, the view argued here is that one cannot even in principle wholly explain what a person and her self are like simply by reference to heredity or environment or to both. Human life is underdetermined by these two influences, either singly or jointly. People have the capacity to think and act independently of both biological and social influences, even if, regrettably, this capacity is not exercised as often as one might hope.

In taking this stance I am not at all endorsing a third traditional view, which also argues against both biological and social determinism, but on a different basis. It is true, this third argument goes, that we have a biologically determined animal nature, and to that extent are members of the animal kingdom. But, in contrast to the brutes, humans have the capacity to rise above their animality into the realm of freedom, the ability to act from choice independently of both the biologically determined part of their nature and the constraints of social convention. This view has its origins in the Christian view of humans as a mixture of the material and the spiritual, part animal, part angel: pieces of clay into which God has breathed his holy spirit. This religious, indeed mythic view, which can be traced back to the Book of Genesis, was secularized, more or less, by Kant, who distinguished between the realm of heteronomy, which is governed by the laws of nature, and the realm of autonomy which, he hoped, humans are capable of entering, and where the human spirit can act freely, ungoverned by the determinism of nature. One form or another of this view is still widely held, despite the well-known philosophical difficulties that arise when its mythic underpinnings are removed. In contrast, the viewpoint argued here is not at all dualist. The point is that the ability to act independently of both biological and social influences is itself genetically implanted as a part of our animal nature. As Rousseau insisted, we are born free and only gradually acquire our chains. We do not rise from heteronomy to autonomy; rather, all too often, we sink from the latter to the former.

The Innate Equipment: Drives, Emotions, and Instincts

The psychological approach adopted here is Freudian. It is, however, over seventy years since the main lines of Freud's theories were set forth, and by now they are in need of modification in a number of places. I shall therefore feel free to depart from his views when the evidence indicates the need for this. In particular, the inborn capacities and proclivities of humans are both more extensive and in some respects of a different kind than Freud and many others have thought. My account will start off in Freud's footsteps, but as it proceeds will depart in significant respects from the picture he draws, under the influence of recent findings on infant development. Many of these findings have been integrated into a Freudian perspective in Daniel Stern's *The Interpersonal World of the Infant* (1985), and I shall draw freely from this work in what follows.

All human thought and action is motivated, that is to say it has a complex meaning for the actor, part of which is a desire or, more usually, a complex of desires. To explain an act is simply to describe this meaning. Such a description is always an interpretation, even when we are describing our own motives. Desires vary in intensity, and we often experience a strong desire as driving or impelling an action, sometimes in opposition to other desires which in the event turn out to be weaker. Nothing more than this is meant when it is said that a motive or desire 'causes' an act.

Desires have objects: things or states of affairs that are desired. Desires also have aims: a specific type of gratification or satisfaction that attainment of the object is intended to achieve. Aim and object are often not intrinsically connected. For example, if one desires an ice cream cone the aim normally is the gratification of hunger, but it could be the satisfaction of an aggressive impulse, as would be the case if one intended to slip the scoop of ice cream down the back of someone's shirt. To some extent this is purely a semantic issue; by simply rewording the case one could distinguish between the desire to eat an ice cream cone and the desire to slip it down someone's shirt, which gives us a difference in both aim and object. The point, however, is that the aim and the object of a desire are different things. It would for example normally be a misstatement to say that one desires to satisfy one's hunger, for taken literally this conveys the complex idea of desiring to satisfy a desire. More probably what is meant here is simply that one is hungry, i.e., that one desires food with the aim of satisfying hunger.

Freud grouped desires into 'drives' (*Treibe*), which are classified by aim, not object. A given drive can manifest itself in desires for a wide variety of objects which, however, always have the same aim. He eventually settled on two such drives: libidinal, whose aim is sensual gratification, and aggressive, whose aim is more obscure. Freud's argument was that although libidinal and aggressive desires can combine, as they typically do in sexual desire, his clinical experience indicated that they cannot substitute for each other, which indicates that their aims are different. Whether or not Freud was correct in this, it is clear that from the start infants exhibit both sensual desire and rage in the most powerful fashion, and that both soon find specific objects, the libidinal perhaps more quickly than the aggressive.

By now it is evident that Freud's list of basic drives was not long enough. When the infant has been fed and is comfortable she does not always sleep, but often stays awake and takes an active interest in and engages the world, following what is going on first with her eyes and ears, then by moving her head, then reaching out to touch or grab, and so on. The aim here is clearly neither libidinal nor aggressive, and we must therefore posit another basic drive, which seeks satisfaction in active engagement with the world. One might call this the cognitive drive, not in the sense of seeking conceptual knowledge, but in the broader sense of seeking to become acquainted with and relate to the world. The existence of such a drive was already affirmed by Aristotle's dictum that humans by nature desire to know. As with the other drives, the vicissitudes of life may eventually cause the motivational thrust to be blunted or diverted, but in infancy and early childhood its vigorous impetus is abundantly and with rare exceptions universally evident.

Doubtless this third drive is activated in response to a somatic stimulus of some sort, but with respect to the external world its most general characteristic is not that it responds to stimuli but that it seeks them. When artificially deprived of auditory and visual stimuli, for example, the infant will proceed actively to search for them. There is therefore no specific object or activity that can be regarded as the natural, appropriate, or prototypical expression of the cognitive drive. It is instead a broad mandate to explore the world. The lack of specificity of the early objects of this drive should not obscure its intensity. For infants the drive has all of the peremptory character of those deriving from the more obvious physiological needs.

From the point of view of the intentional stance all of these drives are simply given. They are present at birth and continue throughout life. In that sense they are innate. To go beyond this and say that they are biologically implanted is doubtless true enough. The connection, for example, between the libidinal drive and its underlying physiological processes and needs is obvious, and it seems highly plausible to hold that all the drives – and hence all desires – have a somatic source, and scarcely less plausible to hold that on some level a drive, and hence a desire, just *is* a special kind of physical process. To establish such claims, however, we would have to leave the intentional stance and move into a field such as psychobiology or neuropsychology, and thus pursue another course than the one undertaken here.

The human emotions are also innate. They are universal and indeed also shared with some other animals. These conclusions were first advanced by Darwin (1872), but fell into disrepute with the dominance of behaviorism and other tabula rasa theories. Recent evidence suggests strongly that Darwin was essentially correct. The basic innate emotions (often called categorical affects) appear to be happiness, sadness, fear, anger, disgust, surprise, and interest. Each of these is associated with and so identifiable by specific facial and bodily expressions. These emotions are readily recognized as such the world over.

As people grow up, the range and quality of their emotional responses expand and ramify. There are many permutations, combinations, and refinements of the basic emotions, and some of these may perhaps be regarded as new emotions. There is a great deal of cultural and individual variability here. The basic emotions, however, remain in being, and provide a transcultural common denominator that underlies these variations.

There is a third type of innate characteristic of mental activity, which is structural rather than motivational. The emotions and even more so the desires may be regarded as engines which push thought and action into motion. Such motion, however, is not random, but moves along certain paths. These paths give thought and action a structure that is not a product of the impelling motivation.

Freud called the basic inherited structure of thought and action 'primary process'. The associative 'laws' of primary process mental activity are the structural characteristics by which one thought leads to another, or to an action. These include condensation, displacement, reversal, and contiguity (similarity). Freud held that the specific paths of such trains of thought are governed by the principle of least resistance, i.e., each step is the one which most gratifies the desire which impels it. His theory of primary process therefore uses a stimulus-response model. The desire itself is a response to a stimulus, and it in turn stimulates an automatic train of successive mental responses (structured by primary process) leading (prototypically) to an action designed to satisfy the desire.

The problem with straightforward stimulus-response models of mental activity is that they cannot account for mental processes that involve a genuine cognitive grasp of the situation, which enables the response to take a variety of paths, depending on the conclusions drawn about the probable consequences of the alternatives. Such levels of performance simply cannot be understood as themselves nothing more than the products of experience. The best known of these theories, that of B. F. Skinner, has been subject to several devastating critiques along these lines.

The story is told about the students in one of Skinner's classes, who decided to conduct an experiment to test his theories. Without telling him what they were doing, whenever Skinner talked about sexual matters, the students paid rapt attention, asked numerous questions, engaged in discussions, and so on. On all other topics they displayed a bored and inattentive indifference. Soon, the story goes, Skinner began to spend more and more class time on sexual questions, and after some weeks that is virtually all he talked about. So far, proof of Skinner's stimulus-response model. However, one of his students tipped Skinner off to what was going on, and of course he immediately stopped talking about sex, even though the students did not alter their behavior. Whether true or not, the story precisely illustrates the decisive weakness of behaviorist models.

Freud recognized the distinction between primitive stimulus-response primary process and the higher cognitively informed levels of thought, which he called 'secondary process'. He saw secondary process as arising out of primary process in a process of conditioning that in itself works on a stimulus-response model. The way Freud attempted to get around the kind of problem that has done in Skinner's theories is highly ingenious, but a careful examination reveals that it does not work. Given the premises from which Freud started (the basic drives, the principle of maximum immediate gratification, and the typology of primary process association) it is simply impossible to account for secondary process.

In recent years, research in a variety of fields has revealed two facts: first, much more of the structure of human mental activity is biologically imprinted than had previously been supposed; and, second, these innate patterns are too sophisticated to be accounted for in straightforward stimulus-response terms. Many innate processes are not specific responses to given stimuli, but ways of dealing with sensory input which are genuinely cognitive from the start. What is biologically implanted is not a pattern of behavior but a pattern of learning. Such patterns, moreover, are not confined to humans, but are widespread in the animal world in general.

Particularly striking have been some experiments with bees. It has long been known that when a bee comes across a good source of food it will return to the hive and communicate the location of its find to other bees, who then proceed to the site and gather food. While this is remarkable, it is readily accounted for by traditional instinct theory. It is supposed that the route by which the bee has reached the food is imprinted as sensory registration, and that this information is transmitted to other bees by instinctually imprinted signalling. Another experiment, however, had an even more surprising result. Two food supplies were placed at sites B and C, both some distance from the hive at site A. Soon the bees found the two sites, and established routes from the hive to both. Then the food was removed from site B, and a group of the bees at the hive were placed in a closed box, transported via a roundabout route to B and let loose. Instead of proceeding back to the hive and then to site C, as might be expected, these bees flew straight to $C!$

One cannot account for this on the traditional instinct model. The bees appear to be able to create a mental map which shows not only the routes from A to B and A to C, which can be understood as the processing of sensory input, but also the route from B to C, for which the bees have no basis in sensory experience at all. In Freudian terms, the bees are here exhibiting secondary process thought. Other species, for example birds, have been shown to possess similar cognitive powers. What is true of these animals is also true of humans. Secondary process does not emerge from primary process via conditioning; instead it is there from the start.

Soon after birth we begin to organize the world into three-dimensional objects firmly located in space and enduring through time, whose activities are organized into recognizable events. This process of organization occurs so quickly, and on the basis of such scanty and one-sided sensory input as to make inescapable the conclusion that it has an innate basis. We do not arrive at the world of objects and events located in space and time by building these out of sensory experience, rather the character of this world is a preexisting interpretive framework in terms of which sensory experience is understood. Perception is a heavily cognitive and conceptual process. In Husserl's terms, perception is 'transcendent'. We always see more than can be accounted for simply on the basis of sensory input. For example, when we look at a building from the front, we see it three dimensionally, as having sides and a back, even if we have never seen it from those angles – even, in fact, if we happen to know that we are looking at a phony facade.

This transcendent character of perception is manifested very early. For example, at five to seven months, infants who have been familiarized with a full-face view of someone will recognize at first sight the profile of the same face. The infant sees the face in the round, as having a character that transcends any particular perspective from which it is viewed, and so is able to recognize it when it is seen from a novel perspective. In that sense, perception is anticipatory; we see objects from perspectives, and as presenting appearances, not yet experienced.

The ability to understand events and relations between events in terms of physical causation appears also to be innate. Already at six months infants expect certain causal relations to obtain between objects, and register surprise at apparent causal anomalies. For example, when one moving object strikes another of similar size, they expect the motion to be transmitted to the second object, but only if actual contact occurs (Baillargeon, Spelke, and Wasserman 1985). This causal understanding is present too early to be accounted for on such theories as those of Hume and Piaget, who (in different ways) see the idea of causation as built up gradually out of repeated experience. Instead, the evidence indicates that our capacity to understand events in terms of physical causation is innate. It does not arise out of experience but instead is applied to and shapes the content of our experience as this experience arises (Leslie and Keeble 1987, Leslie 1988).

The points made above with respect to the transcendent quality of perception and the innate bases of secondary process and our causal understanding of the world can be generalized. Not only does experience transcend its sensory basis, but also in turn knowledge transcends its experiential basis. Moreover, many of the categories in terms of which such knowledge is formulated are pregiven, ready to be applied at birth or shortly thereafter.

In summary, an examination of what is innate in human life reveals two central facts. First, what is given in advance are not only certain basic motivational drives and emotional responses, but also much of the way in which experience and knowledge are formed and organized. Second, this genetic basis does not rigidly determine the content of experience or our response to this experience. Rather it lays down highly flexible patterns of thought and action, which enable the individual to attain a cognitive grasp of the situation and to proceed accordingly. The ability to exercise originality and creativity in our dealings with the world is genetically implanted. As these findings show, the long weary debate over free will and determinism totally misses the point. Freedom of the will, if you wish to use the phrase, is biologically determined.

The World of the Infant

As soon as she is born, if not before, the infant begins to build and relate to her world. When only three days old she can distinguish the smell of her mother's milk from that of others. Not only that, she can recognize and respond in kind to a smile. This astonishing fact illustrates several important points. First, as argued above, the infant possesses advanced and highly specific cognitive skills that are innate. Second, the interaction is not at all on the stimulus-response level. What is responded to is not a stimulus but a cognitively grasped fact: the other is smiling. The response is not automatic, for the infant will not smile back if she is distressed or distracted. The responsive smile is a voluntary act in the full sense. Third, the emotional and the behavioral aspects of the infant's smile are inseparable. It is obvious that the infant who smiles is experiencing pleasure, but it does not quite state the matter properly to say that the smile is an expression of the emotion; rather it *is* an emotion, a visible emotion. Fourth, the ability to communicate with others and interact with them (in the full sense of the word 'act') is not learned but inborn.

Within a few weeks the infant's world is brim full of people, objects, and events, which are readily recognized and sharply distinguished from each other, and to which she relates with passionate desires, emotions, and interest. Her relations with those around her are interactive from the start, and soon build up into complex, coherent, and evolving patterns.

This world is so different from that of an adult or even a six year old that it requires a very considerable stretch of the imagination to grasp what it is like. The principal source of this difference is not the relatively primitive sensory-motor development of the infant, or her lack of the background of experience that comes only with time, but the fact that her world is wholly nonlinguistic. The contents, flow, and objects of adult conscious awareness are so pervasively and deeply saturated and shaped by language that we live quite literally in a different world. The infant's world is another world, the world of the unconscious. Our conscious grasp of it is at best highly interpretive and incomplete. Nevertheless, thanks to the substantial body of research that has recently been done, it is possible to say a good deal about the world of the infant. In addition, our understanding is perhaps aided by the fact that beneath our adult conscious world we all live in an unconscious world which has much in common with that of the infant. Although the unconscious world of the infant is subject to modification and evolution as maturation proceeds, in its fundamental aspects it endures throughout the life of the individual, as the foundation on which all other awareness rests. So also the prelinguistic self underlies the mature conscious self in the sense that the roots of a tree underlie its trunk and branches.

The outstanding fact about the experience of the infant is its global and transmodal character. The ordinary divisions of awareness, such as perception, cognition, desire, and emotion simply do not apply, nor do the subdivisions within these divisions. In perception, for example, infants see (become visually aware) not only with their eyes but also with their fingers and tongues, and hear not only with their ears but also with their eyes. For example, they can recognize on 'first' sight a nubbly nipple which they have previously experienced only by sucking. To take another example, the seen movement of the lips is often perceptually dominant for infants over the actual sound of the voice. They hear better with their eyes than with their ears.

The early objects of awareness are sometimes pictured as 'bundles' of attributes, but this implies collections made up of discrete units. In the same way, a term such as 'synthetic unity' implies an integration of what has already been differentiated. Even the term 'undifferentiated' fails us, for some aspects of an experience are more salient for the infant than others. For example, the outline of an object is initially more important in defining it than its internal features. We cannot help it; willy-nilly, language brings its own categories to the understanding of the nonlinguistic. Perhaps the term 'syndrome' is as good as any to describe the complex unity of a prelinguistic experience.

Another mistake is to characterize infantile thought as 'concrete', in contrast to the more 'abstract' and 'conceptual' quality of linguistically articulated experience. On the contrary, infants definitely use abstraction in forming the objects of awareness. For example, as pointed out above, within days of birth they readily recognize and respond to a smile, and since a smile is an organization and pattern of movement of the features of a face which are invariant across specific differences between smiles and between faces, the act of recognition requires a high degree of abstraction. We can say, however, that infants abstract from experience and conceptualize it in ways very different from how conscious adults do so.

In addition, language ignores or relegates to the periphery attributes of experience which are very significant for infants. For example, drawing on the work of others, Stern (1955, 57ff.) has pointed to the importance of what he calls "vitality affects." In contrast to the traditional Darwinian categorical affects, these concern the expressive qualities that spring from what Stern calls the "activation contours" of experience. He uses terms such as 'rush', 'surge', 'fading', and 'resolution' for these affects, which cut across the usual categories of experience. A rush, for example, could apply to the way someone enters a room, plays a piano, or applies paint to a canvas. One can have a rush of anger, or of sensation (as when one takes a drug). The art forms of dance and music rely heavily on these affects for their expressivity. In our conscious experience, which is dominated by language, such vitality affects move on the whole from the center to the periphery of awareness.

All this is not to say that the infant does not build a clearly defined object and event world, of parent, toy, furniture, meal time, bed time, change time, play time, and so on, or that these do not all have a definite structure and character for the infant. What is the case, however, is that these structures and characters are different from and cut across the structures, modes, and character of linguistically defined and understood experience. Stern summarizes the process by which the infant builds her world as follows:

> Amodal perception (based on abstract qualities of experience, including discrete affects and vitality affects) and constructionistic efforts (based on assimilation, accommodation, association, and the identification of invariants) are thus the processes by which the infant experiences organization. While these processes have been most studied in perception, they apply equally well to the formation of organization in all domains of experience: motor activity, affectivity, and states of consciousness. They also apply to the yoking of experiences across different domains (sensory with motor, or perceptual with affective, and so on). (1965, 64)

The infant is preprogrammed to respond more strongly to people than to other objects, and quickly forms a powerful attachment to important persons in her life, especially the principal caretaker, usually, in our culture, her mother. In order for the infant to make a clear distinction between herself and her mother as separate persons, however, it is necessary for the groundwork to be laid.

The experiential basis for the formation of the self begins to build almost from birth, and has a very special character. There are three main points here. First, the infant's experience of her own body is radically different from her experience of the rest of her object and event world, including her experience of other persons. Perceptually, she can see only a part of herself, and always from the same perspective. Kinesthetically, when she touches herself, the sensation is strongly different from the sensation of touching other people. The sensory awareness of her own movements or position (proprioception) also has a far broader spectrum than her awareness of the movements of others (although this is perhaps mitigated by the cross-modal nature of her awareness). Second, the hedonic tone (sensuous pleasure and pain) of her experience of her own body is different from and generally much stronger than her experience of the rest of the world. Third, her own body is subject to voluntary control, only very minimally at first, but gradually more and more, as she learns to put her thumb in her mouth, reach out and grasp objects, then to crawl, and eventually, in one of life's great triumphs, to walk. The infant learns that there is a repertoire of motor activity that she can employ at will to produce desired results. These three special areas and types of experience of her own person (sensory, sensual, and purposive) are interconnected into a complex but nonetheless coherent whole that forms the basis on which the self is built.

The Formation of the Core Self

Stern places the emergence of what he calls the 'core self' in the second through the sixth months. By the second month the experiential groundwork outlined above has been laid. Stern summarizes this under four headings: self-agency, self-coherence, self-affectivity, and self-history, and describes the self as emerging from this basis through interaction with the principal caretaker(s), who will here be assumed to be her mother. Before proceeding to this account, however, it is necessary to be more specific about how the infant conceptualizes her world.

By the second month the world of the infant is a familiar one, i.e., it is characterized by object and event recognition, coherence, and constancy. Spatially, parents (as well as objects such as toys) are recognized as the same when seen from one side or another, from near or from afar, in bright or in dim light. As mentioned earlier, the object seen transcends the particularity of the experience. Temporally, when the infant sees a familiar object or experiences a familiar event, she recognizes it as having been encountered before. The memory world of the infant is a background against which and in terms of which the present world is experienced and understood. This background consists of a network of prototypical objects and events, which serves to orient and organize present experience.

The notion of the prototype as a kind of preverbal concept or category has emerged as central to the theory of infant and child development. The mother, the toy, the familiar day-to-day events perdure in a clearly defined form in the background of the infant's awareness, built up out of experience via a process of abstraction that is both synthetic and, as always with the objects of experience, transcendent. For example, in one experiment a group of ten-month-old infants were shown a series of schematic face drawings, each different from the others in the size, shape, and placement of the features. They were then 'asked', via an experimental technique which need not be described here, which single drawing best exemplified the series. They chose a drawing which they had in fact not previously seen, but which was a composite average of the drawings that they had been shown. The inference is that the chosen picture was closest to a prototype which they had formed on the basis of the pictures which they had seen. In these terms, the first self is a complex prototype, which the infant builds up out of her experience of herself, in interaction with others, especially her mother.

The nexus of prototypical objects and events that serves as a formative background for the flow of present experience is not only mnemonic, it is also anticipatory: the infant expects that the objects and events with which she is dealing will have a certain character, and behaves accordingly. The most vividly immediate present experience, the overflowing now, is nevertheless saturated by both the past and the future. Freud's statement that time does not exist for the unconscious is incorrect if it is taken to mean that there is no awareness of the past or the future in the unconscious. All three dimensions of time exist for prelinguistic awareness, but they are not separated out. Instead they are telescoped into a single past-present-future in which each phase acts to define the other two.

The typical event for the infant is the interaction with another person, usually her mother. By the age of two or three months the infant is able to engage in a variety of such social interactions. The social smile is in place, she directs vocalizations at others, seeks mutual eye contact, pays close attention to and reacts to the faces and voices of others. The range and complexity of social interaction expand quickly. As with the rest of the world, these interactions come to be understood prototypically. In feeding, for example, the event might proceed as follows: the mother presents the filled spoon, the infant opens her mouth, the mother inserts the spoon, the infant closes her mouth, the spoon is withdrawn, the infant swallows, then opens her mouth. All this is accompanied by eye contact, mutual vocalizations, exchanges of expression, and so on. Alternatively, if she is not hungry or does not like the food, instead of opening her mouth she will close it firmly, avert her head, and scowl. A different scenario then ensues. These are not first-time events: they occur in the context of prototypically organized past and anticipated future feeding interaction. Each step taken by the infant can be understood as the outcome of two sets of variables: first, the infant's own state of mind, i.e., her current desires, feelings, and mood (in the light of remembered and anticipated experience); and, second, her mother's actions, as understood by the infant, once again in context. The interaction serves to differentiate these two sets of variables. The first set acts to define the self, the second set acts to define the mother.

Out of a nexus of many such interactions the infant gradually builds what has been called a "working model" of the mother, as a kind of prototype of prototypes: a person who has (has had, will have) a certain physical appearance, characteristic way of acting, range of moods, and so on. It is the mother conceptualized by this prototype of prototypes who becomes the object of the infant's powerful emotional, sensuous, and cognitive attachments.

In exactly the same way, the infant forms a working model of her own person, with whom she also forms powerful emotional, sensuous, and cognitive attachments. What enables the differentiation is the very different nature of the experiences that she has of her own person, on the one hand, and of her mother, on the other. For example, in the feeding interaction, the infant can control whether or not she opens her mouth, but she cannot control whether or how the spoon is offered, or if she can, only to a very limited degree and by a very different process. If by some miracle the mother were able at all times instantly to gratify her every wish and expectation, the infant would be deprived of an essential resource in making the differentiation, for she would be unable to distinguish the area of experience where she can exercise control from the area where she cannot. Via such interactions, therefore, the invariants gradually get sorted out into those that belong to one's self and those that belong to the other.

Stern emphasizes the importance of variation to this process. Interactions typically proceed via variations on an invariant theme, and this is especially true of playful interaction, for example, the game of peek-a-boo, where the same interaction is repeated in a thousand guises. This helps the infant not only in grasping what is invariant, but also in sorting out self from other. The character of the preverbal core self can be summarized as follows. The infant experiences herself in prototypical terms as a physically existing being who acts and is capable of acting in certain prototypical ways. The self arises via differentiation out of experience of interaction, but transcends this experience. The various traits that define this self are integrated into a more or less coherent whole. The self and its activities are experienced in global, cross-modal, terms. One's action, for example, is not perceived as simply motion in space, but rather is typically heavily laden with categorical and vitality affect, desire, and sensuous tone. These are experienced as inherent to the action itself and/or the part of the body moved.

The Awareness and Communication of Emotion in Infancy

Freud held that there is no such thing as an unconscious emotion, an opinion that is shared by a number of cognitive psychologists. This view seems contradicted by the fact that even very young infants display a full range of categorical affects, such as anger, fear, and joy, which are unmistakably evidenced by facial and bodily expression. It seems impossible to doubt that these physical manifestations are accompanied by their own distinctive mental activity, but these must be unconscious because language acquisition will not begin for some time.

Such preverbal unconscious emotions do not, however, constitute full-scale intentional states; rather, they are no more than modes or aspects of such states. For example, at the age of one week, an infant will respond to a sudden loud noise with unmistakable signs of fear. To say, however, that she is afraid of the noise is to attribute to her a more differentiated level of awareness than she is capable of. Following Schafer (1976), one might say that she is fearfully aware of the noise, or by the same token, that she is angrily aware that she has been stuck by a diaper pin or joyfully aware that her mother has reentered the room. However, this does not yet state the case accurately; for what actually occurs is that the emotion inheres not in the awareness but in its object. In these terms, the infant is aware of a

41

fearful noise, a hateful (and painful) pin, the joyous entrance of her mother. It is the same with desire, which is not separated from the desired object in the field of awareness. In this connection, Freud spoke of a "quota of affect" as spreading over its object, "somewhat as an electric charge is spread over the surface of a body" (1894, 60). For the infant, the desire inheres in the magnetically attractive bottle, the fear in the fearsome tiger. It is the same with the vitality affects, which indeed continue to inhere in the object even for conscious awareness.

It is this fusion of emotions and desires with their objects which explains the 'splitting' that can occur in unconscious awareness. For example, it appears that infants sometimes split their mothers into two persons, a good mother, who is loved and desired, and a bad mother, who is feared and hated. Depending on the occasion, the infant can love and desire intimacy with her mother, or be intensely angry and fearful toward her. In these contrasting situations the mother will appear quite different to the infant, even independently of the different ways in which the mother may be behaving; so there are two prototypes and hence two persons.

A diluted form of this phenomenon is common in conscious awareness. It is well known that how people look to us depends heavily on how we feel toward them. Those to whom we have an affectionate or sensual attachment appear to be beautiful or handsome, and if our feelings toward them change, so does their appearance.

The world of the infant is wholly occupied by people, animals, things, and events, and what we think of as subjective mental states manifest themselves for the infant only as fused into this object world. It is only later that the subjective and objective aspects of experience are separated out. The experience of the infant is heavily charged emotionally, but the emotion itself is experienced only as it shapes the character of its object. This point needs to be kept in mind when dealing with preverbal unconscious emotion.

Nevertheless, like the measles, emotions are highly communicable. This is not communication in the sense of an intended transmission of thought, as in language, but is rather as a rule a spontaneous and unintended emotional contagion. In fact, we generally communicate our emotions whether we want to or not. It is much more difficult to conceal one's emotions from an infant than from an adult, precisely because the infant does not communicate in language. Oscar Wilde once remarked that language was invented to enable us to conceal our thoughts from each other – and, one might add, our emotions. The communicability of emotions rests on their innate transcultural nature, and on their intrinsic connection with their physical expression. The smile may be taken as a prototypical expression and communication of emotion. The infant can recognize a smile and respond in kind almost from birth. Before long the contagious and mutually reinforcing nature of the interaction is highly evident. A slight upturn of our lips produces a response in kind from the infant, at which we cannot help smiling more broadly, and soon both of us are grinning from ear to ear and chuckling. In line with the point made earlier, the infant is not aware of pleasure per se; rather, she is aware of her own and the other's pleasurable smiles. To say that the smile expresses the emotion is not quite accurate. Rather, the smile manifests or actualizes the emotion. One cannot smile without having the emotion (what comes out is a grimace), and it is only with difficulty that we are sometimes able to smile inwardly without showing it outwardly. Usually a twinkle of the eye or a twitch of the lips escapes us. An active muscular effort is required *not* to smile, and if we suppress a smile for long our face begins to ache. I dwell on this point because it so clearly demonstrates the futility of the Cartesian attempt to separate mind from matter.

The intensity and strongly interactive character of the emotional relations between mother and child produce a powerful mutual bonding. Mahler, Pine, and Bergman (1975) have termed this relationship a 'symbiosis' and, following Freud, have identified the infant's state of awareness as one of 'primary narcissism', in which no distinction is made between the self and the other or, for that matter, between the self and the world. This view is only partly justified. From a cognitive/perceptual point of view, the infant makes a clear-cut distinction between herself and others, based on the different character of the experience. This includes a primitive awareness of the self and others as possessing separate agency. Emotionally speaking, however, mother and child form a single unit, for two reasons. First, as has been pointed out, the infant does not experience her emotions as inhering in herself, but rather as infused into the whole field of awareness, and especially into the object (as distinct from the subject) of the emotion. In this respect the infant has not yet differentiated herself from her mother. Second, because of the contagious character of emotion the infant will in many circumstances share the emotions or others, especially her mother, and so experience them as her own, in the global sense indicated. In short, the infant experiences the world as occupied by distinct objects and events, including self and other, but these are infused with her emotions and desires, which do not have any clear location with respect to either subject or object.

The Core Self as Drive Object

In common with the rest of the self, the core self is an intentional object in the sense of the term developed by Husserl. As such, it is the object not only of perception and cognition, but also of libidinal and aggressive desires. Already the infant's early motor activity, such as wriggling and kicking, are the source of sensual pleasure. Soon motor control develops to the point where the infant is able to suck her thumb. This activity is prototypical of the way in which the body can be the object and source of sensual gratification. Because of the global nature of the experience, the desire to suck the thumb is not for the infant anything separate from the awareness of the desirable and pleasurable thumb. Here as elsewhere the desire inheres in its object.

The body is not only a source of pleasure for the infant, but also on many occasions of pain and distress. This is especially the case when the infant is ill. Once again, the infant is not aware of a pain which emanates, for example, from a injured thumb, but rather of the painful and distressful thumb. The thumb is here experienced as something quite different from the desirable and pleasurable thumb of a few minutes before. We have here two thumbs, a "good thumb" and a "bad thumb," corresponding to the contrast between the good mother and bad mother discussed earlier. In this situation, the desire to be rid of the pain from the thumb is not to be distinguished from the desire to be rid of the painful thumb. In general, aggressive impulses typically arise toward objects that are the source of pain or distress, and here in a kind of primary masochism the offending body part becomes the object of an aggressive impulse. By extension, the whole of the body, or more strictly the core self, can become a hated bad self.

The psychic mechanism involved here is illustrated by the story Freud tells about the rich man and the "schnorrer." (In Jewish culture, a schnorrer is a beggar whose job it is to persuade wealthy people to live up to their obligation under the Holy Law to give alms.) On this occasion the schnorrer was particularly eloquent on the subject of the misfortunes that had put him in desperate need of cash. Deeply moved, the rich man summoned his servants and instructed them, "Throw him out! He is breaking my heart" (1905, 113). As it says in the scriptures, "If thy eye offend thee, pluck it out."

The Reflexivity of the Core Self

I have defined the self as one's own person seen reflexively. In the case of the preverbal self, however, the reflexivity is of a highly limited kind, what Chisholm (1981) has called 'nonemphatic reflexivity'. Suppose, for example, that one sees one's own reflection in a mirror, without realizing that it is one's own person, and suppose that one says, "That person needs a haircut." Here the person one sees and refers to is oneself, and in that sense the perception and reference are reflexive. But one does not see and refer to oneself *as* oneself, as 'I' or 'myself'; i.e., one is not aware that the person who sees and the person who is seen are one and the same. In that sense reflexivity is absent.

The self-awareness of the preverbal infant is reflexive only in this limited sense. The infant is aware of herself as a distinct and vitally important part of her world, but is not aware of this person as herself, the very person who has this awareness. In fact, she is not aware of any awareness at all. The world of which she is aware is made up wholly of physically existing objects and the activities of these objects, organized into events. It would be very surprising to find otherwise, for, as we shall see, it is language which makes such full reflexivity possible, and we are here at the preverbal level.

Nevertheless, a number of those working in this field have insisted that by the time the preverbal self is firmly in place, the infant has a firm and clear awareness of herself as subject. When one examines this literature, however, what one finds is that the infant is aware of her own subjectivity only in a highly limited and special way. She is not aware of the inner world of her thoughts, feelings, desires, and emotions as anything separate from her own overt activity. She is aware of her voluntary activity as purposive, but the purposiveness inheres in the act, and is not anterior to it.

The point here may perhaps be clarified by considering the infant's awareness of the activity of other living beings, especially people. The infant is aware, for example, that her mother changes the diaper, fills the bottle, kisses her good night, and so on. These are events that the infant recognizes as being under the purposive control of the mother: they are things that the mother *does*. Only in that sense is the infant aware of her mother as a subject or agent. It is the same with the infant's awareness of her own purposive activity. Stern puts it this way: "Even when we are unaware of [our] motor plan, the sense of volition makes our actions seem to belong to us and to be self-acts. Without it, an infant would feel what a puppet would 'feel' like, as the nonauthor of its own immediate behavior" (1985, 77).

There are two points here. First, the infant is aware of the voluntary behavior of both herself and others as *action:* as an exercise of subjectivity or agency, not as separate from the act, but as integral to it. An act possesses agency in the same sense, for example, that it possesses motion or sound; the agency inheres in the act. Second, her own action has a very different experiential character for her than the actions of others, most importantly because it is under her voluntary control, while the actions of others are not. In other words, the infant is aware of the acts of both herself and others as purposive 'doings'; what differentiates her own acts is that they are under her own purposive control and so feel quite different from the acts of others.

This primitive sense of agency is quite different from the causality in terms of which ordinary physical events are understood. It is true, for example, that when the infant pushes her cup, she understands the push as causing its motion, and will be surprised if the cup does not budge. But the *act* of pushing, i.e., the voluntary motor action, is not experienced as caused in the same sense as the resultant motion of the cup. In contemporary philosophy of mind, the motivational cause of an act is often thought of as causal in the same sense as the causation found in the physical sciences, but for infants the two cases are not at all the same. I think the infant is right about this.

In sum, what marks the self off from others is the unique nature and character of the experience out of which it is built, coupled with the sense of agency that it possesses (Taylor and Fiske 1975). For the infant, one might say, the self is 'mine', not in the fully reflexive sense, for there is as yet no 'I' that can be identified with herself *as* herself, but rather as possessing a special, intense, purposive, close-to-home character, right across the modal range of perception, cognition, desire, emotion, and the other affects.

The Mirror Stage

The process of building the preverbal core self culminates in the period from about twelve to eighteen months with several interconnected developments. Perhaps the most dramatic of these is the emergence of the child's ability to recognize herself in the mirror. The process whereby this self-recognition emerges has been much studied, and reveals a good deal about the genesis of the preverbal self.

At first the infant's image in the mirror is seen as another person. Late in the first year, the infant becomes fascinated by the fact that the person in the mirror copies her actions exactly. Dixon (1957) has called this the "Who dat do dat when I do dat?" stage. As we have already seen, the fact that the infant's motor activities have predictable consequences is of central importance in building the self. What soon is predictable here is that her actions are copied in the mirror. The actions of the mirror image are not, however, seen as self actions, because of the novel perspective from which the infant is viewing herself: from the outside instead of from the inside. She sees herself not as she usually sees herself, but as *others* see her, and so she does not recognize herself.

Eventually (the time is quite variable) the infant recognizes her image as her own. In one telling experiment, a dab of rouge is surreptitiously placed on the infant's nose. When, on looking at herself in the mirror, she reaches up and touches her own nose instead of the nose of the image, one may conclude that she is aware that it is she herself whom she sees.

The realization that the person in the mirror is really oneself can come as a sudden and dramatic revelation, and the observer is confronted with, as Lacan put it, the "startling spectacle of the infant in front of the mirror" gazing at the image enthralled, "in a flutter of jubilant activity" (1949, 1). What is revealed to the infant here for the first time, I am convinced, is that she is a *person*. The argument is as follows.

The infant organizes and distinguishes the objects in her world according to a taxonomy of natural kinds. These objects are picked out not according to any essential or defining traits, but rather according to a syndrome or family of typical traits which, as I have mentioned, form a prototype. Particular objects are identified as belonging to one or another natural kind, not because of their exact sameness with this prototype, but rather because of their general similarity or family resemblance to it. Perhaps the broadest division in this taxonomy of natural kinds is between animate and inanimate objects, and among animate objects by far the most important natural kind is of course 'people'. The infant does not initially realize that she is of the same natural kind as the other persons in her world, because her experience of herself is so radically different from her experience of others. Therefore she does not at first recognize herself *as* herself in the mirror. When the realization dawns, it sometimes comes as a revelation. She becomes aware that she is a person, the same sort of being as the other persons in her world, i.e., a member of the human race. Here we have the first diminution of the initial total self-centeredness of the infant. Not only is she now aware that she is a person like others, but by the same token for the first time she begins to see herself as others see her: not from her own perspective, but from the perspective of the lifeworld.

Access to a mirror is not essential to the emergence of this new perspective, but it hastens the process. The infant has already developed a sense of agency, which is evoked here by the fact that the actions of the mirror image exactly copy hers, and hence are under her control in the same way as the motions which are copied. In this way the 'copycat' image becomes absorbed within the self, sometimes as early as the age of twelve months.

Where such a volitionally steered feedback process is missing, as when the infant sees herself in photographs or video recordings, self-recognition comes later: no sooner than at eighteen months, and generally not before the end of the second year. Since language acquisition is by then well under way, the child is able to point to the image and say "That me," or "That Susie."

In a connected development, at about this time the infant begins to acquire the capacity for empathic understanding of others. This is a step beyond the simple contagion of emotions discussed earlier. Children are inveterate generalizers; in fact they often overgeneralize. They have an innate tendency to attribute to every member of a natural kind those properties that are observed in a single instance. As they become increasingly aware that they are persons like other people, they will generalize from their own case to others. Since, as has been pointed out, in the preverbal stage the modalities of awareness are not separated out, to be aware of another person's emotional state is to *feel* that emotional state. The empathic responses that infants begin to show at this stage are the consequence of the realization that they are persons like others, coupled with the underlying contagion of emotions.

In a connected development at about this time, the infant begins to form the capacity for a kind of primitive identification with others. Hoffman (1977) describes a thirteen-month-old boy who was in the habit of pulling on his ear lobe and sucking his thumb when upset. Once, when his father was visibly upset, he went over and pulled his father's ear lobe, while sucking on his own thumb. Here the capacity to empathize combines with the knowledge that one is a person like others, to overcome, for the moment, the division between self and other, and to produce an early form of identification.

Conclusion

Since this chapter has covered a lot of ground, it may be useful at the close to draw things together a bit under the three categories of self, person, and world.

Self. The preverbal core self begins to form at the age of about two months, as the infant's experience of herself, in the context of interaction with others, begins to assume a coherent and stable structure, and she becomes aware of herself as a distinct entity existing in her world, able to act purposively, someone very special to whom she relates powerfully across the full range of intentional modalities. Awareness of herself as a person like other persons, however, comes only late in the preverbal period. This is the basis for empathic relations with others and a kind of primitive identification with them.

To say that the prelinguistic self is 'objectified' in the sense of reduced to its physical or behavioral manifestations is a mistake; rather, the emotional, cognitive, and motivational states of one's own person (and others) are not experienced as anything separate from the physical existence of the person. One could just as well (and equally one-sidedly) say that the physical existence of the self is 'subjectified', i.e., one's person as experienced is infused with one's own intentionality. For the infant, and throughout life on the unconscious level, with respect to both self and world, we find that subject and object, inner and outer, are not differentiated.

The fact that subject and object are fused rules out the possibility of fully reflexive self-awareness. There is no awareness of an 'I' who is both the subject and the object of one's thought. Reflexivity goes no further than a 'nonemphatic' awareness of one's self as a purposively active being. Nevertheless, as we shall see, much of the groundwork for the evolution of the 'I' has already been laid.

Person. The person is born with a wide range of innate characteristics, many of which are manifest at or soon after birth. These include the basic drives and emotions, and certain ways of perceiving and knowing. Perception and cognition are transcendent almost from the start. Experience transcends sense, and knowledge, in turn, transcends experience. These facts refute the traditional reductive approaches to human personality.

Interpersonal relations and interaction also have an innate basis. They begin almost immediately after birth, and are crucial to personal development. Whatever the vicissitudes of this development, except in rare cases the infant quickly develops powerful and lasting relations with others and with herself, right across the range of drive, emotion, perception, and cognition.

The abstract and conceptual nature of preverbal thought has been widely overlooked, very likely because of its strong differences from verbally constituted thought. Foremost among these differences are the heavily amodal and cross-modal character of preverbal intentionality, and the fact that what are later distinguished as the subjective and objective aspects of experience are fused. When language arrives on the scene, a great deal of development has already occurred. Language and the lifeworld do not construct, but rather *reconstruct* the person and, at least on the unconscious level, this reconstruction is quite limited in extent.

World. The unconscious world of the infant is filled with clearly delineated persons (both self and others), things, and events, to which strong attachments are formed. Objects are sorted out according to natural kinds, which are understood in terms of syndromes of characteristic traits. Because of its very special experiential basis, the self is not identified as a member of the natural kind 'person' until the time of the twelfth to eighteenth month, toward the end of the preverbal stage. For the infant there is no inner or outer world, in respect either to herself or to others. There is only one world, to which the categories subjective and objective do not yet apply.

Sources

Explanation of action. The position taken here is essentially the same as that of C. Taylor 1964, 1971, and 1980. For a recent defense of this view, and a critique of the more widely accepted account of Davidson 1980, see Ricoeur 1990, 56–87. One of the advantages of the position taken here is that thought processes are explained in the same way as overt action, i.e., by describing their motivation. Thought then emerges as a form of action, and the whole problem of the connection between the two is bypassed. The topic of the explanation of thought and action will be taken up again in chapter 7.

Drives and affects. By now it is widely recognized even among psychoanalytic circles that Freud's theory of the basic ('instinctual') drives, and their relation to the affects is inadequate (Kernberg 1882, Kohut 1977). Fairbairn 1941, and more recently Plaut 1984, have called for the introduction of a third basic drive, which they label "ego instincts," and I have adopted this idea (but not the term) here. This expedient has the advantage of enabling one to account for the empirical evidence (Lichtenberg 1981, 1983; Stern 1985, 44–45), at the cost of creating substantial theoretical problems, which I have not dealt with at all. The whole theory of basic motivational drives and their relation to the affects needs to be rethought from the ground up.

For a critique of the way in which Freud saw secondary process as growing out of primary process, see McIntosh 1986a. The real distinction, as I shall argue later, is between linguistic and nonlinguistic thought. Nonlinguistic thought is already 'transcendent' in Husserl's terms. (Husserl's 'transcendent' is not to be confused with his 'transcendental'.) The view that perception, and experience in general, are not built wholly out of sensory registration is argued in Stern 1985, 61–68.

For an interpretation of the experiments with bees described above, as well as similar experiments on other species, see Gould and Marler 1987. The extent to which behaviorism has been abandoned in the field of animal psychology is illustrated by the studies in Roitblat et al. 1984.

Infant perception. In addition to the discussions in Stern, see Strauss 1979 and Fagan 1976 for face recognition, and Field et al. 1982 for smile recognition and response. The studies of object perception conducted by Spelke and her associates have been especially striking (Spelke 1987, 1988; Kellman and Spelke 1963; Baillargeon, Spelke, and Wasserman 1985; Streri and Spelke 1988). Spelke stresses the conceptual quality of perception. In her accounts, the concepts via which objects are perceived bear a startling resemblance to Husserl's *Wesen*, the abstract object which establishes what the empirically given object is seen *as*. For the conceptual nature of infant awareness, see also Mervis 1985, and Leslie 1988. Infant perception of causality is discussed in Bullock, Gelman, Baillargeon 1982; Golinkhoff, Harding, Carlson and Sexon 1984; Baillargeon, Spelke, and Wasserman 1985: Leslie and Keeble 1987; Leslie 1988;

and Poulin-Dubois and Schultz 1988. The evidence presented in these works strongly suggests, but does not firmly establish, the dual-causality interpretation advanced here. The amodal nature of perception is discussed, with extensive citations, in Stern 1985, 47–53 (vitality affects are treated on 53–61). For a discussion of the role of prototypes in infant perception and cognition, see Keil 1987, and Lakoff 1987. Infants understand events in terms of what Fivush (1987) calls 'scripts', which are much like prototypes in character, except that they are organized sequentially.

The core self. The treatment follows Stern (1985, 37–123) closely, except for some of his discussion on (122–23), where it seems to me that he reads verbal level ideas back into the preverbal level. For the development and nature of the infantile self, in addition to Stern see Lewis and Brooks-Gunn 1979, Lewis 1986, and Kagan 1989. For discussions of infants' sense of self as agent, in addition to the above, see Poulin-Dubois and Schultz 1988.

Stern has challenged Freud's theory of primary narcissism, which is still widely held among psychoanalysts (e.g., Mahler et al. 1975), as well as the notion of 'splitting' (e.g., Kernberg 1975). The interpretation advanced here agrees with Stern in some respects and attempts to reconcile the apparent contradictions in others. For a fuller treatment, see McIntosh 1993a.

Emotions in infancy. See Lewis and Michalson 1983; Michalson and Lewis 1985; and Emde 1988. For the contagion of emotions, see Sullins 1991.

The mirror stage. The most thorough treatment is in Lewis and Brooks-Gunn 1979. As with much of the literature in cognitive and developmental psychology, the central notion of self is neither clearly defined nor consistently used in this work. The interpretation of the significance of the mirror stage presented here is my own.

3 LANGUAGE AND THE 'ME'

With the coming of language, the evolution of the self enters a new phase. Overlaying the unconscious preverbal core self there emerges a verbally defined aspect of the self which I will call the 'Me', and then, more gradually, a fully reflexive conscious self which will be termed the 'I'. This terminology is fairly common in cognitive psychology where, following William James, the 'Me' is often described as the 'self as object', in contrast to the 'I', defined as 'self as subject'. These designations are appropriate to the concepts as developed here, but only if properly construed. The 'Me' is the self as object in the sense that here self-understanding is limited to outer physical and behavioral properties, at least initially, while the 'I' is the self as subject in the sense that one is aware of oneself as having thoughts, feelings, and motives, and as acting on these.

Since the influence of language is so fundamental to the development of both the 'Me' and the 'I', a preparatory treatment of the impact of language on the thought processes of the child is needed. In this chapter, I will begin with the lexical level of words and word meanings, and then move on to the fully linguistic (syntactically organized) level. (The term 'verbal' will be used to cover both levels.) A central theme will be the transition from unconscious to conscious-preconscious awareness. The role that language plays in the further development of full consciousness will be taken up in the next chapter.

The Advent of Words and the Evolution of Word Meaning

The first words that the child learns to understand and then to speak are names for the objects and events of which she is already aware. The term 'label' is often used for names, but this greatly underestimates the close and powerful bond which commonly exists between signifier and signified. The term 'handle' is perhaps more appropriate. At the early one-word (lexical) stage of language acquisition, the name is simply added to the attributes that make up the prototypical syndrome in terms of which the thing or event is conceptualized. Henceforth the name is experienced as intrinsic to the thing. Once learned, for example, the word 'cat' is as much a part of the animal it designates as its tail or its meow, and the force of this is even stronger when the cat is given a proper name, e.g., Topsy.

The fusion of word and thing is characteristic of the lexical and early linguistic stages of language acquisition, during which the child's awareness remains wholly unconscious. It is only considerably later (after the age of six or so), when syntactically organized (linguistic) thought has evolved into conscious awareness, that the word may begin to be seen to have a purely conventional relation to the thing, like a label that can be peeled off and replaced by a different label without affecting the thing labeled. Beneath this, however, the intrinsic connection between word and thing is often retained unconsciously, especially for objects to which a strong attachment has been formed.

Moreover, by the alchemy of unconscious thought processes, to pronounce or even to think the name of something has the effect of bringing the whole sharply to attention. I speak the words "Mont Blanc" and immediately a clear memory of the mountain springs to awareness. There is another alp. I have forgotten its name, but it is craggier, more looming. The words help me some, but the recollection is still vague. Suddenly I remember. The Matterhorn! Instantly the mountain is present, sharp and distinct in my imagination. It is almost as if I were once again standing in the valley, looking up at it.

Recent research reported in the *New York Times* (6 March 1993, C1) indicates that language has a strongly stabilizing effect on memory, which may explain why adults retain so few memories of the period before the age of two or three.

Our sharpest, most immediate and vivid awareness of something normally occurs when it is actually present before us. The experience of the object is, as Husserl put it, 'filled'. Hallucinatory experience can share this quality or nearly so. In contrast, the remembered or imagined object usually has only a shadowy, incomplete presence. Language greatly diminishes this contrast by enhancing the immediacy of what is imagined or remembered. When we pronounce or read the name of something that is absent, we are bringing one aspect of its being, its name, into direct perceptual awareness. We hear or see the name. Most of the thing is still absent, but a part of it, its name, is present in immediate sensory experience. To that extent the experience of the thing is filled. The quality of being a 'handle' now comes into play. The immediate presence of the word serves in turn to bring the whole that has been named into more vivid and immediate awareness.

The word evokes the thing. It makes present what is absent. Where there was nothing, there is now something. "In the beginning was the word," says the Bible. By speaking the words, "the earth," "the heavens," "the oceans," "the mountains," on the Biblical account, God brought these into his presence, and hence into being. There is truth here, not only psychological but also ontological. "A thing is," wrote Aristotle, "what it can be said to be." The widely held magical belief that to know a person's name is to have power over her also contains a psychological truth, for to pronounce a name is to possess what has been named, and what we possess we can control. The ability to affix a name to things has a strongly stabilizing effect on object relations. The adage, "Out of sight, out of mind," no longer applies, because one can now bring the object to presence simply by pronouncing or thinking its name. Since the object is more constantly present, so too are the feelings of love, hatred, or fear that we have toward it. The feelings become more tied to the object, less readily displaced elsewhere.

There is an apparent contradiction here between findings of cognitive psychologists and psychoanalysts. The former see object constancy as emerging very early, according to some studies in the first few weeks of life, while psychoanalytic researches put it much later, toward the end of the second year. The contradiction is only apparent, however. Cognitive psychologists place primary stress on perception, cognition, and memory, and in these modes of intentionality coherent stable objects form very early. In contrast, psychoanalysts focus mainly on libidinal, aggressive, and emotional relations to objects, intentional modes whose objects stabilize in character and intensity only with the advent of language.

Language also affects the *quality* of experience. "What's in a name?" says Juliet, "That which we call a rose by any other name would smell as sweet." In this she is mistaken. In our language, the word 'rose' evokes the concepts of sweetness of smell, intensity of blossom coloration, and sharpness of thorn. As a consequence, when we take a rose in hand, our senses concentrate on these qualities, to the relative diminution of others, such as the color of the leaf, the curve of the stem, or the explosive vitality affect of the open blossom. Once we have learned the meaning of the word, the rose smells sweeter, its thorns are sharper, and its color, instead of being simply red is now, as Burns put it, "red, red." All this is lost if we pick it up and say, "This is a grue."

The example of Juliet's rose has taken us beyond the one-word stage of language into the syntactic level. Here perhaps the most basic effect of language, deriving from its universal 'deep structure' is to separate the contents of awareness into subject and predicate, or, as some cognitive psychologists put it, topic and comment. The preverbal world contains roses, but it does not contain redness, sweetness, or sharpness as separately distinguishable. The infant is aware of such properties only as fused into the global syndrome of the experience of the object. It is the capacity to say and think "The rose is red, sharp, smells sweet," which thematizes these properties and isolates them for separate awareness.

Some of the consequences of this thematizing property of language may be illustrated with respect to the emotions. Suppose that a little girl, whom I shall call Marie, becomes aware that her mother is feeling sad, by observing her facial and bodily activity, perhaps because she is crying. Prior to her acquisition of language, Marie will be aware of her mother's sadness only as part of the undifferentiated quality of her appearance. We might say that she sees a sad mother, rather than seeing that her mother is sad. Furthermore, Marie will empathically pick up her mother's sadness, and become sad herself. As a result, the whole world will appear sad. Her mother's sadness will have spread to the whole field of awareness. But with the acquisition of language, if Marie says, or thinks, "Mommy is sad," the contents and objects of her awareness will be significantly different. First, the sadness will be thematized as something that itself can be an object of awareness. Second, it will now be her mother, not the whole world, who is sad. The emotion will be located in a particular person.

Two consequences of these developments for the relationship between Marie and her mother may be noted. First, the personhood of the mother will be even more stabilized than at the one-word level. Instead of a sad mother and a happy mother, a loving mother and an angry mother, all quite different persons, there is now one and the same mother who at different times is sad and happy, loving and angry. A higher degree of object constancy has been achieved. In the process, however, the emotional relation to the mother has become more variable and hence more problematic. As Mahler, Bergman, and Pine put it, at this stage "Fear of losing the love of the object (instead of fear of object loss) becomes increasingly evident" (1975, 78).

In sum, the shift from the preverbal to the verbal level, which Freud identified with the transition from unconscious to conscious-preconscious thought, marks a radical change in the contents and objects of awareness. Freud (1915a, 166) called the translation into the new register a "transformation" (*Umsetzung*), a term which is echoed by Stern when he writes,

> Language grabs hold of a piece of the conglomerate of feeling, sensation, perception, and cognition that constitutes global nonverbal experience. The piece that language takes hold of is transformed by the process of language-making and becomes an experience separate from the original global experience. (1985, 174–75)

The Linguistic Overlay

My picture of the changes wrought by language is still far from complete, for in addition to profoundly changing the contents of experience, language adds a new layer which does not derive from what is already there. What happens is that the lifeworld takes over and shapes conscious-preconscious thought into socially established patterns.

As I have pointed out, the preverbal world of the infant consists wholly of materially existing objects and their actions and interactions. The basic categories into which this world is organized consists of natural kinds such as people, dogs, trees, and rocks; artifacts such as spoons, chairs, and autos; and events, such as lunch, going to bed, taking a bath, or games such as peek-a-boo or patty-cake. Also in this world are parts of such basic objects or events, such as faces, noses, tails, handles, and being put in the high chair preparatory to a meal. Higher order categories are much more thinly conceptualized, although there does appear to be an innately drawn distinction between animate and inanimate objects, which forms the basis for the distinction between motivational and mechanical causation discussed above.

Language brings with it a huge expansion of our categorical understanding of the world, and also eventually strongly changes the basis on which categories are formed, at least in traditional Western culture. Two such changes may be noted here. First, it will be recalled that preverbal and early verbal categories are formed on the basis of bundles or syndromes of features, in which physical appearance is highly important. Categories are conceptualized as prototypes, and specific objects or events are recognized on the basis of their family resemblance to such prototypes. Gradually, in our culture, this approach is altered in a more "scientific" direction, for example from 'characteristic' to 'defining' traits as decisive. In the case of natural kinds this may bring to the fore properties not readily visible; for example, the distinction between animals which are oviparous and mammalian, vertebrate or invertebrate.

In addition, among living things, categorization comes to be laid down on a genetic basis. For example, young children who are still categorizing at the lexical or early linguistic level generally think that you can change a cat into a skunk simply be painting a stripe on its back. It is only gradually that they learn that an animal becomes a cat at birth, and will remain a cat through a wide variation in the outward physical characteristics by which objects were previously categorized.

In the case of artifacts, function often replaces appearance as decisive for categorization. For example a hammer comes to be understood not as an object with a wooden handle and a metal head of a certain shape, but as something that is used to drive in nails and the like, leading to a 'rational' (i.e., functional) subcategorization, e.g., tack hammer, sledge hammer, and so on.

Another change introduced by our culture is the formation of categories into a logically organized hierarchy, according to 'essential' as against accidental or peripheral features. Children innately generalize via collective nouns – e.g., the generalization from trees to forest. The 'scientific' way, in contrast, is to define categories according to features that are transitive across subcategorization – e.g., the generalization from trees to plants. The point of this method is that everything that is true of plants is also true of trees, which is not the case with a forest in relation to its trees (e.g., being a mile wide). Such 'scientific' categorization is not widely used in most cultures, but it is absolutely basic to modern technology and science. Children have a good deal of difficulty learning to think in this way, because it runs against innate methods of categorization.

The evolution of categorization in children is invariably treated in the literature on the topic as a matter of increasing reality grasp and learning "scientific" ways of looking at things. Language is generally regarded as no more than a neutral or transparent medium for transmitting understanding about the nature of reality. This of course is quite correct from the perspective of the naive natural attitude, which all of us take most of the time. Once this naivete is overcome, it becomes more prudent to say that what is going on in the processes studied in this literature is the acquisition of the modes of categorization prevalent in the upper strata of the Modern Western lifeworld. What we have here is a new reality grasp, but is it necessarily a better one? Such questions will be discussed later. The relevant points here are, first, that the lifeworld method of categorization is culturally contingent and, in our culture, more or less at odds with what is innate; and, second, that the new method does not abolish the old, but overlays it. The original preverbal modes of conceptualization remain active, more or less unconsciously, underneath the new ways imposed by language and culture. This situation illustrates a general characteristic of the relation of lifeworld to underworld.

I have pointed out that language thematizes for separate attention properties that were previously fused into global awareness. In addition, it introduces a host of new properties not previously present in awareness at all. These include comparative terms such as large-small, fast-slow, heavy-light, loud-soft, and relational terms such as under-over, before-after, near-far, mother-daughter. Note, for example, that while in preverbal awareness the experience of large objects is different from the experience of small ones, the terms 'large' and 'small' introduce and thematize a comparative idea that is new. There is now a background context in which the thing is large or small relative to something else.

Another whole realm is opened up by the introduction of verbs and verbal terms. The groundwork has previously been laid by the infant's nonlinguistic awareness of events and of purposive action. Verbs now thematize aspects previously fused into global awareness, and they also introduce a whole range of concepts not previously present — e.g., start, stop, enter, leave, look, wait, stay. Verbs designating mental activity, such as think, want, like, and hate, are already in use by the age of three, although, as will be detailed in the next chapter, it will be some years before they are thought of as referring to anything separable from the visible world of objects and events.

In addition to altering the contents of awareness and adding new elements, language also has a filtering effect on prelinguistic intentionality, with the result that important aspects of prelinguistic awareness get translated into the conscious-preconscious very thinly if at all, and so remain largely or wholly unconscious. I have already mentioned the vitality affects as highly underrepresented in conscious-preconscious awareness. Of greater importance, perhaps, is the fact that language initially has a strongly objectivating effect on intentionality, in the sense that the verbal expression of feelings toward an object is confined to a physical description of the object. As has been noted, in infancy the subjective aspects of experience, such as desire, mood, and emotion, are not separated out, and enter awareness only as inhering in the objects toward whom or which they are directed. Consequently, when expressed in language, the feeling emerges as a visible property of its object. A child will say of someone she dislikes, for example, "She is ugly!" The dislike will likely be expressed by the tone of voice and accompanying facial expression, but when put in language the feeling becomes something which pertains to the object, and which can be described in physical or quasiphysical terms.

It might seem that my description of the child Marie, who says, "Mommy is sad," contradicts what has just been said, but in fact it does not. If we ask Marie, "What is sad?" she will reply something like, "Sad is crying." Sadness is equated with its physical expression, and it is this expression that is taken as defining. Children cannot conceive that a person who is smiling is not happy, or conversely that a person who is not smiling is happy.

This reduction of emotions and feelings to their physical expression continues well into childhood. Eventually in our culture this objectivation begins to break down, preparatory to the emergence of awareness of feelings as distinct from their objects. For example, a boy just under ten years old described someone he disliked as follows:

He smells very much and is very nasty. He has no sense of humor and is very dull. He is always fighting and he is cruel. He does silly things and is very stupid. He has brown hair and cruel eyes. He is sulky and eleven years old and has lots of sisters. I think he is the most horrible boy in the class. He has a croaky voice and always chews his pencil and picks his teeth and I think he is disgusting.

This statement is amusing because of its inappropriate mixture of straightforward description with expressions of hostile feeling. Note that the boy stops just short of an explicit statement of his feelings. From the claim that the other is disgusting one has to infer that he is disgusted. The account is characteristic of those nine or ten years old. Earlier (e.g., at age six), the description would have been emotionally much flatter and more 'objective': e.g., "He fights a lot," and "He picks his teeth" (perhaps with a disgusted expression), but not "I think he is the most horrible boy in the class," or "I think he is disgusting." Later (e.g., at age fourteen), he would have been able to separate descriptive and emotional statements more clearly, e.g., "I hate him because he fights a lot and picks his teeth" (but not because he is eleven years old and has brown hair).

To summarize, the acquisition of language has the following effects on the contents and objects of awareness: (1) It separates our global experience into discrete parts or aspects, which can themselves now become objects of awareness; (2) It enhances object constancy with respect to affect, and so greatly stabilizes object relations; (3) It emphasizes certain aspects of experience and de-emphasizes others; (4) It locates our feelings towards objects in the objects themselves, and in doing so objectivates these feelings; (5) It drastically changes the categories and concepts in terms of which we understand and deal with the world; and (6) It adds a host of new categories and concepts not previously in awareness.

Language and the Lifeworld

It is clear from the foregoing that language revolutionizes the world and the way we look at it. It is perhaps no exaggeration to say that the child is born again: born into the lifeworld of the common everyday experience, concepts, and ways of thinking of the society of which she now becomes a member. It is a particular lifeworld, one of many. Modern anthropology has demonstrated how profoundly different one culture can be from another.

The relativism of lifeworlds stands in contrast to the cross-cultural uniformity of the preverbal world of the infant. The main reason for this uniformity is the innate genetically determined nature of the process whereby the infant constitutes and relates to her world, in contrast to the huge variability that language opens up. This is not to say that the social environment does not have a strong influence on the psychic (as well as physical) growth of the infant prior to language. Far from it. But the social world is precisely an environment. It shapes growth in much the same way that the climate and soil shape the growth of an oak. Through all the variations by which an oak comes to terms with its environment, its essential features remain the same.

With the advent of language, the influence of the environment on the life of the individual enters a new dimension. Language creates a whole new level of awareness and a whole new world that opens to this awareness. The child's experience is not simply shaped by this lifeworld, it *partakes* of it. Language not only brings the child into the lifeworld, it brings the lifeworld into the child. Once full conscious-preconscious awareness has been achieved, the lifeworld becomes far more than an environment; it is now embedded in the child's way of understanding and dealing with the world.

The conscious-preconscious lifeworld, and the evolving conscious-preconscious self do not, however, replace the unconscious world and the unconscious self; rather, they constitute a new level that overlays what is already there. It is true that the thought processes on this new level have a significant impact on what happens on the unconscious level, but the basic character and structure of unconscious thought remain unaffected.

The position taken here therefore stands in contrast to that of Jacques Lacan, and in particular to his well-known dictum that "the unconscious is structured in the most radical way like a language" (1966, 234). Lacan's argument (1966, 157–71) relies most importantly on the claim that the basic unconscious processes of displacement and condensation are identical to metaphor and metonomy, figures of speech which play a central role in the constitution of linguistic meaning. But, as Lyotard (1974, 19–55) has shown, the equation does not hold. The most salient point is that to utter or think a metaphor or metonomy is to perform an intentional act, while although displacement and condensation are thought processes (Freud called them 'mechanisms') which shape unconscious thought, they are not themselves intentional acts, much less propositions. They are instead processes by which intentional states are shaped or connected. For example, condensation is the process by which two or more intentional states are combined into a single intentional state.

The basic premise of Lacan's position is that, as Saussure put it, "Without language thought is a vague, uncharted nebula. There are no pre-existing ideas and nothing is distinct before the existence of language," (1922, 112). The whole argument falls through, however, once it is shown, as I have above, that unconscious thought has a distinctive and coherent structure of its own, which it possesses from the very start, and which stands in sharp contrast to the structure and character that language brings to thought.

The Origins of the 'Me'

The self which first appears in verbally constituted awareness lacks the reflexivity of the fully conscious self (the 'I') which eventually emerges, and generally has a very different character as well. So I shall use the term (and concept) 'Me', which was originated by William James, and is now widely used in cognitive and developmental psychology. James's concept was taken up and developed extensively by G. H. Mead, and it has since been the subject of much empirical study. As a result, the 'Me' is the aspect of the self of which we have the firmest and most complete knowledge, at least with respect to our own culture.

The basis for the 'Me' is laid during the mirror stage treated above, which occurs in the child's second year during or slightly before the 'one-word' stage of language development. Here for the first time the child sees and recognizes herself from the outside, i.e., from the same perspective from which others see her. While the self that opens to this perspective is new, there is some overlap with the unconscious core self. One's hands and legs, for example, are recognizably the same, despite the distance (spatial, sensuous, and kinesthetic) that the new perspective brings. Other physical attributes, most notably one's face, are new.

Early in the one-word stage the child learns her own name, and not long after learns the appropriate use of 'Me' and 'mine'. ('I' comes later.) She can point to a picture of herself and say "Me" or "Susie." The child builds up her 'Me' around the nucleus of the mirror self and her name, first under the tutelage of her parents, then in interaction with the larger family and playmates, and finally at school. The self that emerges is her own person seen from the perspective of what Mead has called 'the generalized other'. Virtually all of the characteristics of this self are formulated in terms and concepts derived from the socially and linguistically constituted lifeworld. As such, initially at least, it is located in conscious-preconscious awareness.

It follows that the characteristics of the 'Me' vary widely according to the society and even the stratum or section of the society in which it is embedded. One must therefore be cautious in generalizing from the existing evidence, which is mostly drawn from middle- to upper-middle-class white, urban, English-speaking subjects (often from academic families or university towns). It is frequently the case, moreover, that the evidence is taken in special or even artificial situations which might themselves affect the results. Perhaps the theories worked out in this book may be of some assistance in distinguishing results that are likely to apply only locally from those of wider relevance, but the relatively narrow empirical base from which the discussion of this and the following chapter proceeds must nevertheless be kept in mind.

In our society undoubtedly the most important characteristic of the 'Me' is gender. It is a very different thing to be a girl than to be a boy. The anthropological evidence makes it clear that this is true for all or almost all societies, although gender-defining traits vary widely. Here the relativity of time and place is especially important. Until recently, the studies made have shown that for young children the most salient defining trait of gender was hair length! Clothing is also important, as are characteristic activities. For example, girls play with dolls, while boys play with toy trucks. This is not only what they do, it is what they are expected or supposed to do; indeed, it is what makes them boys or girls. Young children believe that if a girl had her hair cut short and began playing with trucks instead of dolls she would thereby become a boy. They also believe that when they grow up they will become someone else. In this respect the 'Me' at this stage is a primitive form of what sociologists call a 'social role', i.e., it is a set of behavioral traits associated with a given social position, which define that position, and with which the members of society expect the occupants of the position to comply, or else face sanctions. At first, however, the role is not accepted in a normative sense; for example, young children do not consider it improper for boys to play with dolls, but instead unwise, because others will be displeased.

In its early stages the 'Me' is mainly defined in terms of external properties, especially physical features, and characteristic activities, such as riding a bike, which serve to differentiate self from other. One is a 'big boy' or a 'little boy' (or in context both), not only with respect to how big or little one is in size, but also in terms of what one is able to do. Later on, age and family membership are significant. Still later, wider group memberships enter in. Although I have not seen any studies on this, I should expect skin color to be profoundly important. On the other hand, the anatomical differences between the sexes, most notably the genitals, are not at first significant (for the groups studied).

In the main, the properties that define the 'Me' are verbally shaped and not present or at least not separable in the global awareness of preverbal experience. In this respect the contrast between the 'Me' and the core self is striking. This holds true even for activities that have long been familiar. A young boy, for example, may long have enjoyed playing with trucks, but the activity can become a gender, and hence self, characteristic only with the formation of the 'Me'. It was not, and does not become, an aspect of his core self.

As the child's categorical understanding of the world evolves, so also will her self. Initially the traits that define the self are often of an ephemeral or temporary kind, and the nature of the self is seen as readily changeable, as when a girl is thought to become a boy if her hair is cut short, and to become a different person when she grows up and becomes a 'mommy'. The shift to understanding natural kinds in terms of innate biological traits tends greatly to stabilize the self, since these traits are enduring. It is not until about the age of seven, for example, that gender comes to be understood as something that is innate and hence constant throughout life. It appears that the genitals become significant for selfhood only when this stage of the development of categorical understanding is reached. They are the locus of strong sensual feelings and attachments almost from birth, but it is a good while before they become a part of the self. The 'Me' has gender from the start; it acquires sex only later.

The Emotional and Motivational Investment of the 'Me'

It has been noted that the 'Me' is defined in terms of physical characteristics (e.g., little), category membership (e.g., gender, family), and characteristic modes of acting (e.g., playing with dolls). These characteristic modes of behavior constitute a role, which is assigned mainly on the basis of the categories by which the self is defined; for example, if you are a girl, you are expected to play with dolls. From the start children are strongly motivated to act according to their assigned role. There are three interconnected sources of this motivation. First, as already pointed out, beginning in the second year children become anxious not to lose the love of those they themselves love and depend on, principally (in our society) their parents. Since the parents normally want their children to act according to their assigned role, to do otherwise is to incur their disapprobation, which children experience, often rightly, as loss of love. Second, since role defines identity, to act otherwise is to call one's identity into question. If a little boy prefers to play with dolls rather than play baseball, the question arises, is he really a boy?

Third, the child comes to *feel* the same way toward the 'Me' as others do. Suppose, for example, that a boy skins his knee but bravely curbs his tears. In our culture the parent (perhaps here the father) will say something to this effect: "You skinned your knee; yet you did not cry. You are a real boy. I am proud of you." Here, the father has rewarded his son by an expression of esteem and at the same time reinforced the boy's sense of identity. But something more is going on here. When the stage I am describing has been reached, the boy will think the same way about himself, independently of his father's actual presence. He has adopted both the mode of thinking and the standards of his father as his own, and applies them to himself in the same way that his father does. Since he did not cry, he is proud of himself. He rewards *himself* with feelings of esteem. What has happened is that he has *identified* with the parent.

"Identification," Freud said, "is known to psycho-analysis as the earliest expression of an emotional tie with another person" (1921, 105). Here, by "emotional tie" (*Gefühlsbindung*) he is referring not to the basic libidinal, aggressive, and cognitive attachments of infancy, which in Freud's terms are emotional 'investments' (*Besetzungen*), but to the sharing of common emotions and attitudes with the parent which is achieved via identification.

It is via such identification that the child learns to look at the world and herself through the eyes of Mead's "generalized other," as represented most importantly by the parents, and so enters the lifeworld. This identification is not only cognitive; it is motivational as well. In addition to the libidinal and aggressive attachments that the infant formed toward the core self (and which continue to exist) there now come into being feelings of self-love and self-hatred, pride and shame, which spring from identification. From now on these feelings will act as powerful, though often contested, regulators of behavior.

It should be noted that in this first and most basic form it is the *person*, not the self, who is identified with the parent. The *child* adopts the parent's attitudes and applies them to her self. It is also possible for the *self* to be identified with the parent, but at this stage such identification will be necessarily limited and of secondary importance. For example, a little boy is sometimes expected to act bravely, just as his father (supposedly) does. When he succeeds in doing so he may be praised as a 'little man', who is acting 'just like his father'. Most little boys will be sharply aware of the folly of trying to push this kind of identification too far; everybody knows that the differences are too great, and it is a dangerous game to try to step into one's parent's shoes. I shall have more to say later on the topic of identification.

Conclusion

My presentation of the 'Me' has largely followed the lead of Mead, and subsequent work in cognitive and developmental psychology. For Mead, the 'Me' was nearly the whole of the self. His 'I' turns out to be rather transient and lacking in specific character, and since he thought that the self is wholly a product of language and society, he did not admit the possibility of a prelinguistic self.

The position taken here is that, far from being the whole of the self, the 'Me' is not even a part. Rather, it is a *stage* in the evolution of the self, specifically in the evolution of the 'I'. In the chapters that follow, I shall leave Mead behind, but continue to make extensive use of the very substantial and interesting work that has occurred in recent decades in the field of which he was the most important founder.

Sources

The impact of language. The idea that language serves to 'fill' the contents of awareness has been taken from Husserl, although the view is not unique to him. He eventually came to share the prevailing view that all coherent intentionality is linguistic in character. For Husserl's views on the relation of language to intentionality, see Welton 1973; and Reeder 1984, especially chapter 3. The intrinsic connection between word and thing is explored in Snodgrass 1984. The distinction between the lexical and syntactic levels of language use, which plays a central role in this chapter, is well known, and can be found in many of the works on the acquisition of language cited below. The treatment of object constancy is my attempt to reconcile the apparently conflicting views of cognitive psychologists and psychoanalysts.

Lee 1986 is a good nontechnical account of language acquisition in children. Recent empirical work on the subject is surveyed in Wanner and Gleitman 1983. The evidence for Chomsky's thesis that syntactically organized language is a specialized biologically imprinted skill is convincingly marshalled in Gleitman 1986. (An especially striking study is Feldman, Goldin-Meadow, and Gleitman 1978.) Keil 1989 is the most complete treatment of conceptual development in children. For the evolution of categorical understanding from the prelinguistic or early linguistic stages, see Keil and Bateman 1984; Keil 1986; Markman and Wachtel 1988; Gelman 1988; Markman 1987 and 1989; Medin and Wattenmaker 1987; Mervis 1987; and Gelman and O'Reilly 1988. For the expansion of word meanings which language brings, in addition to the above, see Olson and Astington 1986; Schreiffers 1990; and Heibeck and Markman 1987. Call 1980 stresses the importance of affective interaction with the parent for language acquisition.

It must be emphasized that while I have drawn heavily on the works cited above, the findings have been placed within my own interpretive framework. In particular, for reasons discussed above, with the exception of Olson and Astington 1986, Markman and Wachtel 1988, and Heibeck and Markman 1987, very little attention is paid to the theme stressed here, the interplay of culturally contingent factors with the innately given character of language.

The nature and evolution of the 'Me'. For a review of the extensive literature on the development of the self, see Damon and Hart 1982, and Harter 1983. An excellent overall work on the topic is Selman 1980. Damon and Hart 1988 is more up to date and detailed, but conceptually less perspicacious. See also Leahy and Shirk 1985. Lewis and his associates (Lewis and Brooks-Gunn 1979; Lewis and Michalson 1983; Lewis 1986) label the preverbal self the 'existential' self, and the verbally defined 'Me' the 'categorical' self. But in fact the preverbal self is also understood in categorical terms (prototypes). It is just that the categories are different. In a similar vein, Damon and Hart 1982 and 1988, attempt to carry forward the distinction initiated by James and Mead between the 'Me' of self as object and the 'I' of self as subject. The result is not only a confusion between self and person (which indeed pervades the whole literature with the notable exception of Selman), but also a sliding over of the decisive differences between the unconscious prelinguistic self and the conscious 'I'.

For the evolution of the child's concept of gender, see Gelman, Collman, and Maccoby 1986. Other works consulted on the evolution of the categories by which the 'Me' is apprehended include Livesley and Bromley 1973, and Gallup and Suarez 1986. There is a broad consensus in the literature on the character and timing of this evolution. As with the previously cited works, the authors show little awareness of the extent to which the 'reality' which children learn progressively to grasp is culturally contingent.

4

THE
EMERGENCE OF THE
INNER WORLD

So far two worlds that exist for the human person have been identified and described: the underworld of the preverbal intentionality of the infant, and the linguistically articulated lifeworld, which grows out of, overlies, and partially modifies the unconscious underworld. There are two more worlds to be considered: the 'inner' world opened up by reflexive awareness of one's wishes, hopes, beliefs and imaginings; and the 'other' world, the world of supernatural beings and events, whose relation to the first three worlds is both problematic and of the utmost concern. This chapter will undertake an examination of the first of these, the inner world.

In contrast to both the underworld and lifeworld, the emergence of this world is gradual. In the middle and upper classes of Western cultures it undergoes a relatively full development which is usually not completed before late adolescence. In contrast to the first two worlds, inwardness is a matter of degree. The first step, however, is universal and early. It is the emergence of the game of 'pretend', the anteroom of inwardness.

Pretending

Children love to play games that involve pretending. Some are able to do so as early as eighteen months of age, and it is virtually universal by the twenty-fourth month. Many animals besides humans engage in play, but pretending is uniquely human. The reason is that pretending requires linguistic ability. One must be able to perform a mental act that is propositional in character. If, for example, a child wishes to pretend that a shell is a teacup, she must be able, in effect at least, to say or think, "This shell is a teacup." Two objects are involved, an (actual) shell and a (pretend) teacup, and a connection is drawn between them which takes a topic-comment (subject-predicate) form. We have here an interaction between the two main ways in which objects can be brought to vivid awareness: via direct perception (the shell) and via language (the teacup).

Children readily learn to distinguish linguistic from perceptual presence, for they are experientially and, so to speak, 'operationally' quite different. Each has its own character, advantages, and uses. One of the ways in which the realm created by language is quickly put to use is the game of pretend. Suppose, for example, that the child is fascinated by the telephone, but is allowed to hold it and talk into it only rarely and under close supervision. Here, any object which even remotely resembles a telephone, for example a banana, can be pressed into service. She has only to look at the banana and say or think 'This is a telephone' and voilà! the banana is magically transformed into the desired object. The child can then pretend to dial a number and have a long conversation with a pretend person at the other end of the pretend line. The dual character of the object in her hand (actual banana, pretend telephone) is entirely clear to the child; she is perfectly aware that what she has in her hand is not a real but a pretend telephone, and that the person at the other end of the line is a pretend, not a real person. No matter; in fact so much the better, for the pretend character of the game enables the child to build any scenario she wishes. In contrast to the stubborn obduracy of the real world opened up by perception, the pretend world created by language is marvelously subject to volitional control.

Leslie (1987) has pointed out that the propositional acts that establish and maintain the pretense have exactly the logical properties which distinguish statements about the contents of mental states. We have here the distinction between what Leslie calls "primary representations" and "meta-representations": thoughts (or statements) about the world versus thoughts (or statements) about thoughts. The latter exhibit what is known as 'intensionality' (with an 's'), and take a form such as 'X believes (hopes, remembers, etc.) Y'. The logical properties of these two categories of thought or discourse are quite different. In the first case, for example, the statement 'This stone is a diamond' entails 'This stone is made of carbon', because in fact all diamonds are made of carbon. But the statement 'Jones believes this stone is a diamond' does not entail 'Jones believes that this stone is made of carbon'. Statements about what people believe (hope, remember, etc.) are, as Leslie puts it, 'referentially opaque'. They also have the logical properties of 'nonentailment of truth' and 'nonentailment of existence'. For example, the statement 'Jones believes today is Friday' does not entail 'Today is Friday' (nonentailment of truth), and the statement 'Jones believes white elephants have poor memories' does not entail 'White elephants exist' (nonentailment of existence).

Leslie distinguishes three basic forms of pretense, each of which exhibits one of the three logical properties of intensionality: (1) object substitution ('This banana is a telephone'), which is referentially opaque; (2) attribution of pretend properties ('This pretend telephone is ringing'), which involves nonentailment of truth; and (3) nonexistent pretend objects (e.g., a pretend friend with whom one is talking on a pretend phone), which exhibits nonentailment of existence. "The emergence of pretense," he concludes, "is not seen as a development in the understanding of objects and events as such, but rather as the beginnings of a capacity to understand cognition itself. . . . It is an early manifestation of what has been called *theory of mind*" (1987, 416, author's italics). 'Theory of mind' is a term used in cognitive psychology which Leslie defines as "the ability of a person to impute mental states to self and to others, and to predict behavior on the basis of such states" (421). In other words, it is the ability to take the intentional stance. Leslie suggests that the semantic mechanisms which enable the game of pretense, and which lead to the ability to take the intentional stance, may have an innate basis. The significant point for our purposes is that the game of pretend lies at the entry way to the inner world, in which we become aware of our mental states as something separate from their objects.

Here at this early age children make, usually with total clarity, their first ontological distinction. There are now two kinds of being in the world: real and pretend. The modes of being, however, are far from wholly separate. The game proceeds by introducing into the real world certain objects and events in the 'brackets' of pretense. These operate in the context of the real (nonbracketed) world, with its real objects, events, and causal rules. Leslie describes several pretend birthday parties that he held with two year old children and some toy animals as follows (the pretend elements are put in single quotes):

> During the 'birthday party' a regrettable incident takes place in which one of the animals picks up a cup which the child has recently 'filled' with 'water' and proceeds to upturn the cup above the head of another animal, holding the cup upside-down in this position. I ask the child what has happened. The children usually answer that the water has gone all over the victim or that the victim is wet. . . .
>
> One regrettable incident leads to another, and soon the child has inferred that one of the animals has become 'muddy' by rolling on a certain region of the table I have designated as a muddy puddle. I suggest that the animal is in need of a bath (the children never seem to think of this themselves) and make a 'bath' using four toy bricks arranged to produce a cavity. I place the animal in this cavity and roll it around a few times, then remove it. The child might then pick up a 'towel' to 'dry' the animal. I say, "Watch this" and pick up one of the toy cups. I then put the toy cup into the cavity formed by the bricks and make a single

scooping motion. I then ask the child, "What's in here?" pointing to the empty cup. The child replies, "Water." (Leslie 1988, 202–3)

The example illustrates how easily and consistently children are able to integrate pretend events with the causal rules of the real world. In the real world, as children are fully aware, if you pour water over something, it will get wet. So, in the pretend world, when you pretend to pour water over something, you must pretend that it gets wet. Children have no difficulty whatever in keeping one foot firmly planted in each of the two ontological realms, real and pretend.

Play in general is an expression of what I have called the 'cognitive drive', and which could with almost equal justice be termed the 'play instinct'. Libidinal and aggressive motivations of course generally enter in as well, but the purer the play the more sublimated these elements tend to be. This is what lies behind the effectiveness of play therapy. Through play, children are able to express their strongest and most troubling feelings in a defused way, which enables them to be communicated to the therapist and dealt with without intolerably high stress.

With the game of pretend the cognitive instinct takes a new turn, for instead of exploring the world, the child is now creating one. From here it is only a short step to artistic creation, most notably perhaps in drama, but strongly also in many of the other arts. In terms of the polarity introduced by Nietzsche, the Apollonian element in art expresses the cognitive-play instinct, and the Dionysian the more visceral libidinal and aggressive drives, again normally in a more or less sublimated form.

The Imaginary World

With artistic creation we are on the road from the pretend to the imaginary. The step from one to the other is short but significant. Sherlock Holmes, for example, is an imaginary person, but only a few of his most ardent fans like to pretend that he existed or still exists. Because of its dual ontological mode, as pointed out above, the game of pretend requires that we act *as if* what is pretended actually exists in the real world. In the imaginary world, this tie to reality is cut. If I imagine that Sherlock Holmes has entered the room, I need not and probably will not do anything about it. But if I *pretend* he has entered, common civility requires that I get out of my chair and greet him. Pretend objects remain firmly located in the real world, but in the ontological brackets of pretense. Imaginary objects occupy another world, which is not at all the real world. For all but a few of us, it is perfectly clear that Sherlock Holmes is a fictitious person who does not and did not exist in the real world. He occupies another world, the imaginary world created by Conan Doyle, which we enter when we read about him. 'Pretend' and 'imaginary' occupy different worlds.

Despite this, the imaginary world is not yet an inner world, as is often thought. When we imagine, for example, a unicorn, we think of it as having a physical existence in this or at least some world. Unicorns are made of the same stuff as horses, i.e., flesh and blood. One can even imagine a whole world, as did, for example, Tolkien. Like the real world, an imaginary world can be a world of physically existing objects and events. The special nature of the inner world is not a matter of its *mode* of existence, for example, real, pretend, or imaginary, but of its *kind* of existence: mental as against physical. This is the distinction that is required before we can move from the imaginary to the inner world. We arrive at the inner world, not with the unicorn, but with the *idea* of the unicorn, which has a mental, not a physical existence.

From the point of view of the natural attitude there is a further and crucial difference between pretend and imaginary objects, on the one hand, and real objects, on the other. The existence of real objects and events is evident to the senses, not only our own, but anyone else's who happens to be there. As a result, in our everyday awareness, we experience them as given objectively, as having an existence 'out there', quite independent of our own subjective awareness, wishes, and intentions, and as long as we stick to the natural attitude, this judgment is correct. In contrast, it is abundantly clear even to a three or four year old, that pretend and imaginary objects and events do not have such an objective existence, that they are instead, 'made up'. It is equally clear, furthermore, that it is we who make these objects and events up. The conclusion is inescapable and will eventually be drawn: pretend and imaginary objects are created by an act of the imagination, i.e., by a mental act. It is this realization that opens the door to the inner world of wishes, fears, hopes, and fancies. There are thus two distinct steps here: first, awareness of the object as pretend or imaginary, and second, awareness that the object has been made up by a mental act. Only when this second step has been taken can we begin to become aware of the inner world.

When we shift from the natural to the phenomenological attitude, which suspends all ontological judgments, it becomes clear that the real world is 'constituted' by mental activity in the same sense as the imaginary. This insight, which is the very gateway to Husserl's phenomenology, has the apparent effect of considerably blurring, or even destroying, the distinction between the real and the imaginary. And indeed this was precisely Husserl's philosophical purpose. The practice of the human sciences requires, however, that the distinction between the real and the imaginary be drawn, and that our sojourns into the phenomenological attitude be temporary. When we return to the natural attitude, the difference between the real and the imaginary is evident and unproblematic, at least in principle. I will return to this theme later.

In sum, the game of pretend leads to awareness of the distinction between real and imaginary objects and events, and this in turn to the realization that the latter are invented whole cloth by the activity of thinking. Via this route, thought itself begins to become an object of awareness, and the inner world of one's own intentionality begins to emerge.

The Road to the Inner World

We are dealing here with the transition from awareness of the world to awareness of awareness of the world. Since this transition presupposes linguistic competence and is carried through mainly in language, in Freudian terms we have here the transition from preconscious to conscious awareness. As outlined here, there are three stages in this process: (1) awareness of pretend objects and events, beginning at about the age of eighteen months to two years; (2) awareness of imaginary objects and events, beginning at about the age of three; and (3) awareness of mental events *as* mental events, i.e., awareness of the inner world, a very slow process which rarely culminates before adolescence, if then.

This long and complex transition has been much studied by cognitive psychologists, although instead of using Freud's vocabulary, they generally speak of the transition from level one to level two cognition, and I shall use this terminology for the time being.

The central point that emerges from these studies is that the growth of awareness of one's own intentionality is mainly a process of differentiation. Intentionality is present in awareness from the start, but initially only as fused with the world. We are dealing with the separation of a single world, the lifeworld, into an inner and an outer realm. This is to be understood not as a growth in reality grasp (although cognitive psychologists often treat it as such), but as the evolution of a specific way of looking at the world.

As has been pointed out, language initially picks out for verbally articulated awareness objects and events that are already familiar to preverbal awareness. At the one-word stage, these objects and events acquire the handle of a name, without otherwise losing their preverbal character. Specifically, they continue to be experienced both as physically existing and as charged with the infant's intentionality. As the child begins to enter the linguistic stage, and moves toward the construction of complete sentences, words denoting intentional states begin to emerge. For example, if the child says, "Me want ball," the content of what has been said or referred to seems to be divided into three separate components: the person who has the intentional state ('Me'), its modality (desire), and its object (the ball). By the age of two years, most children are beginning to understand and use appropriately a whole range of words expressing intentional modality, including 'see', 'want', 'know', 'think', 'remember', 'dream', 'happy', 'sad', 'mad', 'scared', as well as a variety of words for pain, fatigue, disgust, affection, and moral conformity. The pace of this development goes hand in hand with the overall emergence of linguistic competence and performance. All this led Piaget and others to the conclusion that by the age of three or even earlier (i.e., when the use of language has been mastered) children have learned to distinguish two orders of reality: the world of perceived reality, and the world of imperceptible intentions, desires, and imagination.

But this conclusion was premature. Already in 1980, Selman urged "the need to be cautious in interpreting self-aware–sounding statements of young children at too high a level when the conception of the psychological self may be still undifferentiated from that of the physical self" (1980, 95). As fused with awareness of the world, awareness of intentionality predates language by a wide margin, as we have seen. But despite the fact that the vocabulary of inner states develops hand in hand with language, awareness of intentionality as something truly inner occurs only gradually, and does not enter even its earliest stages before the age of four. A clear distinction between the psychological and the physical self is not established before the age of seven or eight (Broughton 1978; Bretherton and Beeghley 1982; Shatz, Wellman, and Silber 1983).

The recursive power of language, its ability to focus on itself, coupled with its universal subject-predicate structure, plays an important role in the emergence of the inner world (Feldman 1988). For example, suppose Susie, age two and a half, says "Tommy is happy." What has happened is that the happy Tommy, of whom she would have been preverbally aware as a single syndrome, has been divided by the structure of language into a topic (Tommy) and a comment about Tommy (that he is happy). It is now possible to single out the state of being happy for attention, quite apart from its connection with Tommy. At this age Susie will not understand Tommy's happiness as an inner state, but simply as part of his being in the world. He is happy in the same sense that he has red hair and is good at roller skating. If we ask Susie, "What is happy?" she will likely say something like "Happy is smiling." Via language, happiness has been thematized as a topic, but not yet as an inner state. Further discussion with Susie might reveal that she is aware that sometimes Tommy is happy, sometimes not. Happiness has been revealed as a variable property, in contrast to having red hair and being good at roller skating. The first steps have been taken toward the awareness of happiness as a mental state that has a variety of physical manifestations. The subsequent course by which intentionality emerges into awareness as separate and inner will be outlined briefly here for two areas: perception/cognition and emotion.

Perception and cognition. Initially, perception and cognition are not separated out, and there is no reflective awareness of their experiential basis. Suppose, for example, that we ask our two and a half year old to watch us, and that we then empty out a candy box, put a pencil inside, and close the box. If we now ask, "What is in the box?" she will reply "A pencil." She has reached what is called level one competence in reasoning from experience to cognition. She knows there is a pencil in the box even though she cannot see it. However, if you ask, "How do you know there is a pencil in the box," she will reply, "Because there is a pencil in the box." She can reason from experience to cognition but is not reflectively aware of the reasoning process (M. Taylor 1988, Johnson 1988).

Suppose now that we put the box on a table in a glassed off room, and Susie sees Charlie enter the room and look at the box. We ask Susie, "What does Charlie think is in the box?" She will reply, "A pencil." "Why does he think that?" "Because there is a pencil in the box," she will reply. Here two points are to be noted. First, Susie is already capable of a limited degree of projective identification. She is able to some extent to put herself in Charlie's shoes. However, since she is not aware of her own inferential process, she assumes that Charlie will come to the same conclusion as she. Only when she realizes that she knows there is a pencil in the box because she saw it put there, will she be in a position to take the further step of being able to draw conclusions about how he is likely to think and feel, given *his* circumstances, and so to grasp that since he has not seen the pencil put in the box, he will probably believe that the box contains candy. Many children do not reach this level of awareness before the age of six or even later (M. Taylor, 1988).

To put this point another way, while the separation of the self from the other comes early, and empathy with the other is even earlier, it is only gradually that children come to realize that other people see the world from a different perspective, and that therefore what they know and think will be different from what they themselves know and think.

At stage one children are also unable to make the distinction between appearance and reality. For example, even though they know that the object is being looked at through blue cellophane, they are unable to recognize that it only appears blue and in reality is not. They also cannot grasp counterfactuals: e.g., "What if you were a bird?" "I'm not a bird, just a people" (Flavell 1988, 254). (Here the researcher missed the chance to ask, "Can you *pretend* to be a bird?" at which point the child would undoubtedly have cried "Oh yes!" and started to run happily about flapping her arms and chirping.) The distinction between real and imaginary objects is acquired by about the age of three. As I have argued, however, this is not yet on level two (full consciousness), which is reached only when one can become reflexively aware that one is *thinking about* an object, whether imaginary or not.

Emotions. By the age of three, thanks mainly to language, children are able to locate emotions in themselves and others and to thematize them for separate attention. Note however that location of emotion in the subject is not invariable in linguistic expression. One can say, "It is a sad day (or a sad event)." More is conveyed by this than simply the fact that one is sad or even that many are sad. The sentence says something about the day or event itself. Such usage is only occasional in language, but not so in the unconscious, where when an emotional investment is made, one's emotion is (and continues to be) experienced mainly as a property of its object. Language largely conceals this unconscious process, without significantly altering it.

If a three year old tells you that her friend is sad, and you ask her why she is sad, she might well reply "Because she is crying." Some researchers cite this as showing that the child here has the causation backwards. This commits a dual error, first in assuming that the crying is caused by the emotion of sadness, and second in prematurely imposing the outer-inner distinction on the child. More likely she is answering the question by referring to the crying as *evidence* for the sadness. If asked instead why her friend is crying she could just as easily reply "Because she is sad." Here the crying is *interpreted* as sadness. Children generally and quite rightly confine causal explanations, in the sense used by natural scientists and many cognitive psychologists, to relations between physical events. The point is that for the child the behavior (crying) and the inner state (sadness) have not yet been differentiated, much less assigned causal priority.

Two consequences flow from the fact that the inner and outer aspects of emotion are not separated in early childhood. First, young children cannot believe that a person can have an emotion without showing it. The idea of concealing one's emotions is foreign to them (Selman 1980, 96). Here again, the game of pretend can lead to the differentiation of inner and outer, for it is clear that one can *pretend* to have an emotion that one does not really have. This creates the possibility of concealment or deception, which in turn leads to the distinction between an emotional state and its behavioral expression. A clear grasp of this distinction, however, rarely emerges before the age of eight.

Second, children believe that it is impossible to have two emotions at the same time, even when the emotions are quite compatible, for example surprise and happiness. This holds even when the emotions have different objects, for example being surprised to see Charlie while at the same time being happy to see Miguel. This shows that the child is still utilizing a prelinguistic method of categorization. From this point of view, one can no more be happy and surprised at the same time than an object can be simultaneously round and square. It is not until about the age of seven that children realize that one can have two compatible emotions toward the same object, and only at about eleven that they can admit the possibility of having two opposite emotions simultaneously toward the same object, for example happiness that one's friend has won the prize and sadness that one has not won it oneself (Harter 1986).

Anna Freud has pointed out that before puberty children do not usually engage in much introspection, and tend to externalize their conflicts (Harter 1986, 139; A. Freud 1936). For example, instead of becoming aware of hatred toward their mother, they would more likely experience her behavior as hateful. ("She really hates me.") I suspect that what is happening here is that the unacceptable emotion is repressed, and a regression occurs to the prelinguistic (dynamically and topographically unconscious) way of experiencing the emotion as fused with its object. Since the emotion is more acceptable in this guise, it is allowed to find its way into conscious awareness.

The fact that for children in our culture awareness of conflicting emotions does not generally occur until puberty helps explain the psychic turmoil that characterizes this period. It would likely be a different story in cultures in which such awareness occurs earlier – or never.

The Evidential Basis of the Inner World

The above discussion of the evolution of cognitive and emotional awareness shows that the key factor in the transition from what cognitive scientists call first to second level cognition is the emergence of full consciousness from the system conscious-preconscious. At the primary level of awareness, cognition and emotion have people and events as their main objects. The reflexive power of conscious thought, which derives from the structural properties of language itself, enables these processes themselves to become objects of awareness. The growth of this awareness proceeds via differentiation. As I have insisted, it is not the case that originally we are unaware of our thoughts and emotions, but rather we are aware of them only as fused with (into) their objects. The inner world is not 'there' as a separate realm waiting to be discovered; nor indeed does the outer world exist prior to consciousness either. It is consciousness that separates the two from the one world in which they have previously been fused.

The literature in cognitive psychology on the emergence of the inner world in childhood is by now extensive. A wide variety of research seems to show that this development occurs along the same paths for everyone in our culture. There is, however, considerable variation in the pace of this development and in the extent to which it is carried through. In reading this literature, I have been struck by the fact that the researchers seem uniformly to believe that what is going on is simply the development and improvement of the reality grasp of the children. The inner and the outer realms are taken to be objectively there, waiting to be discovered. In one respect this is a refreshing change from the prevailing behaviorism of a decade or two ago, in which the very existence of mental states was denied or discounted. It is one thing, however, to take mental activity seriously and another to assign it to what amounts to a separate category of being. We have here the legacy of the Cartesian split between mind and matter. Once this division was taken as ultimate, a series of intractable problems and dilemmas arose with which philosophy and psychology have had to struggle ever since. It is these difficulties that led to behaviorism in the first place, and unless the Cartesian view is abandoned, a return to the intentional stance will prove to be no more than a shift from one horn of the dilemma to the other.

Once it is grasped that the split between the inner and outer worlds is essentially artificial, a product of language and consciousness, and moreover that the split is only partial, the philosophical problems associated with the division simply evaporate. Given the strong hold that Cartesianism still has in our culture, including many of those working in the human sciences, it will be worthwhile briefly to outline some points in support of this contention, with particular reference to the inner versus the outer self.

Self Evidence

There appears to be a serious problem as to how one is to obtain reliable evidence concerning the content and character of mental states. Originally (from the time of Descartes), it was thought that in contrast to our fallible knowledge of the outer world, knowledge of our own mental activity via direct introspection is intuitively immediate, certain, and complete. As Freud above all has shown, however, our direct awareness of this world is both radically incomplete and highly inaccurate. We can be, and frequently are, wrong about the content of our emotions, desires, and beliefs, and of course we are not aware of our unconscious thoughts at all. What is perhaps even worse, the two most reliable means of testing and correcting our knowledge of the external world – testing by gathering and cross-checking sensory evidence, and submitting such evidence to others for public verification – are unavailable with respect to the inner world.

The problem of evidence assumes a special character with respect to the self. What is at issue here is not the division between the self and the world, but between the inner and outer self. There is solid evidence for the former distinction, for it is based both on the vast differences in the sensory experience of our own bodies from that of the rest of the world, and on our volitional control over our own actions, as against the rest of the world. The distinction between self and world is evident to the senses.

Matters are not so easy when we come to the inner versus the outer self. The distinction is a dual one. First, there are the public and private selves: the self which I present to others and which they more or less accept, and the real (inner) self, what I am for myself. Second, and related to this, there is the contrast between my bodily self, which is physically present in the world for all to see, and my mental self, a network of thoughts, beliefs, desires, and motives, of which I and I alone am directly aware via introspection. I am also aware, although much less directly, that other people also have inner selves and inner lives, and that these have much in common with my own. The question is, what is the evidential basis for my inner self and its life, and those of others as well?

To begin with, the artificiality of the distinction between outer and inner makes the former frequently good evidence for the later. This is especially apparent with respect to the stronger and comparatively direct drive-based emotions and desires. Take for example the emotion of anger. Shifting for the moment from the intentional to the physicalist stance, this emotion consists of a syndrome of activity by virtually the whole body, including a specific pattern of neural activity throughout much of the brain, considerable muscular activity in both the striped and smooth muscles, and strong glandular and vascular activity, all tightly interconnected into an interactive system. The brain receives extensive sensory input from much of this activity. A similar situation obtains for the other powerful emotions and desires, for example sexual desire.

Moving back to the intentional stance in the natural attitude (the main perspective of this work), people are aware of much of this physical activity, and a good deal of this awareness can be conscious. When we are angry we are conscious of the glandular and vascular activity as the vitality affect of the rush of anger, we can feel our cheeks get hot, our muscles tense, even the blood pounding in our arteries. In short, the anger of which we are aware is a fusion of emotional and physical states. We can also conclude from the physical demeanor of others that they are angry, and on that basis feel that anger empathically ourselves.

More generally, mental states typically find expression in overt behavior, and it is often possible to infer the former from the latter. In fact, the position adopted here entails the conclusion that *every* mental act has a physical manifestation. Sometimes this can be quite subtle. For example, for most people telling a lie involves minute physical changes that can be measured on a lie detector. In the polar case, perhaps, mental activity manifests itself only in brain activity, but even in this case it appears possible in principle (and perhaps will eventually be possible in practice) to reason from such activity to the thought involved. In short, it is often possible in practice, and perhaps always possible in principle, to gain knowledge about mental states by observing the physical activity of the subject. The reliability of this method rests on the fact that both aspects manifest the same thing.

There is another method for checking introspective reports about mental activity which does not rely on observation of the correlative physical manifestation, but which instead stays entirely on the mental level. This is the psychoanalytic method introduced by Freud. This method relies on the fact that our thought processes form an interconnected, motivationally shaped nexus. By exploring the connection of one thought with another, and examining their motivational basis, it is often possible to bring heretofore unconscious intentionality to consciousness, as well as to check the accuracy or inaccuracy of existing introspective knowledge. I have already discussed this process (in chapter 1) in connection with the distinction between the natural and the phenomenological attitudes. The general point here is that the phenomenological method can in many instances be an effective method of exploring the content and objects of mental activity precisely *because* it confines itself solely to such activity, without reference to what is or has been going on in the external world.

In sum, there are two methods by which introspective reports (one's own or others') can be checked for accuracy and completeness. The first is by observation of the physical activity that is always manifested by mental activity, and the second is by an examination of the motivational or cognitive interconnections of such mental activity. Neither method is entirely reliable, or always available in practice, but the situation is by no means as hopeless as might at first be supposed.

Conclusion

Since the division between the inner and the outer worlds derives most fundamentally from the universal propositional (subject-predicate) structure of language, it is found everywhere, in all cultures and at all times. It is a characteristic of the human condition. The form that the division takes and the degree to which the differentiation is carried through vary widely, both between and within cultures. In the middle and upper classes of Modernity the differentiation has been relatively fully carried through, even to the point of being taken for a basic ontological division. This is carrying things too far. As with the related distinction between the public and private realms, the division is one *within* the socially defined lifeworld, of which the inner world remains very much a part.

A very common expression of this duality is the division of the self into body and soul. (In contrast, the related distinction between the public and private self is distinctively Modern.) The soul, of course, has been conceptualized in many different ways. It is not always taken to be purely mental or spiritual in nature, but it is always thought to occupy an 'inner' or an 'other' realm. The division between inner and outer self, however, pertains only to conscious awareness; it is foreign to the self of which we are unconsciously aware, which originates before the division between inner and outer has occurred and retains its undivided character throughout.

When it comes to the person, as distinct from the self, the artificial nature of the inner-outer division is especially evident. It is true that almost all of the analysis here has been and will continue to be taken from the point of view of the intentional stance, which focuses on the mental life of the person, but this one-sidedness springs not from the subject but from the approach to the subject. In fact, as persons, our mental lives are not at all separate from our physical existence and activity.

Essentially the same conclusions hold for the division between the inner and the outer world. From a phenomenological perspective, this is a division within the lifeworld which plays a central role in every culture. From the perspective of the natural attitude, the division is only apparent: a fiction that owes its widespread credence to the fact that it derives from the very structure of language.

Sources

This chapter is my attempt to deal with the question of the relation of mind to world, which has preoccupied Western philosophy since Descartes. The basic insight, that the two are not different ontological realms, but different ways of looking at the world which arise from an original undifferentiated lifeworld perspective, derives from Husserl. (In contrast to Husserl, I treat the lifeworld as the penultimate, not the ultimate, ground of awareness.) My main argument, however, is not philosophical, but draws instead on what is by now a rich literature of empirical studies in cognitive and developmental psychology. Most of those working in the field treat the division between the inner and outer worlds as ontologically basic, and hence overtly or tacitly treat the process of coming to think in terms of this division as one of increasing reality grasp. The Husserlian insight allows us to see the matter differently.

As the in-text citations reveal, I have found the researches and interpretations of Leslie (1987 and 1988) especially instructive. Selman 1980 has also been most helpful; subsequent studies have been better on the trees, but not as good, I think, on the forest. The thing to be kept in mind is that the pace of cognitive development, and the degree to which it is carried through, vary widely from one person to another, but the order of progression appears invariant. This testifies to the innate basis of the development. Distinctly disquieting, however, is the narrowness of the empirical base of the literature, which has been confined mainly to children from the upper middle classes of urban British and North American society. There have been some attempts at cross-cultural studies in cognitive science, but these face difficult methodological problems. For a discussion, see Harris and Heelas 1979. Kakar 1978, Roland 1988, and most importantly Kurtz 1992 have begun to move the psychoanalytic theory of psychic development away from its middle-class Western character toward a more global perspective. For a critique of Piaget, see Kelly 1981.

For the relation of play to what I have called the 'cognitive' drive, see Plaut 1979 and 1984. Other works drawn on but not cited in-text include Broughton 1978; Damon and Hart 1988; Flavell, Flavell, and Green 1983; Gallup and Suarez 1986; Lewis and Michalson 1983; Livesley and Bromley 1973; Michalson and Lewis 1985; Olson and Astington 1986; Poulin-Dubois and Schultz 1988; Wellman 1988; and Wimmer, Hogrefe and Sodain 1988. For phical studies which take a position not far from the one adopted here, see Garfield 1989, and Haldane 1988.

5

THE NATURE
AND EVOLUTION
OF THE 'I'

The term 'I' will be used here in its ordinary commonsense meaning, to designate the self of whom we are consciously and reflexively aware. The use of the term 'the conscious self' in connection with the 'I' conveys a double meaning. What is meant primarily, here, is the self of whom the person is consciously aware. It is the *person* who is conscious. But frequently we are consciously aware of ourselves *as being* conscious, in which case the *self* is also conscious.

The 'I' grows gradually out of the 'Me', in the context of the overall development of the personality, and its formation is generally not completed before late adolescence. Indeed, the 'I' continues to evolve through life, in a series of stages that have been examined in detail by Erikson, who conceptualized the process as the evolution of the person's 'identity'. While Erikson was not totally clear about what he meant by this term, from the way it is used in his works his basic conception seems to me much the same as the one used here, where 'identity' is taken to mean 'the character of the 'I', the distinctive and enduring traits in terms of which it is conceptualized. Since the growth of the 'I' is essentially a matter of the development of its character, this chapter could just as well have been titled "The Nature of the 'I' and the Evolution of the Person's Identity."

The Nature of the 'I'

Three characteristics of the 'I' distinguish it both from the 'Me' and from the core self: its inwardness, its reflexivity, and its association with a sense of self as subject or agent. I will take these up in turn. The discussion of the 'I' as agent will include a brief treatment of the topic of freedom of choice. Finally I will take up the relation of the 'I' to the motive of self-preservation.

Inwardness. The inward character of the 'I' is a consequence of the emergence of the inner world, which was traced in the previous chapter. With respect to the unconscious core self, the child is aware of her own intentionality only as fused into the objects and events in her world, a fusion that is carried over into the first stages of conscious-preconscious awareness. Since the 'Me' emerges before full consciousness, it initially has no 'inside' and is built instead out of physical traits and ways of behaving. Only when the child begins to divide the world into an inner and an outer realm can she move toward awareness of herself as someone who has an inner life. In the process the 'I' begins to emerge from the 'Me'.

There are three aspects to the inwardness of the 'I'. The first is the separation of the content of awareness from its object. Anger and desire, for example, are experienced as inner states that are distinct from the objects toward which they are directed. The second aspect is the recognition that the experience is one's own, something that one *has*; that it is 'I' who am angry or desiring. The third aspect is the awareness that the anger or desire is more than something that one has, that it is also something that one *does*, that the intentional state is an *act* that one has performed.

In practice, an 'I' that is fully inward in all three aspects is never achieved. The most important reason is that when unconscious thoughts work their way into consciousness, they are often experienced as alien and inimical to the conscious self, as inner states that are not part of the 'I'. This point will be taken up in greater detail later. Moreover, while volitional impulses that are in accord with conscious standards can generally be recognized as one's own active doing – for example, when one says or thinks, "I am becoming angry," or "I am beginning to want that" – the situation is otherwise in other realms of intentionality, most notably in perception. The lifeworld conviction that what we see, hear, and touch has a character that is objectively there in the world makes perception appear to be a purely passive process of the registration of the preexisting object in our awareness. Only when one adopts the phenomenological stance, as in hermeneutical inquiry or one phase of psychoanalysis, is it possible to begin to grasp the extent to which the character of the perceived world is a product of our own intentional activity. In short, the third aspect of inwardness – recognition that intentionality is an active doing – is never more than partially achieved.

Though inwardness is one of its constituent properties, the 'I' is hardly ever experienced as something *wholly* inner. One's physically existing body is generally a highly important aspect of the 'I', and this is also the case for many of one's worldly activities, such as being a doctor or being good at tennis. A complete divorce of one's worldly existence from the 'I' is to be found only in some mystical states and certain kinds of psychopathology.

Reflexivity. Since reflexivity is a distinguishing trait of full consciousness, the reflexivity of the 'I' follows from the fact that it is an object of conscious awareness. As in the case of inwardness, this reflexivity has three aspects. First, there is an awareness of one's own thoughts, feelings, and desires, i.e., an awareness of one's own awareness. It is true that prelinguistic awareness exhibits a limited and special kind of reflexivity, in that our emotions and desires are fused into their objects, and so enter awareness in this presubjective form. As we have seen, it is language that breaks up this fusion. For example, a sentence such as "I want an ice cream cone" leads inexorably by its structure to a separation in awareness between the *desire* for the cone and the *cone* that is desired. It also leads just as inexorably to the second feature of reflexive awareness, that it is 'I', the person who is speaking, who *have* the desire. We have here the transition to what Chisholm (1981) has called 'emphatic' as against 'nonemphatic' reflexivity. The desire is affirmed as something that pertains to one's self, in the first person. If the reflexive principle is carried all the way through we reach a kind of second order reflexivity, in which one is not only aware of one's awareness as one's own, but is also aware of this awareness of awareness. One could carry the reflexivity still further, in fact in an endless regress, but I will leave that to the philosophers.

In common with the conscious awareness of objects in general, the reflexive element in the awareness of the 'I' is often not at the center of attention, but instead is more or less relegated to the background, as a context which subtly shapes what is at the center without obtruding itself. Nevertheless, in tandem with the separation of intentionality from its object, this reflexivity is responsible for major advances not only in our self-understanding, but also in our ability to deal with the world. One of these advances is the growth of conscious awareness of ourselves as both subject and agent.

The 'I' as subject and agent. In principle there are two steps in the development of subjectivity. First, there is the gradual emergence of the inner world, as the child becomes aware of her desires, emotions, and feelings as things that are distinct from the objects toward which they are directed; second, and along with this, comes the realization that it is she herself who *has* these desires, emotions, and feelings.

Awareness of self as agent requires the further step of recognizing that one's actions spring from, express, and carry out these desires, emotions, and feelings, i.e., that they are motivated, and that both the actions and the motives are one's own. The basis for this recognition is already present in the primitive sense of agency which is present in the core self, and which undergoes a further development in the characterization of the 'Me' as someone who performs certain kinds of actions. Here we go from the action as something that one does, to something that one does out of motives, and for reasons.

Agency and freedom of choice. The awareness of self as subject and agent enables a far-reaching expansion of the possibilities of action, of the freedom with which choice can be exercised. We are not, however, dealing with the transition, in Kant's terms, from heteronomy to autonomy. Even the newborn exercises a primitive form of autonomy. The difference is one of degree, not of kind. This point is supported by the researches in the field of cognitive psychology to which I have referred, which make it clear that the old stimulus-response model is incapable of accounting for even the earliest human activity. Between the desire and the act there always lie cognition and choice, however rudimentary these may be. Well before the inner world begins to emerge, children are aware that acts have consequences, and they are often able to refrain from acting in desired but forbidden ways if they fear they will be caught. For example, a young child may wish to hit a hated sibling, but refrain from doing so in order to avoid punishment. Before inwardness is present it is a mistake to characterize such choice as fitting a desire to an object, or deciding which desire to act on. Rather, the knowledge that hitting one's sister will bring punishment makes the act less desirable. The choice is among more or less desirable objects, not more or less intense desires, and the relative desirability of objects is influenced by cognitive assessment. The fact that infants always choose the most desired object or act does not in the least undermine the possibility that the choice is a reasoned one.

Once we have become aware of a desire as something separate from its object, the desire itself, along with its relation to the act, are now open to cognitive assessment. We can examine its content, discriminate its features, weigh it against other desires. We can consider whether another possible action might serve the desire better, or serve it almost as well and at the same time avoid undesirable consequences. In short, while inwardness does not create the capacity for cognitive assessment, which is already present at birth, it enables a huge expansion of that capacity, and a concomitant expansion of the possibilities open to choice. There is a sense in which choice is always free; now, however, it can be more free by far.

This freedom extends even to the freedom to choose one's desires, but only in a limited sense. Where there are conflicting desires we seek a way out via compromise, modification of the object of the desire, delay of gratification, or some other measure, and here inwardness is of great assistance. But to the extent that such expedients do not succeed, we must decide which we want the more, and that is a matter not of choice, but of self-knowledge, another cognitive capacity whose potential is enormously enhanced by inwardness. Reflective activity cannot create desires, but it opens them up to conscious assessment, and so can influence the ways in which they are expressed.

A further limitation on freedom of choice, at least in the abstract, lies in the fact that especially in our most intense relations with others, the fastening of a desire to an object frequently involves a lasting commitment that is not easily broken. Quite apart from the institutional setting (for example marriage), in emotional terms such a commitment typically grows out of the relationship in an unplanned way; it is not something one chooses, but rather something that happens. I leave it to another occasion to discuss whether such commitments in general constitute an enhancement or a limitation of freedom and, if the latter, whether freedom is the highest personal value.

Hume was only partly right in his assertion that only a desire can check a desire. It is true, as he held, that we always act from the strongest desire. For example, when we act from moral scruples in a way that runs against our own economic advantage, it is simply that our desire to do good has outweighed our desire to do well. But his famous assertion that "Reason is, and ought only to be, the slave of the passions, and can never pretend to any other office than to serve and obey them" (1748, 25) is not, generally speaking, correct, although it is undoubtedly true more often than might be wished. Reason can both alter the intensity and change the object of a desire. It is not itself a motive, but it can be an important part of the process whereby our motives are shaped. Kant was mistaken in his belief, or at least hope, that reason can transcend desire and itself become a motive. Nevertheless, despite the difficulties, the development of our innate cognitive capacity, in tandem with the self-reflective 'I', can produce at least a measure of the freedom of choice and responsiveness to the voice of reason valued by those in the Kantian tradition. The main difficulty, of course, is that most thought is unconscious, and so subject to rational cognition to only a certain degree, and to self-reflection not at all.

Self-preservation. So far I have been discussing the 'I' in which we recognize ourselves as conscious subjects and agents, capable of mediating among desires, and between desires and the world. In addition, the growth of the 'I' results in a formation of an important new set of desires, which pertain to the 'I' itself. The reason is that (with the exception of some transcendental philosophers) we do not think of ourselves as pure subjects or agents, but as persons who have a certain character. In other words, the 'I' that the person creates has a certain identity, and this identity is the focus of intense desires and emotions. In "On Narcissism" (1914), and for a few years after, Freud toyed with the idea of a separate drive or set of instincts which he termed the 'I' instincts. In these writings the sense in which he uses 'the I' (*das Ich*) is the same as employed in this work (not by accident), and it is tempting to conclude (but not so easy to argue from the texts) that by 'self-preservation' Freud meant not only physical survival but also preservation of one's identity, of the *character* of the 'I'.

Whatever Freud's views on this, it is clear that the preservation of one's identity is generally a very powerful motive, to the extent that when this involves risking one's physical existence, the choice can be exceedingly difficult. In fact, there are many instances when people have chosen death rather than compromise the most basic features of their identity.

By the same token, difficulty in achieving a stable, positively invested, clearly defined and centered identity typically produces or is accompanied by intense psychological problems and conflicts, which not infrequently take a pathological form.

The Impoverishment of the 'I'

The 'I' has its origins in, and grows out of, the 'Me'. As we have seen, the 'Me' is not wholly a product of the lifeworld. It inherits from the core self a primitive sense of agency, of being someone who *does* things, and from the mirror stage the grasp that one is a person like other persons. Moreover, the initial way in which the 'Me' is defined utilizes an innately given capacity to understand the world, first, in terms of objects located in space and time and conceptualized via prototypes that are grasped as syndromes of sensorily evident traits, and second, in terms of events that are often 'doings' of such objects. Nevertheless, the specific categories by which the 'Me' is initially defined derive wholly from the lifeworld. The most important of these are name, age, family membership, and gender. All four of these attributes of the 'Me' normally continue through into the emerging 'I', and in the process gradually assume a conscious, reflexive character.

As the inner world and the capacity for reflexive awareness begin to develop, the child also begins to become aware of her own intentional activity, much of which was already well established prior to the formation of the 'Me'. This activity includes desires and aversions, likes and dislikes, habitual ways of thinking and doing things, many of which have little or nothing to do with either the 'Me' or the underlying core self. Major instances of these are the child's libidinal and aggressive attachments to the parents. These have nothing to do with the core self, and enter prelinguistic awareness only as the aura of attraction or repulsion which radiates from the loved or hated object. Nor does the child initially understand her 'Me' as someone who loves (much less hates) her mother or father. Yet the child has these feelings, and as consciousness and inwardness develop, they become potentially capable of being recognized as the exercise of her own subjectivity, as activities or traits of the 'I'.

Where this mental activity does not run counter to external demands and requirements, or the character of the 'Me' that the child already accepts as her own, this potentiality is readily actualized; what has previously been unconscious or preconscious now becomes conscious (in the first instance via the translation/transformation discussed earlier), and enters the domain of the 'I' as one's own activity or traits, as what 'I' do or am. This infusion enlarges the conscious self to something far richer and more extensive than the already established 'Me', which at this time is also assuming conscious form within the 'I'. For example, "I ride a bike" becomes "I like to ride a bike," and "The bike is red" becomes "Red is my favorite color."

But matters are often not so simple. In particular, the child's libidinal and aggressive attachments to her parents which I have mentioned, as well as the narcissistic and masochistic attachments to her own self, are often at odds with or sharply antithetical both to the standards of the world around her and the character of her 'Me'. What is new here is not the desires themselves, but the conscious awareness of them. Previously the child had been aware of them only unconsciously, and in fusion with their objects. Now she is beginning to become aware of them as distinct from their objects, as something she herself *has* or *wants* to do; that is what creates the problem.

By the time the inner world begins to emerge, at about the age of four, the child has learned rather well to control her actions when they are likely to have adverse consequences, as is the case with many of her libidinal and aggressive impulses. Faced with punishment or (what is perhaps worse) loss of love, most children will on the whole behave compliantly. It is one thing, however, to control one's actions and another to control one's thoughts. At this age, in its emotional consequences, awareness of the desire is almost tantamount to acting on it, and so subject to the same prohibitions.

Two things combine to make the situation especially threatening. First are the fantasies of the dire consequences of the forbidden deed, which generally far outrun the actual threat. Second is the fear of the loss of control over oneself. The wish to do the forbidden thing comes to awareness spontaneously, as if of its own accord, which only intensifies the anxiety caused by its appearance. In response, the child moves from controlling her actions to controlling her thoughts, by repressing them. The forbidden wish is cut off from conscious awareness and relegated to the preconscious or the unconscious.

In psychoanalytic terms, repression is called an 'ego defense'. The term 'ego', however, confuses the issue, and is best avoided. It is the child, i.e., the *person*, who is doing the defending, and what she is defending is her *self*, especially her 'I'. In part the threat is external: the real or fantasied punishment that the child believes the wished for and therefore prospective deed will evoke. But the danger is also internal. Before the birth of the inner world, real or imagined adverse consequences simply lessen the attractiveness of the deed. Now, however, the child becomes aware of two opposing motivations, the desire to do the deed and the fear of acting on this desire. The birth of the inner world makes possible both psychic conflict and its awareness. Moreover, the more intense the desire, the greater the fear that it will be acted on. The powerlessness of the 'I' in the face of the conflict brings its own integrity into question. The fear of the desire escalates beyond the fear of the consequences of the deed, and extends to fear that the 'I' will be overwhelmed by the forbidden desire. At issue are not only physical well being, and the need for parental love and protection, but also the maintenance of the very identity of the 'I'. Repression not only removes the external threat, it restores the mastery of the 'I' within its own domain, and reestablishes its integrity.

It is possible to overestimate the extent of repression in humans. Freud did so, for example, with respect to the most powerful of all prohibitions, that against incest, which in fact occurs a good deal more often than he thought. The early Puritan settlers in America are often thought of as an especially repressed group, but the evidence indicates that on the whole they had active and enjoyable sex lives (mostly, of course, within established bounds), and the same point has been made about the alleged widespread repressions of the Victorian era. Moreover, a great deal that is repressed does eventually find conscious expression via indirect routes which provide at least a partial gratification of the forbidden wishes via acceptable substitutes.

But these qualifications all concern matters of more or less. The basic fact is that the repression of a substantial portion of intentional activity is universal, and these repressions extend far beyond the original infantile libidinal and aggressive impulses that evoked them. Like the ripples on a pool when a stone is thrown in, repression tends to spread via association until the whole surface of conscious awareness is affected, although the disturbance lessens as the distance from its source increases. Repression impoverishes both the 'I' and the conscious world open to it. Only a part of the human self is ever conscious. Much of the core self cannot find translation into conscious awareness, and there are many things about our later selves of which we become unconsciously aware, but refuse to admit consciously to ourselves. It is the same for the whole inner world of our thoughts, feelings, beliefs, and fantasies, only a part of which comes within the domain of the 'I'. There is a profound sense in which we are all strangers to ourselves.

Yet what is cut off is still a part of us, a part that often has a strong effect on our actions. Freud had this to say on the subject:

> If I seek to classify the impulses that are present in me according to social standards into good and bad, I must assume responsibility for both sorts; and if, in defense, I say that what is unknown, unconscious and repressed in me is not my 'I', then I shall not be basing my position upon psycho-analysis, I shall not have accepted its conclusions – and I shall perhaps be taught better by the criticisms of my fellow-men, by the disturbances in my actions and the confusion of my feelings. I shall perhaps learn that what I am disavowing not only 'is' in me but sometimes 'acts' from out of me as well.
>
> It is true that in the metapsychological sense this bad repressed content does not belong to my 'I' – that is, assuming that I am a morally blameless individual – but to an 'it' upon which my 'I' is seated. But this 'I' developed out of the 'it', it forms with it a single biological unit, it is only a specially modified peripheral portion of it, and it is subject to the influences and obeys the suggestions that arise from the 'it'. For any vital purpose, a separation of the 'I' from the 'it' would be a hopeless undertaking. (1925, 133 – I have rendered Freud's *Ich* and *Es* as the more literal and idiomatic *I* and *it*, instead the *ego* and *id* used in Strachey's translation.)

The effect of this passage is to shatter the confinement of the 'I' to what is revealed to reflexive awareness. If I use the term honestly and truthfully, my 'I' must refer to my whole person, much of whose mental activity does not and cannot become conscious. Freud was not the first to point out that we have depths within ourselves which are hidden but which are nevertheless wholly our own.

Citing Freud's *Civilization and Its Discontents* (1930), some thinkers have argued that repression is the price we pay for civilization. This claim is highly questionable if by 'civilization' is meant social orders of the 'higher' kind, for these are quite compatible with, and indeed often depend on, relatively high levels of murder, rape, and mayhem, as long as a certain discrimination is observed with respect to the victims. As Freud himself put it, all too often "the state has forbidden to the individual the practice of wrongdoing not because it desires to abolish it, but because it desires to monopolize it, like salt and tobacco" (1915c, 279).

The argument is stronger if by 'civilization' is meant culture, especially the high culture of art, literature, and the pursuit of knowledge and understanding. Freud held that such pursuits are motivated mainly by derivatives of repressed primitive impulses. No repression, the argument goes, no high culture. But in view of the deficiencies in Freud's instinct theory discussed in the second chapter, this view is also open to question, or at least substantial qualification.

In any event, repression seems here to stay, a part of the human condition which can be mitigated but not eradicated. If there is a culprit, it is not civilization in either sense, but language, which opens up the inner world of our thoughts and desires to conscious awareness. The basic fact is that both as young children and as adults some of this awareness is inimical and intolerable to our conscious selves. It is not civilization that represses us, but we ourselves, and for good reason.

The Evolution of the 'I': The Case of Gender

As mentioned above, the principal characteristics in terms of which the 'Me' is initially defined are name, age, family membership, and gender. Of these, gender identity is perhaps the most basic, not only for the child, but even more so for the adult. In order to simplify my treatment of the complex and lengthy process of the development of the 'I', I shall focus mainly on this crucial element, and let the part stand as exemplar for the whole.

As mentioned earlier, gender is initially defined by essentially arbitrary socially assigned characteristics such as hair length or playing with dolls (girls) or toy trucks (boys). This raises the question of the relation of gender to genetically given characteristics, especially the genitals.

Gender and genitals. Because of the high sensory (erogenous) salience of the genitals, it would seem safe to assume that they are an important part of the prelinguistic core self, what Freud called the 'bodily self' (*Körper Ich*). In contrast, they are ignored or downplayed in the initial definition of the 'Me', at least in a broad stratum of Western middle-class culture. In the face of this, it must be noted that the first order of business when a baby is born is to determine its gender, and that is done by observing the genitals. Gender is socially defined, but it is assigned by society according to the biological fact. It is inevitable, therefore, that for most people the genitals, as well as the other visible characteristics of sex, come to play a central role in the identity of the 'I'.

By the age of three most children are aware of the anatomical differences between the sexes, most notably having a penis or vagina, and have connected these differences with gender. However, as was discussed earlier, prelinguistic and early linguistic categorizations do not conceptualize natural kinds such as people or animals in terms of innate and immutable characteristics. These early categories are made up of syndromes of characteristics which are subject to change, and when such change occurs, the categorical attribution also changes. For example, as pointed out earlier, young children believe that they will be a different person when they grow up and become a mommy or a daddy. By the same token, three year olds think it quite possible to change their gender by changing their hair style and mode of dress, or by acquiring or losing a penis. This early mode of conceptualization readily leads to fantasies that often persist in the unconscious into adulthood.

It is only gradually that the genitals, as well as gender as a whole, come to be seen as permanent attributes of the conscious self. In

our culture this evolution is partly a matter of the growth of biological knowledge. As discussed earlier, the original categorization
of natural kinds in terms of syndromes of visible traits evolves in
the direction of what cognitive psychologists like to call a 'scientific'
understanding based on immutable inborn features or processes.
Other cultures work this out differently, but the end result is usually
the same. Gender becomes a fixed and highly important part of the
'I', a permanent part of one's identity. The earlier ways of understanding the matter, however, typically remain active in the unconscious. Underneath the firmly fixed gender identity of the 'I' lie the
unconscious fantasies in which one's gender, and the things that go
with it, can have a shifting or ambivalent character.

Gender and identification. My main discussion of identification must
await the next chapter, but here its importance for the development
of the 'I' must be noted. In *The Ego and the Id* (*Das Ich und das
Es*) Freud went so far as to assert that "the character of the 'I' is a
precipitate of abandoned object-attachments and . . . it contains the
history of these object-choices" (1923, 29 – I have substituted 'I'
for Strachey's "ego" and 'attachments' for his "cathexes"). This is a
puzzling statement. On the one hand, it is clear that by the 'I' he
cannot intend (at least primarily) the predominant 1914–17 meaning
of *das Ich* as the self, so that one should not read "the character of
the 'I'" as referring to one's identity, in the sense used here. This
is evident both from the context of his discussion in this work and
from the extended treatment of identification in *Group Psychology
and the Analysis of the Ego*, published two years earlier. On the
other hand, it is equally clear that Freud cannot intend primarily the
main meaning assigned to '*das Ich*' in *The Ego and the Id:* the 'structural ego', which refers to a division within the psychic system which
is characterized by conscious-preconscious thought processes, and
which performs certain functions, such as reality testing and control
of motor activity.

The puzzle is resolved when it is grasped that Freud is here using
das Ich in the sense that predominated prior to 1914: the person as
subject. This meaning is quite close to the structural ego, which is
the "agency" (Freud's term) that plays the leading role in organizing
and directing the activity of the person as subject. The notorious

difficulty of much of the discussion in *The Ego and the Id* is much lessened once it is understood that Freud is constantly switching back and forth between the two closely connected meanings, often intending both ideas simultaneously. The relation of this work to *Group Psychology* is also much clarified when it is grasped that in the earlier work Freud alternates between *das Ich* as the person-as-subject and as the self. In the process, he distinguishes between two different kinds of identification: first in which one's *person* is modeled on the other, and second in which one's *self* is modeled on the other. It is the first kind that Freud saw as central in building the character of the 'I', i.e. (here), the character of the person as conscious subject.

Children typically identify in this way with both parents, by picking up and adopting some of their characteristic ways of thinking and acting. Both maternal and paternal identifications are attended by difficulties, but I wish to focus initially on the identification with the parent of the opposite sex. As the capacity for reflexive awareness develops, the growing child begins to be cognizant of attitudes and traits that are at odds with the socially defined gender of the 'Me'. One thinks of oneself as male or female, but finds elements of the other gender within oneself. The consequence is to shed doubt on the gender identity of the evolving 'I'.

Perhaps an example will help clarify this point. Suppose that a young boy's mother is terrified by spiders, and that, by identification, the boy picks up the same trait. This trait cannot be an attribute of his core self, because on the unconscious level he is not aware of his fear of spiders, but only of the dangerous horrible spider. Fear of spiders will also not be a part of his 'Me', for, as everyone knows, boys are not afraid of spiders. One the contrary, real boys can pick them up and play with them without compunction, and have even been known to frighten little girls with them. As inwardness develops, however, the boy will begin to become aware of his fear. This raises the question of whether he is a real boy. Here we have a little identity crisis.

In nearly every society we know of, men and women are supposed to exhibit quite different behavior and attitude patterns, and by and large they do. In the face of this, children identify to some degree with both parents, and the identification with the parent of the opposite gender is often quite strong. As self-consciousness emerges, via realistic self-assessment, such children will begin to become aware that their actual personality differs significantly from the person they are supposed to be, and had thought they were. Here we have not a little but a big crisis of gender identity.

There are a number of ways in which this problem can be handled. A common pattern is the 'machismo' male, whose attitudes and behavior display an exaggerated and highly sexualized masculinity. What is involved here is a reaction formation against the 'feminine' elements of the personality, which are so threatening that every trace of them must be extirpated. The underlying fear of femininity pervades the whole personality. Women must be dominated, and stress is placed on the superior physical power of the male in exercising such domination. The pattern is unfortunately a familiar one and I need elaborate no further. The female counterpart of the machismo male is the 'total woman' whose exaggerated femininity is an attempt to repudiate the masculinity within her personality. In both versions, the gender identity that is worked out is highly inauthentic, because so much of the personality is denied awareness or expression.

At the opposite extreme are those who repudiate their socially assigned and genetically established gender: the male who sees him/herself as a woman, and the female who sees her/himself as a man. This case is perhaps based more on acceptance of the identification with the parent of the opposite sex than on repudiation of the identification with the parent of the same sex, because the attitude toward those of the same sex is generally less demeaning and underlain by fear than it is in the previous case. It is a mistake to regard this kind of gender identity as inherently more pathological than the machismo/total woman pattern, but the blatant contradiction between the gender identity and the biologically given genitals creates a situation of the utmost difficulty. Sometimes a sex change operation is undertaken: a desperate remedy for a desperate dilemma.

Various compromise formations are possible in the situation where the character traits springing from the prevailing identifications do not accord with established gender standards. A good example is the 'tomboy'. Here the gender identity established by the biological facts is not repudiated, and the rejection of identification with the

mother in favor of the father instead takes the form of a rebelliousness against the socially established gender traits. "I *hate* playing
with dolls," she may say, "I don't *want* my hair long; I want it cut
short, like boys." Accordingly, she becomes (and sees herself as) a
tomboy: a girl who acts as boys are expected to act. The deviance
of a tomboy is itself socially defined and even socially accepted,
although in a rather ambiguous way. Tomboys are in part treated with
derision, but on the other hand may be accorded a kind of grudg-
ing respect. The point here is that her identity has been worked out
within the framework of the socially defined boy-girl gender division. She has achieved a rather precarious compromise, in shaping
an 'I' that expresses the dominant traits of her character, while still
remaining (ambiguously) within the confines of social acceptability.

The invidious nature of our socially established gender standards
is clearly shown by the fact that the same pattern in the boy, that of
being a 'sissy', is the subject of unmitigated scorn. Since the male
gender is regarded as the superior one, the girl's aspiration to be like
a boy is accorded a certain legitimacy. It must be noted, however,
that because of different psychological problems faced by girls and
boys in our culture during the Oedipal period, gender ambivalence
is more common during latency among girls (Plaut and Hutchinson
1986). The greater frequency of the tomboy as against the sissy may
at least partly explain the more tolerant attitude.

To generalize on the above discussion, as the capacity for inner
self-awareness grows, children find themselves faced with an anoma-
lous situation. On the one hand, they have accepted a stereotyped
socially defined gender as a part of the 'Me'. On the other hand,
the actual personality of which they are becoming aware exhibits
a highly complex pattern of traits, fantasies, and self-attributions,
much of which is unrelated to, or diametrically opposed to, the con-
ventionalized 'Me'. In trouble-free areas, which will not evoke psychic conflict or run against the character of the socially defined 'Me'
or other standards imposed by the external world, growing children
can allow these aspects of their personality into conscious awareness
and accept them as their own. In the process, the gender attribution
of the 'Me' will be enriched, enlarged, and perhaps modified into a
gender identity that conforms to social standards and yet constitutes

a genuine expression of the person's own individuality. With respect to these unproblematic aspects of personality, the 'Me' has grown into a socially *and* psychologically acceptable 'I'.

Obviously, things are never wholly that easy. The human personality is a highly complex and diverse affair, with a number of strongly felt and touchy areas. Clearly not everything can be brought to conscious awareness and accepted as one's own. Always, and for everyone, the task of working out a coherent, stable identity which is psychologically viable and which also enables the person to get on in the world in one way or another, is one of great difficulty.

Matters are of course comparatively easiest when the identification with the parent of the same sex is relatively strong and not too conflicted. A good deal of conflict is, however, virtually inevitable in childhood because of rivalry with one parent for the affection of the other. Freud stressed the difficulties of the Oedipal period (roughly ages four to six), but such problems are also highly salient in adolescence; indeed, for females this period is more critical than the earlier one (Plaut and Hutchinson 1986). In any event, a stable and secure gender identity of the conventional sort is hardly possible before adulthood, and depends on at least a partial abandonment, on the unconscious level, of the direct (aim uninhibited) libidinal attachment to the parent of the opposite sex, and also of the hostile and rejecting components of the relation to the parent of the same sex.

Gender and Biology

Obviously the genitals and other anatomical sexual characteristics are biologically determined, and just as obviously such gender traits as having long hair and playing with dolls are socially established. There remain a number of gender-related features where the issue is in doubt. Freud thought that active strivings were innately male in character, and passive strivings female. Since everyone has both to some degree, he thought that bisexuality was genetically embedded in everyone.

Perhaps the most persuasive case for the biological determination of gender traits has to do with the duality of the aggressive man and the pacific woman. In this connection, the aggressive-pacific dichotomy is not to be confused with the active-passive. Aggression always has a competitive or destructive element. One is always getting the better of someone or something. An aggressive personality, for example, is more than self-assertive; the self is asserted *against* others, the attempt is to drown them out. A person with an active orientation toward sexuality might well make the first move and would certainly participate actively in a sexual encounter. In contrast, for someone with an aggressive sexual orientation the object of the encounter is *conquest*, which in fact might be achieved by passive means. Indeed, 'passive-aggressive', far from being a contradiction in terms, designates a well-known personality type.

In these terms, while the view that the male is innately more active than the female has little going for it, the argument for the innately greater aggressiveness of the male has more substance. It rests mainly on two facts: first, it seems to hold for most if not all cultures; second, it holds for most (but not all) mammalian species. On this argument, the fact that aggressiveness is *attributed* to males as a gender characteristic, and accepted as part of their identity is no more than a simple recognition of the biological truth.

But a counterargument is possible. The fact that males on average are bigger and stronger than females undoubtedly explains why they are assigned tasks that require the greater strength, such as hunting and fighting. Success in such pursuits, in turn, generally requires an aggressive approach. Aggressiveness will therefore be encouraged in males, then expected, and finally attributed. The socially defined 'Me' of males will include the trait of aggressiveness, and they will on the whole behave aggressively, and accept this as a part of their identity, not because this is biologically implanted, but because it is socially expected. This example illustrates the difficulties in separating nature from nurture in the formation of the character of the 'I'.

This issue carries a heavy load of ideological freight. If a trait such as aggressiveness or a particular sexual orientation is held to be innate, for example, then it might be (and often is) argued that departures from this standard are pathological or wrong. Freud himself was not above falling into this trap.

The 'Me', the 'I', and the Person

In this section I will focus on a theme that has cropped up sporadically in the discussion so far: the mutually shaping interplay of the 'Me', the 'I', and the person in the development of the individual.

The assimilation of the 'Me'. As we have seen, the 'Me' is initially defined by society, acting through the parents, and accepted by the child as a set of categories and ways of behaving that establish who the child is. Usually the child 'accepts' this characterization in the sense that she thinks of herself in terms of these categories and is motivated to conform with the associated behavioral expectations.

Initially, this motivation is what could be called 'utilitarian'. For example, when four-year-old boys and girls are asked why they do not behave like members of the opposite gender (e.g., play with dolls/trucks), they will cite the likelihood of disapproval and the possibility of sanctions at the hands of others. The reverse side of such fear is the desire for the approval bestowed on correct behavior. While I do not recall having seen the point made in the literature, my own observation of children leads me to suspect an additional motive which rests on what Lévi-Strauss called one of the two basic rules of all social organization: the binding force of the rule as a rule. Although they are often eventually taught otherwise, children initially have an omnivorous curiosity about the world. For example, they will eagerly point to one object after another, asking its name, and of course they accept the name without question. Once they have learned that the animal is called, e.g., a zebra, they wouldn't think of calling it anything else, e.g., a horse or a deer. Children are also quick to learn and use the rules of grammar, for example that plurals are formed by sounding an 's' at the end of the word. It never occurs to children to challenge such rules: the rule is the rule; that's simply the way things are. It is plausible that they also accept without question the prevailing rules of behavior, both those that apply to everyone, and those specific to their own case.

We are dealing here with what sociologists call social roles: rules of behavior that go with the various positions in the social order, both those that are assigned (e.g., gender), and those that are achieved (e.g., being a doctor). In these terms the 'Me' is a role definition and assignment that has been accepted in the sense just described.

In childhood and throughout life, the relation of the 'Me' to the 'I' can take a variety of forms. On the one hand, the socially defined self can be partly or even wholly rejected as inimical to the 'I', as with the biologically and socially defined male who thinks of him/herself as a woman. To the extent that the 'Me' is not rejected, its relation to the 'I' can take or admix three forms. First, the 'Me' can be experienced as exterior to the 'I', so that the socially required behavior becomes a role that one plays, as on a stage. The role is accepted, but not as a part of the 'I'. Second, the role can be assimilated in such a way that the obligation to obey the rule is experienced as coming from the inside, not as a part of the 'I' but as an active force that stands over the 'I', watches it, commands it, blames or praises it. Here the 'Me' is incorporated within the superego, in a process that will be considered at length in the next chapter. Third, the 'Me' can be accepted as a part of one's identity, as a genuine and appropriate expression of one's own talents, proclivities, and needs, something which springs from and is a part of one's 'I'. It is this third sense that I have had in mind when stating that the 'I' grows out of the 'Me'. This assertion, however, rests on more than the fact that a good deal of the 'Me' usually becomes incorporated into the 'I'. More than this, the 'Me' is generally the nucleus out of which and around which the rest of the 'I' grows.

Personality and the 'I'. Let us take as an example a young boy who has accepted his boyhood as part of his identity. This means that he sees the requirements and prohibitions involved in being a boy as a part of the expression of his own selfhood. Not only does he dress appropriately and not play with dolls, but he *wants* to act or not act in these ways, and, moreover, he sees such desires, and the actions that follow from them, as expressions of his own selfhood. In short, his identity as a boy is well established. Now in addition to the behavior which is obligatory, and that which is prohibited to boys, there is a wide range which is permitted but not mandatory. He may become engaged in one or more of a variety of such activities: for example, sports, music, nature, science, stamp collecting, and so on. When these activities are heavily invested and pursued for some length of time, they often become part of the 'I', as the boy begins to see himself, at least in anticipation, as a musician, athlete, scientist, and so on. Here the 'Me', which has been accepted as defining the 'I', acts as a kind of framework or nucleus, within or around which the already existing proclivities of the person can also become incorporated within the 'I'. This in turn can lead to further role assignment by society, as the person in time *becomes* an athlete, musician, or scientist. What we have here, in sum, is an evolving and mutually shaping interaction among three elements, the socially defined 'Me', the 'I' which emerges in relation to the 'Me', and the personality. In the process, the 'I' is progressively enlarged from the 'outside' by society and from the 'inside' by elements of the character of the person.

Nevertheless, only a fraction of the personality ever becomes incorporated within the 'I'. We are born with distinct personalities and these very quickly become hugely complex and diverse. The human mind is a swarming beehive of thoughts, desires, perceptions, memories, emotions, ideas, fantasies, hopes, and fears, all of the most variegated kind, and all shaped into a vast, complicated, ramified, and shifting structure. It is a universe. Only a fraction of this whole finds its way into consciousness, and a further selective process allows only a fraction of this to be incorporated into the 'I' of the conscious self, as a part of one's identity.

The 'Me' plays a major role in this filtering process. Those parts of the personality that are inimical to the 'Me' will often be denied access to consciousness, and much of what does become conscious will be experienced as alien to the 'I'. In this way, the 'Me' has a strong shaping influence on the 'I'. But it is an error to see the 'I' as nothing more than an assimilated 'Me' to which have been added only some aspects of the personality which fit in comfortably with the 'Me'. As we have seen, it is perfectly possible, via compromise formations or even outright defiance, to work out an 'I' that is in important respects at odds with what is socially prescribed. Moreover, even in the simplest societies, the lifeworld has a diverse, rather than a monolithic character, and an 'I' that is out of place in one socially defined niche may find itself at home in another. Although the 'Me' is its original nucleus, the 'I' is the product of the interaction of the 'Me' (and for that matter, society as a whole) with the personality, and the outcome can be quite variable.

Self-improvement

As Freud pointed out, in addition to the 'I' of the person we believe ourselves to be, there is the 'ideal I' of the person we would *like* to be. This ideal self includes both modes of behavior (e.g., punctuality, truthfulness) and inner states (e.g., bravery, modesty). The presence of such an ideal indicates the existence of a motivation to act like, and indeed as far as possible to *become*, this ideal person. If the motivation is strong enough, it will affect the person's actions, and to that extent the actual personality will come to resemble the ideal self. It is easier to shape outer behavior than inner personality – easier, for example to *act* modestly than to *become* modest; nevertheless, the scrupulous observance of the one may lead in time to the other. In short, the ideal 'I' can, and sometimes does, have an effect on one's personality.

Usually the ideal 'I' reflects the generally accepted standards of society, the ways that everyone knows one should act, and the kind of person everyone knows one should be, even though, as everyone also knows, few people live up to these standards in practice. The ideal 'I' is often held to be closely related to the superego, but in fact it is close to something quite different, the conscience. One might say that the conscience holds up the ideal 'I' as a model. The topic of the superego and its relation to the conscience will be addressed in the next chapter. The point being made here is that not only does the personality influence the development of the 'I', but also the 'I', and especially the ideal 'I', can influence the development of the personality.

The Relation of the 'I' to the Unconscious Self

The original self, the unconscious core self which is formed in infancy, remains in place underneath the 'Me' and the 'I' which grows out of the 'Me'. With the advent of consciousness, much of this core self is capable of becoming incorporated within the 'I', in a suit-ably altered form of course. For example, the infant's unconscious awareness of her hand as a part of herself is readily translated into a conscious awareness of it as a part of her 'I'. Other aspects of the core self may be cut off by repression from conscious expression, and hence from the 'I' – for example, the 'bad' self of one's own person as the object of angry or self-destructive feelings, which was discussed earlier.

In addition, the arrival of consciousness and the conscious self bring with them an enormous expansion of the unconscious self. The main agency of this expansion is repression, which wards off un-wanted thoughts and feelings about the self, which do not thereby vanish, but remain active in unconscious intentionality.

To some extent the unconscious self may be a more accurate ex-pression of the actual personality than the conscious. Earlier I cited the example of the boy who was afraid of spiders, but who could not admit this to himself because of his conviction that real boys do not fear them. In such a case the quite correct awareness of him-self as someone who is afraid of spiders will be relegated to the unconscious.

The salient point, however, is that the unconscious self is heavily, one might even say predominantly, a creature of fantasy. True enough, the conscious self is always to some extent a product of wishful thinking as well as realistic self-assessment, but, except in some psychotic states, the fantasy element is always much greater on the unconscious level. To continue the example of the boy who is afraid of spiders, his awareness of this fear, in conjunction with the knowledge that real boys are not so afraid, raises the question: Is he really a boy? When the fear is driven into the unconscious, so also will be the fear that he is really a girl, where the fear will become a fantasy.

For this to assume any importance in the boy's psychic economy, there must be reinforcing elements. Suppose further that the boy has a sister, of whom he is intensely jealous, because he thinks she is getting the lion's (or better lioness's) share of his parents' atten-tion and love. This emotion may well take the form of a wish, which is quickly repressed, to be a girl, like his sister, and so receive a greater share of their love. On the unconscious level, the wish to be a girl and the fear that he is a girl will readily combine (very likely with other reinforcing formations) into the pleasurable and dreadful conviction that he is really a girl.

The feelings and fantasies that surge around the unconscious self often have a marked and sometimes direct effect on conscious life. The syndrome called 'narcissistic personality disorder' provides an example. On the unconscious level, this syndrome is characterized by weak libidinal and powerful aggressive ties to the self. The 'bad Me', so to speak, heavily outweighs the 'good Me'. On the conscious level, these can take the form of a grandiose self ("I'm the greatest"), which does not reflect a genuine narcissism (self-love), but rather a desperate attempt to ward off the unconscious negative feelings. This grandiose self often collapses into periods of intense self-denigration ("I'm no good"), in which the unconscious self-hostility finds a relatively direct expression.

The contents of the hidden unconscious self grade off from shallowly repressed materials, which retain a coherent verbally articulated character (e.g., the belief that one is not competent enough to perform one's assigned tasks), to more deeply repressed and primitive contents (e.g., fantasies about one's genitals). At these lower levels the unconscious self hooks into the early preverbal self, and the feelings and attitudes toward this self which derive from infancy. It must be emphasized that most of the self is unconscious. The 'I' of which we are consciously aware is no more than a fraction of the whole.

The 'I' is a part of the lifeworld; the categories by which it is understood and the ways in which it is thought about are lifeworld categories and ways. It is true that the 'I' is influenced in a thousand ways by unconscious thoughts and ideas, and many of these have the character of prelinguistic and hence prelifeworld intentionality. But the ticket of admission of such intentionality to the 'I' is that it be translated/transformed into conscious-preconscious, and hence lifeworld terms.

As for the unconscious self, the deeper we go, the less it partakes of the lifeworld, and at the lower levels the lifeworld is absent, and thought operates according to genetically established and hence

universal modes of unconscious intentional activity. The division between the lifeworld and the underworld cuts across the human self,
which partakes of both.

Sources

For a discussion of the various senses in which Freud used "*das
Ich*," see Kernberg 1982 and McIntosh 1986b. The term 'I' is used
here in the sense which predominated in the period between 1914
and 1920. As such, it designates exactly what Husserl (1925, 1929)
called the 'empirical I'. See also Chisholm 1981.

The treatment of identity developed here is intended to supplement, and provide a sounder theoretical basis for, Erikson's pio-
neering work on the subject (1950, 1958, 1968). There is by now a
substantial philosophical literature on identity, but with the exception of Tugendhat 1986, I have found these studies rather formalistic
and empty.

The section on agency and freedom of choice represents my attempt to revise the theory developed in Freud's early and foundational *Project for a Scientific Psychology* (1950) which, however,
was published only posthumously. Freud saw cognitively informed
'secondary process' thought and action as evolving via conditioning
from 'primary process', which he conceptualized on an ingenious
stimulus-response model. This theory fails on purely theoretical
grounds (for an analysis, see McIntosh 1986a), and is also contradicted by the empirical findings discussed earlier. Evidently, cognitive processes that transcend a stimulus response model are innate,
and do not have to be accounted for ontogenetically (phylogeneti-
cally is another story). In terms of Freud's theory, they act as 'side
cathexes' from the start. But the introduction of this idea, in turn,
would require a revision of Freud's drive theories. The fact is that
the whole theoretical edifice of Freudian psychology needs rethinking from the ground up. Meanwhile, it remains, as the saying goes,
the only game in town, and we are not likely to have another of
comparable stature soon.

The discussion of repression follows Freud, except that greater
emphasis is placed on the threat to identity as a source. For a critique on the views of Habermas and Marcuse on the relation between

civilization and repression, and in particular their idea of "surplus repression," see McIntosh 1977a. The treatment of the emergence and evolution of the 'I' is an attempt to integrate the findings of Freud and Erikson with work on the development of the self in cognitive psychology, which generally completely ignores the role of the unconscious. On the evolution of the concept of gender in childhood, see Carey 1985; Lewis 1986; and Gelman, Collman, and Maccoby 1986.

The final three sections attempt to apply the dual distinction between person and self, lifeworld and underworld in a systematic and integrative way to the area of the developmental psychology of the self, in the hope of injecting some clarity into the conceptually muddled situation generally found in the literature of both psychoanalysis and cognitive psychology.

For a discussion of the ideal self, see Blos 1974. Kernberg 1976, and Kohut 1971 and 1977, have attempted to work Freud's scattered and often cryptic treatments of the relations between the conscious and unconscious selves into a more coherent account. My own treatment is more reconstructive, and draws on the cited materials in cognitive and developmental psychology.

6

IDENTIFICATION,
AUTHORITY, AND
SOCIAL ORDER

The focus shifts now from the individual to the relations among individuals which create and sustain organized society. The main emphasis will be on a crucial aspect of human relations which is widely misunderstood or even ignored in the human sciences. If one examines the literature, it will be found that much of social psychology and sociology, most of political science, and virtually all of decision theory proceed from the assumption that the relations among people are wholly external. The underlying premise might be called the 'anti-Donne' principle: every person is an island. People may be seen as relating to each other, influencing each other, shaping each other's attitudes, preferences, and perspectives; but the possibility that they can *partake* of each other is ignored or denied. The truth is, however, that one cannot understand what it is to be a person in the world unless one understands how, and to what extent, the world, and in particular other people in the world, are found *within* the person (and the self).

The fact that no person is an island, that we are all part of the main, does not mean that there are no boundaries between us; rather, it means that these boundaries are permeable. We infuse into each other, to an extent that we generally do not realize because most of the processes are unconscious. These processes intermingle and interact, but for the sake of clarity I must treat them as more separate than they really are.

I have already pointed out that in our prelinguistic awareness of and attachments to other people the character of the investment is fused with its object, so that how we feel toward others cannot be separated from what we take them to be. Once we begin to enter the lifeworld a new set of processes arises, in which person, self, and other intermingle in new ways.

Various terms have been used for these processes. Freud's overall term was 'identification', and I will follow him in this. In accord with the distinction used throughout this work, there are two main subcategories: identification of the other with one's *self*, and identification of the other with one's *person*. Freud used 'identification' for both, sometimes in ways which cut across this distinction, but the term 'introjection', which occurs with some frequency, always conveys a special case of the second of these senses (identification with the person), and here I shall follow his usage. For reasons set forth below, I will call the other kind of identification (identification with the self) 'lateral identification'.

The term 'internalization' was used by Freud only three times in all (the first instance being in 1927), and always in the sense generally employed in sociology and social psychology (e.g., when one speaks of the internalization of a social norm). In the more recent psychoanalytic literature, the term is often used in a much wider sense – as in Roy Schafer's *Aspects of Internalization* (1968) – but I will stick with Freud's usage. As such, 'internalization' designates a secondary process, built on but different from the two basic forms of identification. I shall approach these topics via a review and extension of the concept of personality discussed earlier.

Personality and Early Forms of Identification

By 'personality' I mean the person's character and style – how and what the person typically thinks, does, feels, and desires; in short, what the person is like as a person.

Despite the fact that much has been written on the subject, it is still far from clear how much of adult personality is innate and how much has been acquired in the course of the vicissitudes of life. Some aspects of this question have become the focus of hot and ideologically tinged debate – for example, the issue of the origins of one's sexual orientation (homosexual, heterosexual, or bisexual). It seems safe to say, however, that the truth lies somewhere between the extremes staked out by those who believe in the biological determination of personality, on the one hand, and the social determinists, on the other. To this it needs to be added that the concept of the 'determination' of personality by one or more factors inappropriately imports from the physical sciences a notion of causation that is out of place when one takes the intentional stance.

The position taken here is that (1) both heredity and environment are major factors in the evolution of personality; (2) these factors can be looked at alternatively as influences on this evolution or as resources on which the individual draws in the course of building her personality; and (3) the interaction of the two factors is so complex and pervasive that the question of which is the more important is pointless.

In infancy the term 'environment' refers principally to the main caretaker(s), who are here assumed to be the parents, especially the mother. The personality of the infant develops in and to a major extent via relatively constant interaction with them. From the start, how the infant acts affects how the mother acts, and vice versa. For example, a colicky or frequently restless baby will cause a very different reaction in the mother than a placid and happy one. Since both the conscious and the unconscious emotions of the mother are quickly transmitted to the baby, an interaction will be set up that will be quite different in the two cases. It is in such contexts that the personality of the infant evolves.

In some respects the early personality will mirror that of the mother. Genetic inheritance may play a role here. In part this will also be the product of deliberate action by the mother, who will teach the infant to do things the same way she does – for example, the way in which a spoon is held and used. In part the transmission will be unintended. It is striking, for example, how infants pick up some of the mannerisms of their mothers, such as a way of cocking the head, or looking out of the corner of the eyes. More importantly, the infant will usually acquire many of the attitudes and feelings of the mother. If the mother is afraid of dogs, it is likely that the infant will be too, and if the mother has a favorite game, we can expect the infant to enjoy it highly as well. While the infant's responses are perhaps far enough beyond mere imitation to merit the term 'identification', they fall well short of the full scale identifications that occur later.

The communicability of emotions plays an important role in these early identifications. Earlier I described an incident reported by Hoffman (1977), in which a thirteen-month-old boy appeared to identify with his father via an empathic sharing of his distress. It would appear that a two-phase interaction occurred here. First the awareness of the upset of the father caused the boy also to become upset, by the familiar contagion of emotions. The boy is now aware of both his upset father and his own upset self. The similarity produces an identity: boy = father, and the boy acts accordingly. However, we do not yet have here a full identification in the form of a generalized and enduring sense of identity with the father. What happened was an episode of the moment, and it would have been the same with others to whom the boy had a strong attachment, such as his mother or even the family pet. The identification is not yet an ongoing structural (characterological) part of the personality.

The feelings, attitudes, and ways of behaving of the other become a part of the child's personality, not her selfhood. Identification with the self (lateral identification) becomes possible, at least in principle, at the mirror stage of self-recognition, where, as I have argued, we first recognize that we are persons like others. Awareness of our common membership in the human race produces an underlying sense of identity with our fellow humans. However, this sentiment is usually not strong enough to overcome the passions and interests which divide us.

The relations just discussed (the tendency to pick up attitudes and behavioral traits from the main caretakers, the temporary fusion with the other based on shared emotion, and the awareness that one is a person like others) lay the groundwork for the full-scale identifications that begin to form during the second year of life, as the child begins to enter the lifeworld under the parents' guidance.

Despite idiosyncratic elements, the outlook of the parents will usually be closely similar to that of others in the same social class, and much the same as that of society in general. As she picks up the new perspective, the child will normally have little difficulty in building up relationships with peers and adults (including teachers) of the same social class, and perhaps only moderate difficulty with those from other sectors of the overall society. The child now sees the world, as it were, through the eyes of others, not only the parents' eyes but also the eyes of what Mead has called the 'generalized other' – the 'they' of the social whole. It must be emphasized that from the point of view of a participant the lifeworld is not a perspective: it is seen as reality itself. The lifeworld is the world as it 'really is' for the members of society, including the newly socialized child. It is in this sense that such terms as 'reality orientation' or 'reality grasp' are to be understood. They refer to reality as it exists from the point of view of the lifeworld perspective.

Entry into the lifeworld orientation involves far more than adopting a particular cognitive set. Also strongly affected and shaped are the attitudes, emotions, and desires of the child. The lifeworld transforms the child's personality. This of course is most true on the conscious-preconscious level, but the previously existing prelinguistic (unconscious) personality is also affected, in ways which will be discussed briefly later in this chapter and at greater length in the concluding chapters.

The term 'socialization' is often used for the process in which the person acquires the lifeworld perspective. However, the deepest and most powerful forms of socialization are effected by additional processes, which usher in two kinds of full-scale identification, which I will now take up.

Identification of the Self with the Other

I have already discussed the emergence of the 'Me', the first lifeworld self. It might be thought that for this self to emerge, an identification with the parents and through them with the generalized other must already have occurred, because this is presupposed by the idea of the child seeing herself as her parents see her, of looking at the world through the eyes of the generalized other. However, while the early identifications just discussed probably play an important role, it must be kept in mind that we are *born* seeing the world as others see it. Prelinguistic conceptualization and categorization is the same for everyone. The lifeworld mode of understanding takes this common prelinguistic basis as the starting point on which it builds through progressive addition and modification. The fundamental point is that both personality and selfhood are products of the *interaction* between the lifeworld and what is innate.

For example, as conceptualized in the prelinguistic stage, a cat has whiskers and a tail, meows, and hunts mice. When the child first learns to understand the word 'cat', it is such a bundle of characteristics that defines its meaning. Gradually the word assumes its lifeworld meaning, in which the identity of the cat is defined in terms of a set of characteristics which are in part are the same and in part replace the prelinguistic meaning. Learning to see the world in lifeworld terms does not require identification any more than does learning to eat with a spoon or to tie one's shoelaces.

In fact, with respect to lateral identification it is just the other way around. The specific content of the initial 'Me', the set of characteristics that establish the socially defined identity of the lifeworld self, is not formed primarily via identification; rather, it is the basis on which the main lateral identifications are built. Those who share any of the defining properties of our selves are in those respects the same kind of person as we are. To that extent self and other are perceived as identical and we therefore identify the two. In this kind of identification, self and other are equated, and stand on the same plane as equals. That is the reason for the use of the term 'lateral identification' for identification with the self.

To some extent we form a lateral identification with anybody who shares a property with us, with people who have the same color of hair or skin, for example, or who dress the same as we do, or are the same age. The strength of the identification depends on the importance to our selfhood of what we have in common, as well as on the strength of the emotional ties (positive or negative) with the other. As we have seen, the most salient attributes of the original 'Me' are generally name, gender, family, and age. As a result, we initially identify most strongly with the other members of our family, especially those of the same gender and age.

The prototypical lateral identification is among siblings of the same gender, and the terms 'brotherhood' and 'sisterhood' are widely used for groups in which such ties are strong. Lateral identification finds its most powerful expression in the male or female adolescent band, where many of the traits that define the members' identity (such as gender, age, ethnicity, religion, and geographical location) combine with common likes and dislikes, and especially a common rejection of parental authority (which greatly lessens any countervailing elements of sibling rivalry), to establish powerful ties of group solidarity and conformity.

Lateral identification usually operates in both directions. On the one hand, I am the same as the other. I think of myself as having the same character as the other. On the other hand, the other is the same as I am; I assume that the other shares my character. A dual shaping ensues. I model my self after the character of the other; and at the same time I model the other after my self. If the other also identifies with me, the net effect of the mutual shaping of selves is that we will tend to become alike. Note that self and other are both 'intentional' objects in the sense discussed earlier. Just as the self is what I believe, hope, and fear myself to be, so the other is what I believe, fear, hope the other is. As with the self, it is this intended other, not the actual other with whom I form the relationship.

While this kind of identification pertains to the self, it has an impact on the personality. As I pointed out earlier, the character of the self tends to spread to the personality, as we begin first to act, then to think in accordance with what we believe ourselves to be. Hence, as first the self is modeled on the other, so then the person is modeled on the self, and all three take on something of the same character.

Identification creates a powerful emotional tie to the other. The other's misfortune or triumph is experienced as one's own. Strong libidinal or even aggressive ties are often accompanied by identification. The complexity of the human relations which can result is strikingly illustrated by Freud's account of the psychodynamics of a sado-masochistic relationship in his paper "Instincts and Their Vicissitudes" (1915b).

Freud builds the relationship up in stages. The first stage is what one might call simple sadism. One achieves pleasure (prototypically sexual pleasure) by inflicting violence or more generally by exercising power on the other. The second stage is just the opposite: one achieves pleasure by submitting to the exercise of pain or power by the other. This involves a double reversal: the aim of the relationship is turned from aggression toward the other to aggression toward oneself, while at the same time, via projective identification, one puts oneself in the place of the other who is exercising the aggression. In such a masochistic relationship, the person gets satisfaction not only by being punished, but also, via identification, by being the punisher. In the third stage there is yet another reversal: the original identification with the other as punisher is replaced by an identification with the other as sufferer. Here the person gets the sadistic satisfaction of being the punisher, and vicariously, via identification, the masochistic satisfaction of being the sufferer as well. This third stage differs from the simple sadism of the first stage in that the punisher participates pleasurably in the feelings (real or imagined) of the other. It *matters* how the other person feels. A full-fledged sado-masochistic relationship is thus a cooperative interaction in which one person is oriented in the second stage and the other in the third.

In common with many other intense interpersonal relationships, sado-masochism is characterized on both sides by a nexus of interacting identifications combined with powerful libidinal and aggressive drives, both active and passive. It is impossible to overestimate the complexity of human relations of this kind.

Introjection and the Superego

I move now to the second form of identification in which it is the *person*, not the self, who is identified with the other. Here the person incorporates into her personality certain attitudes, preferences, ways of behaving and speaking, and so on, of the other, without necessarily being aware that she has done so, or even without necessarily being aware that these traits are now her own. Such identification takes place throughout life, and can take a variety of forms, which have in common the shaping of one's personality on the model of the other.

A special form of such identification was labeled "introjection" by Freud. He saw introjection as a result of the break-off of an intense libidinal (or aggressive) attachment to another person. This break-off can be the result of a death, a prolonged absence, or a voluntary renunciation. Freud especially stressed the theme of renunciation. The famous passage in which he discusses the "fort-da" game played by an eighteen-month-old boy, provides a telling example. In the game, the child would make a toy disappear ('fort') and then triumphantly cause it to reappear ('da'). Freud argued that the toy stood for the boy's mother, whose absence he was able to tolerate without becoming visibly upset. In making the toy disappear, he was saying, in effect, "All right, then, go away! I don't need you. I'm sending you away myself" (1920b, 16).

Though Freud does not explicitly say so, in causing the toy to reappear, the child was also in effect asserting, "And I can bring you back whenever I wish, too." As I pointed out earlier, at about this age the same effect can be produced more directly simply by saying or thinking the absent person's name. In that way the boy's mother can become a constant presence, whether she is there or not. The sequence is: absence, loss, renunciation, reappearance of the renounced person as a constant presence.

In the final stage, the character of the lost person is adopted and incorporated as a part of one's own personality, and the attachments to the other person, which have been renounced, are now redirected toward one's own self. In dealing with this theme, Freud, as usual, is thinking primarily in dynamic and economic terms. From that perspective, what is most in need of explanation is not the identification itself, but the searing intensity of the motivational impetus that accompanies it. Freud's answer is to see these powerful motivations as libidinal and aggressive object ties which have been transformed via displacement into narcissistic and masochistic investments in the self.

The most important instance is the Oedipal renunciation, caused by the anxiety provoked by the dangerous and forbidden libidinal and aggressive strivings toward one or both parents. A second pattern reinforces this process. During the Oedipal period, when children are struggling to control their libidinal and aggressive strivings toward their parents, the parents typically come to the child's aid in prohibiting or restraining the uninhibited exercise of these dangerous wishes. Unfortunately, they are not wholly reliable allies in this project. They are absent part of the time and, moreover, generally have their own problems with the relationship; for example, they may have their own incestuous feelings toward the child. Usually such feelings are wholly or largely unconscious and not acted on, but the child will nevertheless inevitably be unconsciously aware of them. This produces a vitiating undertow to the parent's assistance in fending off the child's own incestuous feelings toward the parent. The process of identification eliminates such countervailing parental traits, and the introject takes the form of an idealized parental substitute, which can more effectively control the child's forbidden impulses than the parents themselves. Indeed, the more lenient and permissive the parent, the stricter and harsher the introject is likely to be.

What distinguishes introjection is that the identification results in a structurally distinct and motivationally very powerful subsystem of the personality, which Freud called the 'superego'. The superego is thus essentially an internalized and idealized parent. Its character will always depart more or less from that of the actual parents, often in the direction of being more harsh and punitive.

Most of the processes just described are unconscious. Usually, all that enters conscious awareness is a powerful aversion to the forbidden impulses, and strong feelings of guilt and worthlessness when these are indulged in or even thought about. Everything else is repressed. Since the activity of the introject is largely unconscious, it readily hooks up regressively with early unconscious memories of the 'bad' destroying father and devouring mother. Here we have the harsh, repressive, largely unconscious primitive superego.

In addition to these essentially masochistic activities of the super-ego, there is also a narcissistic side, which rewards virtuous activity with a glow of self-esteem. Here the superego also hooks into early prelinguistic elements as the child unconsciously feels herself to be praised and loved by the primitive 'good' mother or father. The topic of self-esteem has been the subject of a great deal of research in cognitive and social psychology. These studies generally stress the importance of situational factors, especially the attitudes of others, in enhancing or diminishing self-esteem. One should not, however, discount the importance of the basic character of the superego established in childhood, most especially with respect to where the balance stands between the masochistic and the narcissistic sides of the superego.

Freud often spoke of the superego as an "agency," sometimes almost as if it were a separate person within the psyche. In non-metaphorical terms, it is a subsystem within the personality that is structurally more or less separate from the rest. The structural separation consists, first, in the fact that the psychic activity within this subsystem – thoughts, wishes, desires, beliefs, and so on – operate in some independence from the rest of the person's intentional activity; and second, in the fact that the motivations in this subsystem are often in themselves capable of eventuating in action. The divisibility of the personality into structurally distinct subsystems is of course most readily evident in the case of multiple personality disorders, in which the person forms two or more entirely separate personalities, which alternate in possession of conscious awareness.

To the extent that superego activity does enter consciousness, it is often experienced as self-alien, or at least disconnected from the self. The tendency of the motivation to infuse its object plays a role here. What is decisive is not that we do not want to do the forbidden deed, but rather that such action would be disgusting or abhorrent. The commandments of the superego are located largely outside the volitional complex that we recognize as our own.

Identification as the Basis of Social Organization

I have distinguished two kinds of identification: first, identification of the self with the other, via awareness of common traits, especially those basic to the self; and second, identification of the person with the other, in particular a special kind of such identification, the introjection of the idealized character of the other, as a structurally separate division of one's own personality. The first kind is with siblings or sibling surrogates, and the second with parents or parent surrogates. These two kinds of identification form the basis of every social order.

Stated in the vocabulary used here, Freud defined a primary group (by which he meant a social group that has not reached a high degree of formal organization) as a group of people who have formed a superego identification with their parent or a parent surrogate, and as a consequence identified their selves with the other members of the group. The prototype of social organization is the family. In larger social groupings, the leader of the group takes the place of the father or mother by a dual process: first the introjection of the parental figure(s) into the superego, and then the reexternalization of the introject onto the leader. As a result, the members of the group identify with each other as brothers and sisters, i.e., as peers. These two ties – hierarchical (vertical) superego identification with the leader, and lateral identifications among the selves of the followers – form the main pillars of identity and motivation on which social organization rests. The members of a social group pursue their own interests only within the boundaries of these ties, and when the ties of identification break down, so too will the group as a social organization.

The question of what is the basis of social order, of what holds society together and keeps it from disintegrating into a chaos of warring interests, is a perennial one in political theory. The answer adopted here has much in common with those of Plato and Rousseau: What holds any social organization together, from the family on up, are ties of interpersonal solidarity strong enough to overcome the centrifugal pull of the hostilities, competing interests, inequities, and burdens which, in one form or another, infest every social order. What is added here is a specific theory of the nature of the most important of these ties: lateral and vertical identification.

It is true that one group can rule another and establish order purely by force (e.g., an occupying army). In that sense, social order can be established by external coercion rather than the inner force of interpersonal ties. But to be an effective ruling force, the group that does the ruling must be knit together into a cohesive whole by ties of identification, in the case of an army by the lateral identifications among the comrades at arms and their vertical identification with their leader.

Externalization and the Authority of the Other

Identifications form the basic ties among self, person, and other which hold social orders together. To a considerable extent, these ties take the form of interpenetrations. Self, person, and other form a single interconnected nexus. I have treated the basic processes whereby other people's characters become established within our selves and personalities; now I will take up the reverse process, in which the self and the person migrate outward, to other persons and the social collectivities to which we belong.

It is usual to divide social orders into three broad categories, pretraditional, traditional, and Modern. I will focus mainly on traditional societies, because the features I wish to discuss are found there most clearly and directly. Later, I will extend the treatment to Modern society in a sketchy and speculative way.

It must be emphasized that I am not here attempting to present even the elements of a concrete historical analysis of the evolution of social orders. Instead, two theoretical claims are being developed and illustrated. First, an adequate analysis of the evolution of social orders cannot be made on either a purely sociological or a purely psychological level. What is needed is an approach that draws from both levels in an integrated way. Specifically, once the superego has been externalized and institutionalized, it undergoes an evolution in which sociological processes such as the differentiation and rationalization of social action move to the fore. Second, as the evolution of social orders occurs, it feeds back and alters the prevailing psychological patterns on which the social institutions were originally based. Specifically, once it has been rationalized, the externalized and institutionalized superego feeds back and alters prevailing patterns of superego organization, content, and motivational impetus.

In early childhood, social rules are experienced as entirely external. They represent the way in which others expect the child to act. In part children obey simply because they are taught that is the way things are done. They pick up the established rules in the same way that they pick up the grammatical constructions special to the language. In addition, children soon learn that disobedience or non-performance is invariably met by disapproval, punishment, or (what is a terrible fear for infants and children) withdrawal of the supports on which their emotional and even physical survival rests. The child complies because it is expedient to do so.

Additional motives soon begin to enter in. As described above, the self is defined in terms of certain categories and characteristic activities. Once these have been accepted as one's own, to live up to these prescriptions is an affirmation of one's own identity, to violate them amounts to a denial. The desire to affirm and maintain one's identity provides a powerful motivation to live up to the established character of the self. To the extent that the self is defined by its group membership, the individual is thereby motivated to act according to the characteristics that define this membership.

In traditional societies, the basic rules of behavior generally pertain to a larger unit than the family: a clan or tribe, or even a nation. The rules that define the character of such groupings are primarily behavioral: they prescribe how one is to act in various circumstances. Some of these rules apply to all, others pertain to particular social roles. Taken together, they define not only what the members of the group do, but also who they *are*. Social norms not only prescribe how people are to behave, they establish the group identity.

Ritual activity is particularly important in traditional societies, for it is above all ritual that defines both the group identity and the identity of the individual as a member of the group. We have here what Durkheim called "mechanical solidarity," which binds people together not by the functional interdependence of differentiated roles, but by their common identity as members of the group.

Note that, as I have described it, the superego has not yet entered into this process. We are dealing with lateral identifications that define one's identity as a member of the group, and in terms of one's role in the group activities. The consequence of breaking the social code is not guilt, but loss of identity, of which the most common expression is shame. Superego violation calls for the scourge: "I have sinned," one says to oneself, "therefore I should be whipped, indeed I shall whip myself." In contrast, a typical expression of shame would be to heap ashes on one's head: "Ashes to ashes, dust to dust," one says to oneself, "I am as dirt." Even more typical, and more direct, is the act of hiding one's face in one's hands. The term 'loss of face' exactly captures the damage that is done to one's identity when it becomes known that one has violated the traditional norms.

So far I have been dealing with only one side of traditional authority, the authority of the social norms which Weber described as based on "the sanctity of immemorial traditions" (1923, 215). The other side is the authority of the traditional ruler, in which "the obligations of personal obedience tend to be essentially unlimited" (1923, 227). Clearly, the second side brings in the superego. In the simplest case, the authority of the ruler is established by a dual process. First, in childhood the members identify with someone who plays a parental role, and so form a superego introject. In the second stage, the introject is reexternalized by displacement onto the traditional ruler. Just as the superego is a parental surrogate, so the traditional ruler is a superego surrogate. The motivation for this second shift is essentially the same as the motivation for the first: it mitigates psychic conflict.

In this connection, I am reminded of my experience when I was in the army. My outfit had a first sergeant who was intelligent, alert, and a strict disciplinarian. In the eyes of the members of the outfit these attributes were exaggerated to the extent that he was seen as someone almost godlike: all seeing, all knowing, terrible and swift in punishing the least infraction. As a result, his commands were obeyed to the letter, even in situations where backsliding or disobedience would almost certainly have gone undetected.

Since I was already familiar with Freud's work, it was clear to me that what was involved was an externalization of the superego on the part of the members of the outfit, motivated by a need to avoid the conflict between a desire to obey and a desire to disobey the rules. The externalization served to alleviate the conflict, while at the same time maintaining the wished for control of the forbidden impulses. The soldiers were able to say to themselves (and sometimes to me), in effect, "I would like to disobey, but if I do, Sarge will surely find out, and I will be punished drastically. Consequently, I will obey." Just as the motivation for adopting a harsh superego is the desire to suppress dangerous impulses, so the motive for its extremely common externalization onto an authority figure is the desire to lessen the psychic conflict which superego controls produce.

Beneath the authority of the ruler lies the harsh primitive superego, and beneath this, deep in the unconscious, lie the remembered angry destroying father and fierce devouring mother, who have always been feared and hated, and who are now incorporated within the introject and thence externalized. The psychodynamics of the enforcement of social and political authority reflect this constellation. The angry punitive feelings which the enforcers have toward their own selves are displaced onto those they punish. They are doing unto others what they had wished to do unto themselves. At the same time, via lateral identification with the punished, they can vicariously suffer the retribution they unconsciously believe they deserve. This explains the savagery with which social and political authority has been exercised through history (and still is today). The operation of the primitive superego impulses combines both sadistic and masochistic wishes, and results in a brutal, senseless, destructive treatment of the victim, whose only fault may have been the ability to arouse these feelings in the punisher. This kind of behavior is not found elsewhere in the animal kingdom, because only humans have superegos. The cat that plays cruelly with the mouse enjoys doing so, but its enjoyment does not derive from the fact that the mouse is suffering. Humans alone are capable of such enjoyment.

Such processes also serve to explain the powerful charismatic appeal the most savage exercise of political authority so frequently engenders among those who witness or are aware of it. In common with the enforcer, the spectators have it both ways; in identifying with both the attacker and the attacked, they can vicariously satisfy simultaneously the desire for justice, the sadistic pleasure of punishment, and the masochistic, guilt assuaging pleasure of being punished – all without actually suffering or doing harm. This is the source of the otherwise inexplicable hypnotic power of a Hitler or a Stalin to subject a whole nation to the most ruthless and total tyranny.

The Interplay of the Two Poles of Traditional Authority

I have located the source of the two poles of traditional authority – the inviolable sanctity of time-honored custom, and the absolute unlimited right to command of the ruler – in the two types of identification, one lateral and the other vertical. The contrast between these two aspects, as well as their similarity, emerges clearly if one asks in each case, "Why should I obey?" In the case of authority based on lateral identification, the answer is, "Because that is the way we do things." This is not an empty answer, for the 'we', referred to are the members of the social group. If (and only if) I am a member of the group, therefore, is the group way *my* way of doing things. It is my identity as a member of the group that validates the group norm *for me*. The full reply is therefore, "Because that is the way we do things, and you are one of us."

In the case of authority based on vertical identification, the answer to "Why should I obey?" is "Because I said so." This is of course the prototypical reply of the parent to the child. I can recall being enraged by this response when I was young. It struck me as a terrible reason, in fact no reason at all, but by now (perhaps because I have since had children of my own) the meaning of this reply is clear to me, and the reason implied is by no means wholly worthless. Obviously the answer "Because I said so" would have been invalid if said to me by someone else's parent, and equally invalid if my parent had said that to someone else's child. It is the fact that you are my parent and I am your child that validates your command. The authority derives from the nature of the parent-child relationship. The full reply is therefore, "Because I said so, and I am your parent." As with the previous case, the validity of the reply rests on the nature of the identification invoked.

The connection between the two sides of traditional authority is shown by the fact that the members of the society are almost invariably thought to be descended from a mythical progenitor. The ruler is usually regarded as inheriting the progenitor's authority, often by direct descent. The brotherhood and sisterhood of the group members implies a common parent, and the parental authority of the ruler implies the sisterhood and brotherhood of the group members.

Despite this connection, as Weber pointed out, the two defining principles of traditional authority stand in potential conflict with each other, for what if the ruler commands what custom forbids? In a successfully operating traditional system, such a situation will not often arise, for, being a member of the group, the ruler shares the common identity and so reveres the traditional customs. He knows, moreover, that if he violates the traditional code, the effectiveness of his rule may well be undermined. In practice, therefore, the authority of the traditional ruler is much more limited than appears at first glance. Weber saw authority as inherently hierarchical, but it is clear that the lateral identifications among group members are capable of generating a normative system which possesses an authority which is independent of, and in an important sense more powerful than, that of the ruler. The traditional norms circumscribe and confine the authority of the ruler. On the other hand, the ruler is the most visible and effective enforcer of the norms, and in enforcing them, to a certain extent he defines them. Traditional authority systems are bipolar. The successful maintenance of the system requires a kind of balance or equilibrium of the two principles, and hence between the two kinds of identification.

Authority in the Modern Era

As the size and organizational complexity of traditional societies increases, the task of maintaining the social order becomes more demanding, and the psychological formations on which they rest ramify in many directions. When we come to Modern social and political organization the complexities are compounded. A full treatment would be far beyond the scope of this work, and I must content myself with a very brief discussion of some ways in which the patterns of authority in the Modern era are similar to those found in traditional society.

Some Modern institutions retain the duality between inviolable group norms coupled with the absolute authority of the leader to command. A good example is the army, with its esprit de corps and code of honor which unites it into a band of brothers, coupled with the strongly emphasized principle of unquestioning obedience to one's superior. Military effectiveness requires that both principles be maintained, and that they relate to each other in a relatively harmonious way. The Roman Catholic Church provides another example. On the one hand, the Church is a community of believers, the Corpus Christi, in whom the Holy Spirit dwells, and whose members are children of God, who form a community of equals bound together by ties of love, belief, and ritual observance (sacrament). On the other hand, the authority of the Pope, as the vicar of God and heir of Peter, is supreme and may not be questioned on matters of faith. The authority system of the Roman Catholic Church is thus straightforwardly traditional in character. However, at present, as at a number of times in the past, these two basic principles are not so easy for the Church to reconcile.

The authority system found in the Modern state also has important points of resemblance to traditional authority, although this is by no means as evident as in the two previous examples. By the Modern state I mean the Modern nation-state. A nation is a group of people who constitute a community, in the sense, first that they share a common culture, common values, common traditions, and so on, and second, that its members are aware of themselves as a distinct group. Although Modern nations differ from pre-Modern traditional communities in important respects, they share the property of being a social unit which shapes the identity of its members. Via mutual identification the common nationality of the members defines a part of their selves. The nation thereby becomes something with a real social and historical existence.

A number of studies of Modern nationalism have shown that these communities often have a rather fictitious character, in the sense that the common culture and traditions that are supposed to define the nationality have a distinctly shadowy existence. The often used term 'imagined community' reveals what is going on here. Despite a relative lack of common traditions, a common culture, a distinct ethnic character, and so on, the members of these groups *identify* with each other because they *believe* that they are members of the community that defines the nationality. An imagined community is like the fictitious self discussed earlier. It is this community that is invested with belief, desire, and emotion, with identifications and aspirations. In a psychological (phenomenological) sense, the community is perfectly real, and hence can have a profound effect on peoples' actions. An imagined community may need to be taken as seriously as an imagined self.

While a nation is a *community*, the Modern state is an *organization*, whose members are citizens. The state possesses political authority when and to the extent that its citizens recognize its right to formulate rules and make decisions which are legally binding and which they have the obligation to obey. The term "nation-state" points to a dual membership, first in the nationality (by birth), and second as a citizen of the state (in principle, by choice).

The Modern nation-state is considered to be sovereign, by which is meant not only that it alone has the right to use force, but also that its authority is supreme, absolute, and unlimited. It might seem that we have here the same duality as in traditional authority, in that from the point of view of the underlying identifications that support the institution, the nation has inherited the role of the traditional community and the state the role of the patriarchal father. While I would argue that this is to a considerable extent true, there is a counterargument that needs to be met.

Most educated citizens of Modern liberal-democratic nation-states, and many political theorists as well, would bristle at the idea that the exercise of political authority in their country is in principle absolute and unlimited, in fact or in right. The key doctrine among those who hold to the limited and contingent nature of political authority is the idea of popular sovereignty. This doctrine holds that it is the people, joined together into a body politic, who are sovereign. For the sake of mutual convenience and welfare, via a constitution which they have established, they have delegated certain limited powers to those who govern, and the authority of this government is valid only to the extent that, and as long as, it acts within the bounds so established.

From a psychological point of view, we have here the triumph of lateral over hierarchical identifications. Understood in this way, the democratic nation-state is a band of siblings who have risen up and overthrown their parents (the traditional leadership) and chosen some among them to govern along strictly defined lines. The exercise of political authority represents and is accountable to the will of the body politic: a group of equals who belong to the same nationality and share a common citizenship. The hierarchical parental element has been eliminated from political authority.

While the point of view just briefly characterized should not be dismissed out of hand, it appears to have a rather tenuous basis in the actual political life of Modern nation-states, even those few with firmly embedded and effectively operating constitutionally based rational-legal systems. Especially when the integrity of the state organization is threatened, by dissension from within or threat from without, the ordinary restraints and limits on the exercise of political authority are regularly cast aside. In such situations, as history has shown over and over, the state will stick at nothing in order to maintain itself.

Perhaps even more to the point, the state itself as an organization, as distinct from the nation as a group of people, can become the object of the most intense loyalty and fealty. Indeed, the very existence of the Modern state depends on the willingness of its citizens to die for it if need be. These facts are hard to square with the idea of the state organization, with its governing elite, as no more than a means by which the spirit of the nation is expressed and implemented.

I would like to suggest a possibility, which I believe to be more in accord with the way the Modern nation-state operates in practice. This alternative rests on the hypothesis that it is possible to identify not only with a person or with a group, but also with an *organization*. On this view, the nation-state would rest on two kinds of identifications, lateral identifications among the members of the nationality, and hierarchical superego identifications with the state as an organization. The identifications, in short, would be essentially the same as those found in traditional systems.

By far the greatest ideological force of this century, nationalism, on which much of the power of the Modern state rests, can from this perspective be seen as combining two elements: loyalty to the nation as essentially a group of siblings, and to the state which fills the role of the parent. But the two principles are not always in harmony with each other. It is not rare for the maintenance of state security to run counter both to the moral principles on which the nation is held to be founded, and to the welfare of the citizens it is supposed to serve. Where this is perceived, the motivational force of nationalism can be weakened.

The force of nationalism is often also mitigated by the fact that Modern society exhibits a high degree both of division of labor and of formal organization, and as a result contains a multiplicity of more or less well organized and competing interests. These groups are themselves based on common identifications, which have the effect of weakening the identification with the nation as a whole. On the theory advanced here, the underlying tectonics of the political process in the Modern state can be seen as the interplay of three factors: the network of competing partial interests, the general interest of the nation, and the interests of state security.

I raise these issues not to settle them, but to illustrate some of the ways in which the identifications that shape the self and the personality may continue to play an important role in modern social and political institutions, and to suggest the kind of questions that arise when matters are looked at this way. It must be emphasized that I am not trying to reduce the activity of these institutions to their psychological dimensions. On the contrary, while all social institutions have psychological roots and reflect psychological constellations, once a social order is established it has a life and logic of its own, quite apart from the psychological dimension. Moreover, as the following discussion is intended to show, the character of the social order in turn feeds back and alters the underlying psychological factors. We are dealing with the *interaction* of psychological and social forces in shaping the human condition.

The Evolution of the Superego via the Rationalization of Traditional Authority

While traditional authority rests on and expresses unconscious processes, the rules, precepts, and commands in which it is embodied are fully conscious. In the process of externalization, the superego has partly shed its unconscious character and taken on a conscious lifeworld existence. Since they are conscious, these aspects of authority are able to participate in the evolutionary processes that social orders undergo. One such evolutionary theme is the rationalization of society. As it participates in the rationalization of institutional forms, the externalized superego can lose a good deal of its primitive character. While it is the superego which makes society possible, it is society which acts to civilize what might be called the upper levels of the superego. What follows is a brief summary of some of these processes.

The integration of lateral and vertical authority. Both the traditional norms and the authority of the traditional ruler are a part of the lifeworld, and are therefore experienced as having an objective existence that is wholly independent of the wills or purposes of any particular individual or group. Rather, they are a part of the order of things, like the cycle of the seasons or the fact that the sun rises in the east. The particular commands of the leader form an apparent exception, for the content of his binding commands depends on his particular and contingent will. This discretionary area, however, is strongly circumscribed by three factors. First, as has already been pointed out, the traditional norms place strong limits on what the leader can and cannot command. We can indeed expect the leader to support the traditional norms by various enforcing and clarifying decrees. The will of the leader blends into and fuses with the normative order, which thereby controls his actions. Second, the leader will be bound by the precedent, not only of his own previous commands, but also of those who ruled before him. To act otherwise, once again, is to undermine his authority. Finally, as traditional social organization evolves in the direction of increasing complexity, it becomes more and more necessary for the ruler's commands to be issued in the form of generalized regulations or laws, which eventually become institutionalized and so resistant to change.

As a result, over time the authority of the leader will tend gradually to devolve into a set of rules which he himself is powerless to change. He is the source of the authority of the rules, but their content is no longer under his control. There will always remain an area of discretion, but this will become smaller and smaller in relation to what is fixed and unchangeable.

The authority of the traditional leader is invariably seen as divinely or supernaturally legitimated, and this will extend to the laws the leader lays down, which will be seen as originating in a divine will of which the leader is agent, not author. This acts to reinforce the legitimation of the traditional law. Such factors produce a tendency in traditional societies for the law to float free from the particular will of the leader, or even of the deity, and to be seen as objectively given, in the nature of things. The law is not right because God wills it, but rather God wills it because it is right. Here the content of the law is no longer seen as a product of will, and its volitional character is reduced to the fact that it requires an act of will to put it into effect.

To summarize, the arbitrary, unchecked authority of the traditional authority tends eventually to become embodied in a set of general rules, the content of which, while formally a product of the will of the ruler, in fact is integrated with and supported by the traditional social norms. The rules are seen as having their source, not in the particular will of the ruler, but in the divinely sustained order of things. The question "Why should I obey this command?" becomes "Why should I obey this rule?" and the answer is not "Because I am your ruler, and I say so," but rather, "Because so the rule is written."

The differentiation of traditional authority. While early traditional societies are often able to achieve a relative integration between the two poles of authority, these tend to pull increasingly against each other as such societies evolve historically. Weber has traced the vicissitudes of the relation between vertical and lateral authority in his treatments of patrimonial, feudal, and sultanic systems. In Modern society the two have undergone a rather extensive differentiation, which is most clearly exhibited in the separation of criminal and civil justice into two separate systems.

In criminal justice, the crime is always against the state. The decisive fact about murder, for example, is not that one has killed another intentionally, but that in doing so one has violated a law which forbids this. Justice is meted out in the form of punishment: the infliction of harm or deprivation on the guilty. In a rationalized system, the severity of the punishment is in accordance to the gravity of the offense. The main determinant of this is not the extent of the harm done (though this often figures importantly) but the moral standing of the act. For example, a premeditated murder is considered a much graver offense than simple manslaughter committed in the heat of the moment, and is punished more severely, even though the effect on the victim is the same. The worst of all crimes is generally considered to be not murder (even multiple murder) but treason, which is often punishable by death, even where the damage done to interests of state is negligible. The point of course is that while lese majesty is always the underlying offense of a violation of criminal law, here it takes its most blatant form.

Civil justice operates on wholly different principles. Typically, the parties to a legal action are both private citizens, one of whom petitions the state to redress a harm done by the other. The moral standing of the act is usually not at issue: in fact whether the damage was done intentionally or not is often irrelevant. Justice is administered by assigning recompense, not punishment. The injurer must bestow on the injured a benefit equal to the harm done, thus, to the extent possible, restoring the situation that existed prior to the offense.

Here we see a further stage in the rationalization of justice. First the two poles of traditional authority, the inviolability of the traditional normative system and the absolute authority of the ruler, were integrated, and in the process modified. Then a differentiation occurred, and what was combined is now separated, but on a different basis. The fundamental principles remain the same: the group members as sibling surrogates to whom the law applies equally, which is based on lateral identification, and the hierarchical relation between ruler and ruled, which is based on vertical identification. But the two are now combined in different ways, and further ramified. In the process a further rationalization occurs. The resultant social formations are a far cry from the psychological constellations from which they originated and which continue to underlie them.

Generalization. Another basic principle of the rationalization of the externalized and institutionalized superego is generalization. This can take two forms. First, a series of specific rules can be generalized into a single rule. In the simplest case, the discrete commands of the parents form a pattern which can be formulated as a general rule. This normally occurs as a part of an institutionally sanctioned normative system. The Ten Commandments are a good example. "Honor thy father and mother," combines into a single rubric a wide variety of ways in which children are expected to behave toward their parents.

Note that 'parents' and 'children' are highly general terms. The rule applies to all those within the purview of the law who fall within these broad categories. The generality of the law feeds into the other basic principle, equality before the law (the peer principle). In addition, generalization can act to extend the size of the group to whom the law applies. Originally, traditional norms (or laws) apply only to members of the group (tribe, clan, family, etc.). In time the area may widen, especially if traditional rule takes on an imperial character. An important further generalization occurs in the Modern idea of citizenship. Finally, the way in which governments rule their citizens can be seen as subject to certain moral rules which extend to all humanity, as in the contemporary idea of human rights.

The Internalization of the Externalized Superego

The materials of the previous sections have laid the groundwork for a treatment of the process of internalization in which the already existing superego is reshaped. This process is much more variable in importance than the original formation of the superego, both among individuals and among societies. It has been fairly widespread in Modern Western bourgeois culture, although perhaps less so than is often thought.

Let us assume that we have before us a society in which at least a modest degree of rationalization has been achieved, at a minimum that there is a set of rules which its members are consciously aware of and recognize as rightful, and that the enforcement of these rules has been institutionalized at least to the extent that specific people are charged with specific tasks in the administration of justice. These people may be heads of families or clans, kings, policemen, judges, and so on.

As they mature, children will gradually become aware of this normative system and its institutionalized expressions. Generally, this will first occur in connection with the parents. Earlier, before the child has begun to enter into the lifeworld, commands and prohibitions of the parents will not form any clear general pattern. At most the generalization will extend to the awareness that the parents prohibit certain acts and require others. It is these arbitrary dictators with whom children identify in order to control their dangerous impulses. With the growth of conscious awareness, children begin to enter the lifeworld, and to understand what is going on in lifeworld terms. In particular, the parents can *explain* why they command some things and prohibit others. Mark Twain once remarked that at the age of fifteen he thought his parents were idiots, but by the age of twenty-five he found that their intelligence had improved markedly. The way in which one's parents change must be even more striking between the ages of three and thirteen.

In addition, children become aware that the rules taught them by their parents did not originate with them, but rather are believed in and more or less observed by all grown-ups and even older children. The rule loses its personal quality and becomes a part of the ordained order of things. It then becomes possible to believe that these rules should be obeyed not only to avoid punishment, but also because they are rightful in themselves. The legitimacy of the rule itself, as distinct from its perceived coercive backing, may begin to effect its observance. Here the rationalized externalized superego begins to become reinternalized as a conscience. The rules are incorporated within the motivational system of the individual, and acquire a binding force which operates independently from the social incentives and sanctions which support them.

The conscience is often mistakenly identified with the superego, but in fact, though interconnected, the two are quite different. Freud made the distinction, but did not work it out in any detail, and at one point said that it was not of great importance (1930, 136). Schafer, I think, is more on the mark when he writes,

> now we are able to see that superego is not morality at all, nor can morality grow out of it alone, for superego is fierce, irrational, mostly unconscious, with vindictiveness against oneself for wishes and ambitions that threaten to bring one into archaically conceived, infantile danger situations. . . . It is mostly a demonic aspect of mind. (1974, 465)

In traditional societies, the content of the normative system is always a far cry from what is found in the primitive unconscious superego. We may take the Ten Commandments of the Pentateuch as an example. Although there is a generalized prohibition of killing, there is no specific commandment not to murder one's parents, and the transgression of incest is not even mentioned. The basic prohibitions of the primitive superego against such acts are already presupposed, to the extent that they need not be explicitly stated. The main lines of the primitive superego are laid down in the four- to six-year-old period. The introject is something that the *child* sets up, in order to defend against intolerable anxiety. In contrast, socialization in the sense of the internalization of established social values rarely begins before eight, and the decisive period is generally in adolescence. Internalization is a secondary development, and the resulting motivational system is a conscious formation which overlays, is connected with, but is not the same as, the largely unconscious superego. It is, so to speak, a superstructure built on top of the superego, a partially autonomous system of motives, which guides, or seeks to guide, the individual's action along paths of morality and rectitude. The autonomy is only partial because the motivational impetus is derived from the superego, and so subject to its influence. For this very reason, however, the conscience can lead to actions which run counter to wishes and desires which derive from that part of the personality which lies outside the superego.

It is easy to overestimate the extent to which, in the general run of humanity, behavior is governed by such internalized norms. In all social orders, the mainstay for obedience to the normative order and the commands of those in authority is fear of divine or human retribution. The conscience is not an inevitable or universal result of human psychological development, but instead arises as a widespread pattern only where social and political authority have undergone a fair degree of rationalization. Conscience is the product of a journey, in which the primitive superego is externalized, rationalized, and then reinternalized.

There is no doubt that in some strata of some societies the conscience is a motivational force which operates independently of the socially defined sanctions. However, because it draws its motivational strength from the primitive superego, the conscience comes under its influence. Out of the frying pan into the fire: as the internalized standards shake free of the fear of external sanctions, they come to be enforced by the fear of the punitive primitive superego. On the conscious level, transgression of the dictates of conscience evokes powerful feelings of guilt and worthlessness. The unconscious superego has taken back the task of enforcement.

Since the conscience arises as an internalization of prevailing social norms, it motivates the individual to comply with social and political authority independently of external sanctions. This has major consequences for social organization, for it enables much more far-reaching processes of social coordination and control than is possible through external sanctions alone. This theme has been developed by a number of authors, stretching from Plato to Talcott Parsons, and I shall not pursue it further here.

The conscience takes its most common and potentially its strongest form in a religious guise. For many, of course, obedience to the divinely ordained code is motivated by fear of retribution and hope of reward, which is still at the level of the externalized superego, now rationalized into a set of generalized rules of conduct. From the point of view of a more sophisticated religious sensibility, however, true belief requires the inner acceptance, in addition to the outer observance, of God's word, an attitude that reflects at least a partial internalization. The voice of God, moreover, is not infrequently experienced as a "still small voice" from within (an experience that is also found in the purely secular conscience).

I have emphasized the social origins of the conscience; it consists of the norms of a social group grafted onto the individual's superego, which thereby assume a motivational force independent of outer compulsions and sanctions. This holds even for those who resist established political or religious authority in the name of conscience, for the value they uphold is always a group value, often a value professed but not practiced by those against whom they rebel. Even the extreme individualist who stands alone against the crowd is no exception. The story is told, for example, of a visit of Emerson to Thoreau, who was in jail for refusing to pay his taxes, in protest against the U.S. invasion of Mexico. "Henry," Emerson is reported to have asked, "what are you doing in jail?" to which Thoreau is said to have replied, "Ralph, what are you doing *out* of jail?" The point is that the values for which Thoreau was in jail were also held by Emerson, and many others besides, though with a lower priority. A conscience that does not reflect the internalized values of some social group or other must be regarded as exceedingly rare, and very likely a pathological symptom.

The degree to which the externalized and rationalized superego is internalized as a conscience varies from society to society and individual to individual. Even where a substantial internalization has occurred, the conscience is often unable to draw sufficient motivational support from the superego to produce the prescribed behavior. Normally, external reinforcement is required as well. Freud recognized this point. He drew a distinction between the basic superego prohibitions against murder and incest, and the prevailing socially established standards of good behavior. The former, he thought, are generally observed,

> But the case is altered when we turn to the other instinctual claims. Here we observe with surprise and concern that a majority of people obey the cultural prohibitions on these points only under the pressure of external coercion – that is, only where that coercion can make itself effective and so long as it is to be feared. . . . There are countless civilized people who would shrink from murder or incest but who do not deny themselves the satisfaction of their avarice, their aggressive urges or their sexual lusts, and who do not hesitate to injure other people by lies, fraud, and calumny, so long as they can remain unpunished for it; and this, no doubt, has always been so through many ages of civilization. (1927, 11–12)

Freud underestimated the extent to which incest takes place, but his general point is valid. The motivational force of the conscience is much weaker than the basic superego prohibitions that were established earlier. He failed to realize that even the latter are far from infallible in their operation.

The degree to which the conscience is integrated with the rest of the personality is also generally quite limited. The fact that most of us so often feel a conflict between what we want to do and what we know we ought to do (and perhaps also want to do), clearly shows the structural division within the psyche between the two aspects of our personalities. Even the most saintly character can feel such conflict.

Usually the conscience is also experienced as alien from the self. Sometimes it takes the form of a voice, either from the outside or, more usually from the inside, as the inner voice that I mentioned earlier. Socrates is a famous example. In the case where the voice is speaking from 'inside me' a partial integration has taken place.

However, it is generally not 'I' who speaks, but a voice inside me that speaks *to* me.

More often, the conscience asserts itself as a belief that certain things are right or wrong in themselves. The way in which this is conceptualized can take many forms, but what these have in common is the view that there is some objective or authoritative standard that is outside the self. This does not mean that the conscience is not internalized: it is a part of the personality, but not experienced as a part of the self. On the other hand, the act of standing firmly for what one believes to be right, against the opposition of others, and even against one's own desires, can be experienced as an affirmation of one's selfhood, a way of upholding not only one's integrity but also one's very identity. Here the conscience is experienced as one's true self.

The concept of the conscience, as developed here, is not to be confused with the idea of the autonomous superego, as developed in the post-Freudian psychoanalytic literature. Here 'autonomy' can mean independence either from the surrounding lifeworld or from unconscious ideas and motivations. In both cases, the degree of autonomy that is possible in practice is quite limited. With respect to the outer world, as I have argued, while the conscience can achieve substantial independence from the influence of external coercion, its content always reveals its social origin. Basically, the individual conscience is a set of internalized social norms. All that is possible for the individual is a modest amount of idealization, rationalization, and selectivity. On the motivational side, if the conscience is to achieve more than a minimal strength, it needs to be backed by the primitive superego. Underneath the conscious desire to do right 'for its own sake' always lie both fear and desire: fear of punishment by the angry introject and desire for the affection of the loving introject. It is this stratum that must be tapped if the individual conscience is to become strong. The notion that one can be wholly autonomous either from the lifeworld or from the underworld is a chimera. Both of them enter too deeply into our inmost being. It is the human condition to be both in and of both worlds.

—— Sources

Identification and the superego. Freud's treatments of identification, which are scattered through a number of his works, are often difficult to understand in themselves, and even more difficult to square with each other. There is an extensive subsequent literature on the topic (see Meissner 1970–72, and Brenner 1982), which in my opinion has not improved matters noticeably. The main culprit is the widespread and inappropriate use of 'internalization' (e.g., Loewald 1962; Schafer 1968; Meissner 1980; and McDevitt and Mahler 1986). As mentioned in the text, I have stayed with Freud's much narrower sense of that term, which accords with the meaning generally assigned in sociology and social psychology. Sandler 1960 distinguishes between introjection, by which the superego is formed, and identification, which shapes the ego, but the exact nature of the second process is not clear, because Freud's discussions are difficult to square with each other. For example, in the passage in *The Ego and the Id* discussed in the previous chapter (1923, 29), it seems that the identification processes that shape the ego are the same as those that shape the superego.

The interpretation presented here is my own, and has cost me much effort. It was the distinction between the person and the self that finally unlocked the puzzle, and enabled Freud's scattered discussions to emerge for me as a coherent whole. It must be emphasized that this distinction is made explicitly by Freud only in a few passages in the 1914–1915 essays (see McIntosh 1986b). It is usually only implicit at best, and often needs to be read in. Once the distinction is firmly grasped, however, it seems to me that what Freud is saying is always perfectly clear.

For the purposes of this work, the main source is *Group Psychology and the Analysis of the Ego* (1921), in which Freud describes the two forms of identification, and argues that they are the basis of all social organization. In that work, however, he had not fully worked out his theory of the superego. His later discussions (especially in *The Ego and the Id*) need to be read in the light of the *Group Psychology*, and vice versa. The whole picture does not emerge until one has also factored in the 1914–1917 essays.

The theme of the pre-Oedipal precursors of the superego has received a good deal of attention in the post-Freudian literature (e.g., Jacobson 1964), but the term 'precursor' strikes me as too strong. As discussed in the text, some degree of identification with the person undoubtedly begins very early, but the central characteristic of the superego, the judgmental attitude toward the self, cannot begin to take shape before the syntactic level of language is achieved, for it is this that sets the stage for the Oedipal period. On this view, the undoubtedly very important primitive (pre-Oedipal) aspects of the superego can be accounted for as a result of the regressions that follow the massive repressions of the Oedipal period.

Externalization and the authority of the other. This section is an attempt to integrate Freud's theories of identification with the views of Weber and Durkheim on the nature of the basic ties that hold social orders together and give them their character. The best known attempt to understand the basis of social order in psychoanalytic terms is that of Talcott Parsons, who also draws heavily from Weber and Durkheim. Parsons's account, however, is flawed by a serious misreading of Freud's theory of the superego, which he sees as formed by the internalization of social norms (e.g., 1952). But the existence of such norms *presupposes* the superego. The problem is not Parsons's account of internalization, which is much the same as the one developed in this chapter, but his view of the superego as the product of internalization. In fact, what gets internalized is a system of values which overlays the *already existing* superego, is *more or less* integrated with it, and which draws its motivational force from it *to a greater or lesser degree.* Freud made this clear in the passage in *The Future of an Illusion* (1927, 11–12) in which he first used the term 'internalization'. This conclusion is supported by the developmental timetable that emerges from the literature in cognitive psychology cited in previous chapters (stage one: development of the superego, stage two: internalization of social norms). For a good critique of Parson's views, see Lavine 1981, and Golding 1982. Lavine's treatment of the superego is excellent, except that he sees archaic objects such as the bad mother as internal, which they are not (McIntosh 1993). For a defense of using psychological ideas in sociological analysis, see Harris and Heelas 1979.

As Parsons has pointed out in his introduction to Weber 1923b (24–27), Weber's ideal typical analyses lack but invite a psychological underpinning. Weber saw the system of legitimacy that underlies traditional social systems as bipolar in nature, and the theme continues in his analyses of all other systems except the Modern. My strategy has been to ground this bipolarity on the two types of identification set forth by Freud, and to extend the analysis to Modernity. For a more detailed treatment of this theme, see my 1970 article.

The evolution and rationalization of systems of authority. Here again I have drawn on Durkheim (1893 and 1912), and Weber (mainly *Economy and Society,* 1923a, and the papers in *From Max Weber,* 1946). Weber's analysis of the ideal typical basis of rational-legal authority in the Modern era was never carried through, however, and here I have struck out on my own in a speculative way.

The literature on Weber, in my opinion, is more notable for its quantity than its quality. Weber himself must take a good measure of the blame. With the exception of *The Protestant Ethic and the Spirit of Capitalism* and his twin lectures, "Politics as a Vocation" and "Science as a Vocation," his writings present severe difficulties for the reader. The main line of the argument is typically buried beneath a mass of illustrations, qualifications, exceptions, and digressions. Often his main point emerges only fleetingly in a subordinate clause. Moreover, Weber's methodological works are distinctly misleading. As a student, I once heard Marcuse say that Weber was a great sociological analyst but a second-rate methodologist, and it was not until the force of this remark had begun to sink in that Weber's works started to open up for me.

In particular, it is a mistake to take Weber at face value when he says, "All serious reflection about the ultimate elements of meaningful human conduct is oriented primarily in terms of the categories 'end' and 'means'" (1949, 52). Schluchter's (1981) well-known critique of Weber makes this mistake. Habermas's (1981a) treatment follows Schluchter closely. The result is a seriously one-sided account of his thought. For example, they completely misunderstand the important concept of *Gesinnungsethik* (inappropriately translated by Parsons as the "ethic of ultimate ends") and, largely as a result, conflate the quite different distinctions between formal and substantive rationality, on the one hand, and value and goal rationality, on the other.

In practice, Weber's use of the key concept of rationalization is far more flexible and multifaceted than the methodological discussions would indicate. As a result, while Weber's discussions are often brilliant and insightful, they are not contained within a fully coherent overall theory. Any attempt to make sense of Weber as a whole must of necessity be reconstructive. My own reconstructive interpretation is presented in my 1977b and 1983 articles. In the present work I have employed this interpretation without any further defense.

On balance, despite the criticisms that have been leveled at them, I have found Parsons's treatments of Weber the most helpful, especially his introduction to *The Sociology of Religion* (1923c). Tenbruck (1980) has also been influential. See also Max Rheinstein's excellent introduction to Weber 1954.

For the 'imagined communities' on which nationalism is often based, see Anderson 1983. It is common to understand nationalism as permeated by myth and mythic thinking. The phenomenon, however, will never be understood as long as myth is taken in the vulgar sense of an untrue story without substantial factual basis (e.g., Hobsbawm 1990).

On the evolution of the externalized superego, see Jung's *Answer to Job* (1954), which traces how Jehovah's character changed over time as a response to the ever deepening moral insight of the Jews.

7 THE WORLD OF THE SACRED

The central theme of this work is the interaction between the unconscious and the conscious-preconscious levels of human experience. In chapters 2–5 I traced the role that this interaction plays in the growth of the human person and the human self, examined the division between the conscious and unconscious levels of person and self, and explored some of the interrelations among them. These chapters described in some detail how two worlds arise for the individual: the underworld, which opens up to unconscious intentionality, and the lifeworld, which presents itself to conscious awareness as something already objectively there, which the individual enters and partakes of. In chapter 6 the scope of analysis was enlarged via a treatment of the ways in which persons and their selves are tied together into collectivities by two kinds of identification. In addition, the notion of the lifeworld lost its static given quality, and was pictured as evolving historically. In this chapter I will enlarge the canvas still further. The underworld, the world of the unconscious, will be treated not only as something that pertains to the individual, but also as an evolving social phenomenon, and the issue of how the lifeworld itself arises and interacts with this collective underworld will be addressed.

On the social level, the main interface between the unconscious and the conscious-preconscious lies in a special region of the lifeworld, which is experienced by its members as the other world, the world of the sacred. The division between this world and the other world, between the profane and the sacred, is at the core of all magical and religious thought and action, and the most basic expression of these, in turn, is the myth and the mythic symbol. It is in myth and mythic thinking that the unconscious shines through and expresses itself in the lifeworld as a social, not an individual, phenomenon. I will begin with an analysis of the experiential basis and the characteristic modes of thought of magic and religion. Next I will examine the unconscious roots of these. Then I will discuss the basically interpretive stance of magico-religious thought and practice. I will close with a treatment of the role of myth and mythic thinking in building a two-way bridge between the unconscious underworld and the conscious lifeworld.

The Experience of the Sacred

It is widely believed that religion has moved to the periphery of our contemporary lifeworld, at least in advanced industrial society. The most powerful expression of this idea has been Max Weber's thesis of the demystification (*Entzauberung*) of Modernity, which, he held, began with the Enlightenment and has become a central feature of the rationalized social, political, and economic institutions of the West, variations of which are now spreading worldwide. Despite the popularity of this view, nothing could be further from the truth. As Durkheim, Eliade, and Ricoeur, among others, have pointed out, religious thought and action, and with them the central division between the sacred and the profane, have assumed a secular disguise, and in this relatively concealed form remain as fundamental to the life of society as ever.

Durkheim has described this division as follows:

> All known religious beliefs, whether simple or complex, present one common characteristic: they presuppose a classification of all the things, real and ideal, of which men think, into two classes or opposed groups, generally designated by two distinct terms which are translated well enough by the words *profane* and *sacred*. . . . This division of the world into two domains, the one containing all that is sacred, the other all that is profane, is the distinctive trait of religious thought. (1912, 52)
>
> In all the history of human thought there exists no other example of two categories of things so profoundly differentiated or so radically opposed to one another (53). . . . [T]he sacred and the profane have always and everywhere been conceived by the human mind as . . . two worlds between which there is nothing in common (54), . . . which embrace all that exists, but which radically exclude each other. (56)

Despite the path-breaking nature of Durkheim's treatment of religion, his account is one-sided, not only because he reduces the sacred and hence religion purely to their social dimensions, but also because he understands them almost entirely as a set of beliefs and practices, which ignores the most fundamental aspect: the *experience* of the sacred. The classic treatment of this aspect is Rudolph Otto's *Das Heilige* (1917) (rather inaptly rendered in the English translation as *The Idea of the Holy*), which adopts a more phenomenological approach, by focusing on the sacred *as experienced*.

Otto's term for the sacred is 'the numinous' (*das Numinose*), which draws attention to the peculiar quality or aura that emanates from the sacred. This aura can be possessed by almost anything: a person, an animal or plant, a rock, a mountain, a place or locale, a flag, a written or spoken word, a book, an activity. What is never numinous is the human (earthly) person. It is true that numinosity can enter into a person, but it comes from the outside, entering as a spirit, force, or presence which dwells within the person but has its origin elsewhere. The numinous, as Otto says over and over, is "the wholly other" (*ganz andere*).

In fact, as Durkheim points out, the sacred is foreign to whatever it enters. The numinous presence is not indigenous; the sacred grove is sacred not because of the nature of the trees, but because a spirit has entered from outside. A given numinous presence, moreover, can enter a variety of objects. A totem, for example, is a spirit which can enter into a group of people, an animal species, and a plant species, which are thereby bound together and become the same by virtue of their common possession. So when a member of the totem group says, for example, "I am an eagle," what is meant is that, as an initiate, he has been entered by the same spirit that has entered the eagle, and that the two therefore share a common identity.

Numinosity is an active principle; it *does* things, it is a *force*, often a force of great power. Once again, this power springs not from the object but from the spirit that inhabits and infuses the object. The idea is universal, and every culture has its name for such sacred power: mana, orenda, oki, megbe, wakan, charisma, the holy spirit, patriotism. It is common to term this kind of power and the beings or forces that possess it 'supernatural', but this term conveys a widespread Modern conception of the 'natural' that is foreign to most pre-Modern thought. Words such as 'sacred', 'uncanny', or 'otherworldly' express the idea better.

The numinous can manifest itself in a variety of forms. Often it is personified, and the sacred power is seen as embodied in a deity. Usually the idea is worked out in religious terms, but it can assume a character generally thought of as secular, as in Modern nationalism. But while the sacred can be conceptualized in many ways, the way in which it is experienced is everywhere the same. My description will follow Otto's account.

The most salient feature of the sacred is its awfulness, in the full connotation of the word. On the one hand, we find the sacred object mysterious, dreadful, eerie, weird, uncanny. We are filled with the 'fear of God'. On the other hand, as Otto says, we also find ourselves in the presence of something wonderful, shining, glorious, majestic, worthy of the profoundest adoration. We are filled with awe (1917, 12–24). The two sides of the experience are well expressed in the title of Mary Douglas's study of totemism, *Purity and Danger* (1969). In the presence of the sacred, our own selves are experienced as insignificant, worthless, powerless. We abase ourselves before the marvelous, terrible, and powerful presence.

Speaking of the 'wrath of Yahweh', Otto says,

> In the first place, it is patent from many passages in the Old Testament that this 'wrath' has no concern whatever with moral qualities. . . . It is, as has been well said, 'like a hidden force of nature', like stored-up electricity, discharging itself upon anyone who comes too near. It is 'incalculable' and 'arbitrary'. Anyone who is accustomed to think of deity only by its rational attributes must see in this 'wrath' mere caprice and willful passion. But such a view would have been emphatically rejected by the religious men of the Old Covenant, for to them the Wrath of God, so far from being a diminution of His Godhead, appears as a natural expression of it, an element of 'holiness' itself, and a quite indispensable one. And in this they are entirely right. (1917, 18)

Modern nationalism exhibits exactly this duality. The waving flag, the national anthem, the Fourth of July Parade well exemplify Otto's description of the sacred as wonderful, shining, glorious ("old Glory"), majestic, worthy of the profoundest adoration. On the other side, the exercise of the military power of the Modern state is often terrible in its might and wrath. The ultimate expressions of such holy wrath, in our age, have been the nuclear holocausts visited on Hiroshima and Nagasaki, acts identical in character but on a far larger scale than the wrath that Yahweh wreaked on Sodom and Gomorrah.

The sacred, Otto continues, is full of energy and urgency. "It everywhere clothes itself in symbolic expressions – vitality, passion, emotional temper, will, force, movement, excitement, activity, impetus. These features are typical and recur again and again from the daemonic level up to the idea of the 'living' God" (23). Over and over Otto stresses the contrasting and yet intrinsically joined elements of the experience of the sacred, especially the combination of fascination and "daemonic dread."

> The daemonic-divine object may appear to the mind an object of horror and dread, but at the same time it is no less something that

allures with a potent charm, and the creature, who trembles before it, utterly cowed and cast down, has always at the same time
the impulse to turn to it, nay even to make it somehow his own.
The 'mystery' is for him not merely something to be wondered at
but something that entrances him; and beside that in it which be-
wilders and confounds, he feels a something that captivates and
transports him with a strange ravishment, rising often enough to
the pitch of dizzy intoxication; it is the Dionysiac-element in the
numen. (31)

Otto draws a comparison between the experience of the sacred
and the experience of music (49), and the comparison can be pushed
farther than he was willing to take it. The story goes that when asked
to name the greatest composer in the Western tradition, Einstein
replied, "Beethoven." When asked why he had not named Mozart,
of whom he was known to be especially fond, Einstein is said to
have replied, "Mozart didn't compose that music; *God* composed it;
Mozart just wrote it down."

In the presence of great art we often are filled with awe and wonder at the uncanny and even frightening power of what we see or
hear, which seems to transcend the ordinary humanity of the artist.
The notion of the muse who inspires the artist expresses this idea in
a rather diluted form. Especially in the case of powerfully expressive art, it more accurately reflects the experience of both the artist
and the spectator to say that the artist has been possessed by a dae-
mon, an idea that is a central theme, for example, in Thomas Mann's
Dr. Faustus. The kinship between the experience of great art and
the experience of the supernatural derives from the fact that in both
cases we are in the presence of the unconscious shining through into
the world.

Magic and Religion

In analyzing the relationship between the human and the sacred it
was once common to make a more or less sharp distinction between
magic and religion. As recently as 1985, Pearson could define magic
as "any technique or formula aimed at achieving control over the
forces of the supernatural, in contrast to religion . . . , which involves

attempts to placate such forces" (1985, 161). Durkheim stressed the communal character of religion, in contrast to magic, which he saw as an activity of individuals, and in a similar vein Weber distinguished between the magician as a person who acts alone or with a small coterie, and the priest as a communal leader.

Yet religion is typically shot through with magical ideas and practices; indeed, Weber held that the magical element is essential, and saw movements from which magic is largely missing, such as Confucianism, as "on the borderline" between religion and ethical philosophy.

It is of course perfectly legitimate to set up analytic categories as polar types and to treat actual human activity as a varying combination of these types. At least I hope it is legitimate, for, following Weber, I have made extensive use of that strategy in this work. Weber's point, however, is that it is impossible to separate the two because *as an ideal type* religion inherently has a magical side.

A main reason for the attempt to separate the two, I suspect, is the bad press that magic has gotten, as an irrational and at bottom childish practice, proceeding from ignorance and the baser emotions and interests, whereas religion is accorded far more respect from all but hard-core heirs of the Enlightenment, such as Freud and Habermas. Indeed, it is not uncommon to find vigorous efforts within religious movements to extirpate magical ideas and practices in the name of spiritual purification. In practice, however, what is opposed is only the vulgar, basely motivated side of magic. The most advanced doctrines of salvation of the great world religions, for example, retain a heavily magical character, but in a deinstrumentalized, sophisticated, sublimated (Weber would say 'rationalized') form far removed from vulgar thought and practice.

Religion typically has an ethical side to it, and this side can become the predominant one. But the magical side is always there, and at bottom it is the more basic. In the previous chapter I treated the role that religion can play in the creation and evolution of moral or ethical standards in society. In this chapter the emphasis will be on the magical side of religious thought and experience.

The Magico-Religious Stance

As Weber insisted, the search for meaning is as fundamental to the human condition as the search for survival. Religion is such a search.

In *The Roots of Civilization*, Marshack (1971) analyzed what appear to be the earliest examples of writing known to us, which were discovered in southern France. He concluded that the inscriptions are a calendar that depicts the phases of the moon throughout the year. Marshack speculated that the calendar probably had both a utilitarian and a mystic significance. In practical terms it might have informed these early hunter- gatherers, for example, when to move into the nearby valleys in time to take advantage of the spring run of salmon up the streams. In addition, the inscriptions very likely provided the outline of a story in which the cycle of the phases was accounted for as the activity of some sacred power or being.

Throughout history, and undoubtedly prehistory, humans have looked up at the heavens and observed the motions of the sun, the stars, the planets, and especially the moon, with awe and wonder. Experientially, we are in the presence of the sacred, and witness to the activity of sacred powers.

According to Plato, philosophy begins with wonder, and both the Greek and the English word convey that combination of awe, fascination, and curiosity that is so basic to the human stance toward the world. The same attitude stands behind both science and religion, both of which for Plato were a part of philosophy. Our prehistoric calendar makers were surely not so different in this respect from contemporary cosmologists and astrophysicists. They looked at the heavens and they wondered: What is going on? Why do things happen this way? How did it all start?

It is above all the experience of the sacred that evokes wonder, and the explanations which magic and religion find are an attempt to find a meaning that is true to that experience. Since the sacred is experienced as the activity of otherworldly powers, the explanation consists of a description of the nature and mode of action of these powers, and the reasons why they act the way they do. In other words, the explanation is mythic in character.

At the center of every religion is a body of myth, which relates a story that describes the origins of the world and its inhabitants as a result of the actions of sacred beings. This story explains the nature of humanity, its main divisions, and its relation to the world. Such a myth or myth complex is the very heart of all religious and magical thought and practice. More than that, as Ricoeur has put it, a body of myth is the "foundational nucleus" of every society, including our own, the "constitutive kernel" which establishes the "ratio of distribution" between the different functions of society, "political, economic, legal, etc." (1984, 462–63).

Lévi-Strauss held that myths are essentially metaphorical in nature, but this view, correct though it may be, looks at myth from the outside, rather than in terms of its meaning for the community. In its original meaning, as Eliade points out, 'myth' means 'true story', and here we may reinterpret this to mean 'true to the experience of the believers'. A myth is true in this sense if it squares with, illuminates, and explains the life experience of the believers, and so gives meaning to their existence. Only when it fails to do this does a myth assume its pejorative meaning of an untrue, made-up story. When this happens to the foundational myths, it is a sign that the religion will not be present much longer on the stage of history.

Magico-religious explanation is always motivational; the event is interpreted as the action or the result of the action of otherworldly power, although the result is not always what was intended. The ordinary commonsense mode of explaining human and much animal behavior is motivational in exactly the same sense. We understand human action when we understand the motives that impel it, along with the framework of beliefs within which the motive operates. From this viewpoint, both divisions of the lifeworld, sacred and profane, are understood in motivational terms, and every worldly event can in principle be interpreted and explained as the outcome of either earthly or otherworldly agency.

Despite the fundamental nature of the division between the sacred and the profane, the split is not total. Through proper rites of initiation, humans can enter into the world of the sacred, and participate in its activities or, alternatively, sacred powers can enter their persons and inspire them. Moreover, while in principle the two worlds are foreign to each other, in practice, as Lévi-Strauss has pointed out, the ritual observance of sacred practices can be carried out in intermixture with or as a part of ordinary mundane activity. The familiarity of a sacred rite can lead to a loss of most or all of its numinous aura, as for example in the perfunctory mumbled grace before the meal.

The body of myth provides a framework within which particular events can be understood and dealt with. As a rule it is the extraordinary or highly significant, rather than the ordinary routine humdrum, which brings the mythic attitude into play. Above all it is the aura of the uncanny that typically emanates from such events which creates the need for magical explanation. There has been a great storm, or a drought, an illness, a death. What is the cause or reason for this event? The overall system of myth and ritual provides the context within which the answer is sought. Suppose, for example, that there has been a drought. Ordinarily there is a ritual procedure, carried out by or via a soothsayer, oracle, or the like, whereby the reason for the drought is ascertained. Suppose that it is discovered by such means than the drought has been caused by a powerful deity, who is angry because a ritual performance has not been properly carried out. The nature of this deity, and the outlines of its relation to the community, will already have been set forth in the mythic system, and the proper way to handle the situation will also be known, or be ascertainable by further divination. Perhaps it is determined that what is required is a ritual atonement, carried out by the community. Thus, the religious system provides a way for the meaning of the event to be divined and the proper mode of response to be undertaken.

This example provides the opportunity for a further point. The members of a traditional or archaic community will not in general believe that the ritual atonement is capable of efficaciously causing the termination of the drought. Rather, they *hope* that it will have this result. If it rains, that will show that the deity has been mollified, if not, it will be clear that the deity is still angry. So also, if a spell cast to cure an illness fails to have the desired effect, that simply shows that the spell which caused the illness was the stronger. These examples illustrate the often noted post hoc character of magical thinking. A magical belief is impossible to falsify, because whatever happens can be fitted into the framework of interpretation.

It follows that the results of magical action cannot be predicted with any degree of certainty, a fact of which most pre-Modern cultures are well aware. Douglas (1969, 58), reports that the !Kung Bushmen will be much amused at the suggestion that the performance of their rain ritual might cause it to rain. Everyone knows, they will tell you, that you can't make it rain just by dancing around in a circle. To adopt a purely means-end approach to magic is a vulgarization, which I suspect is more typical of Modernity than of cultures less obsessed by instrumental thinking. The underlying reason for the unpredictability of the result is that magical causation is motivational in character, a 'doing', far removed from what Douglas calls the "external efficacy" of the causality dealt with, for example, in the physical sciences.

Another major characteristic of the magico-religious stance is the belief in the magical power of symbols, which arises from an equation between the symbol and the thing or event symbolized. What is done to or with the symbol is thereby done to the thing, and the distinction between saying something and doing it is often not drawn. To know a person's secret name, for example, is to have power over that person, and one can exact vengeance on one's enemy via ritualized symbolic activity, such as laying a curse, casting a spell, or sticking a pin into an effigy. Magical action is typically – one is tempted to say invariably – symbolic in character.

Finally, the magico-religious stance is characterized by a belief in the contagiousness of the sacred. The magical quality is seen as readily spilling over into anything that is associated with the sacred object or event, either symbolically or by physical proximity or resemblance.

The Unconscious Roots of Magico-Religious Thought and Experience

The experience of the sacred as an uncanny awesome double-edged force of great power which is alien to the conscious self, but which can enter and even possess this self, clearly points to its unconscious origin. More generally, it is by now widely recognized that magico-religious thought has important unconscious roots. The pioneer work in this field is Freud's *Totem and Taboo* (1913). Unfortunately this work is seriously flawed not only by overhasty anthropological conclusions, but also, on the psychoanalytic side, by the treatment of magical thought as regressive and neurotic, in line with the then prevailing view of magic as childish and irrational. Over a decade later, in *The Future of an Illusion* (1927) Freud leveled the same sort of charge against religion, which he described as a kind of universal neurosis.

While his specific conclusions need to be used with care, and his dismissive attitude toward magic and religion is unjustified, Freud's work points in the right direction, and his followers have supplied the needed correctives. For example, Erikson says that "Primitive societies are neither infantile stages of mankind nor arrested deviations from the proud progressive norms which we represent: they are a complete form of mature human living" (1950, 96), and his treatments of Sioux and Yorok tribes that follow this remark are conducted in that spirit.

The position taken here will be that magico-religious attitudes and practices utilize modes of thought that originate in the early stages of the development of conscious-preconscious intentionality, and so stand relatively close to the unconscious. These modes of thought continue to operate through life, sometimes covered over by what comes later, sometimes not. They are a part of the human stance toward the world, and not at all inherently pathological or regressive. In psychoanalytic thought, it is axiomatic that *all* thought and action derive from and express unconscious motives and ideas. When applied to magic and religion, phrases such as 'closeness to the unconscious' indicate not that the unconscious influences are greater, but that they are more transparent.

Freud is on firmer ground when he moves from magical thought to its experiential basis. His comparatively neglected essay, "The Uncanny" ("Das Unheimliche") (1919) provides a striking comparison with Otto's *Das Heilige*. Though the examples Freud uses can be regarded as trivial from the point of view of a serious religious sensibility, and his terminology is somewhat different, the substance of the treatment corresponds to Otto's account of the experience of the sacred almost point by point. Freud summarizes his conclusions as follows: "an uncanny experience occurs either when infantile complexes which have been repressed are once more revived by some impression, or when primitive beliefs which have been surmounted seem once more to be confirmed" (1919, 249). As amended in the light of the above discussion, I read this passage as saying that the special quality of experience of the sacred (the uncanny) derives from the fact that it brings to conscious awareness material which has been repressed, or which is ordinarily overlaid and hidden ("surmounted") by everyday conscious-preconscious intentionality. This insight will provide the theme for the account which follows.

The experience of the sacred involves a kind of limited breakthrough of the unconscious into consciousness. As I pointed out earlier, in unconscious awareness our emotions and desires are fused with the objects toward which they are directed. The object radiates the feelings we have toward it. Freud's description of mental activity as entering into its object and spreading over it, "somewhat as an electric charge is spread over the surface of its body," corresponds exactly to Otto's comparison of the numinous to a powerful electric charge that radiates both danger and attraction from the objects in which it dwells.

With the advent of consciousness, this tendency is ordinarily greatly diminished, and what Freud termed the 'psychical intensity' comes to be recognized as one's own, i.e., as emanating from the self as subject. In the experience of the sacred, however, the quality of the unconscious experience shines through into conscious awareness and suffuses its object with a powerful numinous aura. The uncanny power which radiates from the object is thus nothing else but the power of one's own unconscious intentionality, which, however, is experienced as 'wholly other' in origin, and indeed with respect to the conscious self this perception is quite correct.

The intensity of the experience of the sacred derives from the power of the unconscious motivation in comparison with which our conscious impulses and feelings are usually pale shadows. Such motivations are often capable of being mobilized, for example by charismatic leaders. The sacred aura which radiates from the leader can inspire the most intense devotion among the followers, which can readily be harnessed to earthly purposes.

The double-edged quality of the sacred reveals that we are dealing with repressed impulses whose objects are as desirable (shining, pure) as their expression is dangerous (poisonous, unclean). The underlying ambivalence can be dealt with in a variety of ways. In the case of many taboos, for example those concerning incest or the touching of excrement, the positive feelings reach awareness only via reaction formation, and so reinforce, rather than weaken, the strength of the aversion. Alternatively, it is sometimes the case that foods which are normally taboo are eaten on certain ritual occasions. One both eats the cake, so to speak, and eats it not. In other cases, the two sides of ambivalence can find separate conscious objects, for example between a beneficent and just deity who stands in opposition to an evil or unclean supernatural power: a Baal or a Satan. This solution undoubtedly reflects the infantile split between the 'good' and 'bad' parent discussed earlier.

The closeness of magical thinking to the unconscious also explains the notorious contagiousness of the sacred, for unconscious (primary process) intentionality is readily transmitted by association to other objects, especially in the case of repressed intentionality, which tends to spread via progressive displacements much in the way that ripples spread when a stone is thrown into a pool.

In the experience of the sacred, and in magical thinking in general, the translation of what is unconscious to consciousness is subject to the full range of transformations found in unconscious activity, including displacement, condensation, reversal, splitting, and various defenses and compromise formations. Freud found such processes to be the same as those exhibited by very young children and his neurotic patients. This is true enough, but to characterize magical thought as neurotic or childish, as he did, is to ignore his own dictum that *all* thought and action is unconsciously motivated. In adult 'civilized' thought, such processes do not go away, but are instead overlaid by 'rationalizations' in the dual sense of being made more rational while at the same time serving to cover over and conceal the underlying motivation.

The faith that magic typically has in the ability of purely symbolic means to produce worldly results was characterized by Freud as the 'omnipotence of thought'. For him, this trait represented a regression to primary narcissism. I would instead use the phrase 'the efficacy of the symbol', and trace it to different sources. There are two strands to the efficacy of the symbol. First, purely symbolic means are obviously appropriate in communicating with the supernatural. As was emphasized earlier, magical practice is not in essence an attempt to cause a result in a physical sense. Rather, it aims to mobilize magical power in much the way that an orator mobilizes a crowd by an effective speech. The second strand is the identity, in magical thinking, between symbol and thing symbolized. I suggest that this trait has its origin in the early presyntactic level of language development, where the word is an integral part of the thing. At this stage the power of words over things is quite real, for to know the word is to be able to bring what it names to presence at will, and by the same token to describe an event is to make it seem to happen, a power, we may note, which artistic creativity continues to exercise, because art speaks not only to the conscious but to the unconscious as well. As I pointed out earlier, the power of the word to bring the thing to vivid awareness is responsible for the first true object constancy, which develops during the second year, when the child, for example, can bring her mother to presence simply by pronouncing her name.

We are here at the early stages of language use, in the borderland between conscious and unconscious, before the arrival of syntactic organization, which is required for full consciousness to emerge. It seems clear that the preoccupation that magic has with words and symbols derives from the persistence of this early linguistic mode of thought in later life. While the identification of word and thing is mostly absent from conscious, syntactically organized thought, it persists in the unconscious and achieves conscious expression in magical thought and action.

The tendency of magical thinking to read purposiveness or agency into all of nature, especially moving things, can be explained in terms of two unconscious sources. First, as has been noted, infants tend to attribute a primitive agency to any activity. Here we may note that even 'motionless' objects such as mountains exhibit activity via their vitality affects: they loom, or soar, or brood. It is not wholly correct to use the term 'animism' to characterize this tendency to read a motivational impetus into all sensibly evident activity. Animism sees moving and especially living things as inhabited by their own specific purposive spirit, i.e., each possesses a separate agency. The earliest stage of infant awareness of purpose more resembles what is sometimes called 'pre-animism'. Here the world is seen as pervaded by a universal force or power ('mana', 'orende', 'charisma', etc.) which is not personified, and which enters into particular objects from time to time, investing them with extraordinary power for good or evil. The idea of 'the force' in the *Star Wars* movies captures this theme exactly. Such pre-animism corresponds to the very early stage in which the infant sees a kind of agency in anything animate, but has not yet learned to attribute such activity to specific agents. As with the identification of word and thing, this way of looking at things is not replaced, but instead lies underneath later modes of thought, ready to be activated by the magical stance.

The second way in which magical thought reads intentionality into nature is via projective displacement, on the model of the child who is holding a kitten in her arms during a storm and says, "The kitty is afraid of the thunder." For example, when the volcano erupts and people say, "The gods are angry," the anger of which they are aware may in fact be their own. This is often called 'anthropomorphism' (the reading of human intentionality into nature). I shall have more to say later on this theme.

Finally, the closeness of the 'other' world of the sacred to the unconscious underworld applies strongly to the prototypical form of magico-religious thought, the myth. Eliade (1957) has pointed out the similarity of mythic thinking to dreaming, a similarity which derives from the fact that both are relatively direct expressions of unconscious thought. The outstanding difference is that while dreams are an expression of the individual mind, myths are social products and typically lie at the heart of the communal lifeworld. Just as the dream is the royal road to the unconscious life of the individual, as Freud held, so the myth is the royal road to the collective unconscious. I shall address this topic later.

I close this section with a speculation. From our distant ancestors pictured by Marshack as looking in wonder at the heavens, to the desperate quest of Estragon and Vladimir in Beckett's *Waiting for Godot*, the search for meaning seems to be a fundamental and universal part of the human stance toward the world. There is a huge reservoir of meaning in the unconscious, both repressed and nonrepressed, which is in active existence, but which is cut off from the 'I' of conscious awareness. In this respect, lifeworld and underworld are estranged. I suspect that the universal search for meaning is precisely a quest for the buried unconscious, a realm of meaning which we cannot find, but which we sense is there somewhere. From a psychological point of view, the main function of myth is to bring the unconscious into the lifeworld in a way which fits in with and makes sense of our conscious lives and experience. It is above all myth that fulfills the quest for meaning, and so reconciles lifeworld and underworld.

Magic and Religion as Interpretation

Both in thought and in action, the approach of magic and religion to the world is essentially interpretive. A myth is an interpretation which translates the unconscious lives of the members of a community into conscious terms. It is true that this translation is also a transformation, but this is so for all translation of the unconscious into consciousness. Taken as a whole, in turn, the body of myth provides an interpretive framework within which magico-religious action is carried out. Such action often has an instrumental quality, where those participating in the ritual or rite hope thereby to achieve some purpose, such as success in battle, a bumper crop, relief from illness. But such an instrumental meaning is by no means always present, and where present not always paramount. Moreover, even for magical action which is oriented primarily around ends and means, the means by which the end is to be pursued is typically discovered via interpretation. For example, Evans-Pritchard (1937) has described the use of the poison oracle among the Azande. If they want to know if it is a favorable day to go on a hunt, for instance, they will perform a ritual in which poison is fed to a chicken. If the chicken lives, that is interpreted as a favorable omen, while the chicken's death means the opposite. The interpretation of the outcome of the ritual determines the course of action.

It is probably a mistake to hold that such a way of doing things is inherently irrational, even on a purely means-end level. Evans-Pritchard, for example, conducted his affairs according to the poison oracle for some time, and reports that he found it as good a way to live as any. Of course, he conducted this experiment while he was living among the Azande, not after he had returned to England, where the results would likely have been quite different. The point

169

is that an action which seems to us clearly irrational may not be irrational when understood in the context of the total life of the society in which it takes place.

The most important magico-religious interpretations concern motivation: important events of the world, past or present, are interpreted as actions (i.e., motivated behavior) or the results of actions by otherworldly powers. While such actions are understood as the exercise of agency, they need not be for a specific coherent purpose. The main body of myth, and the derivative interpretations, however, generally see things in terms of organized purposive action: the lightning bolt is Thor's hammer, the sun is the chariot that Apollo drives through the sky, the crescent moon is the bow of Diana the huntress, and so on.

The interpretation of motive also plays a central role in the human sciences, and it will prove instructive to make a comparison (and contrast) with the practice of psychoanalysis which, like myth, concerns itself with the interpretation of the unconscious.

Insofar as an interpretive or hermeneutical approach is adopted in the human sciences, explanation necessarily exhibits the same 'post hoc' character as magico-religious explanation. Those working in such fields are not always aware of this, but Freud was quite explicit on the point:

> So long as we trace the development [of a mental process] from its final outcome backwards, the chain of events appears continuous, and we feel we have gained an insight which is completely satisfactory or even exhaustive. But if we proceed the reverse way, if we start from the premises inferred from the analysis and try to follow these up to the final result, then we no longer get the impression of an inevitable sequence of events. . . . We notice at once that there might have been another result, and that we might have been just as well able to understand and explain the latter. . . . [I]n other words, from a knowledge of the premises we could not have foretold the nature of the result. . . . Even supposing that we have a complete knowledge of the etiological factors that decide a given result, nevertheless what we know about them is only their quality, and not their relative strength. Some of them are suppressed by others because they are too weak, and they

therefore do not affect the final result. But we never know before-hand which of the determining factors will prove the weaker or the stronger. We only say at the end that those which succeeded must have been the stronger. (1920a, 167–68)

This passage shows a firm grasp of the nature of psychoanalytic explanation. Those who would make a predictive science of the discipline on the model of the 'hard' (instrumental) sciences are engaged in exactly the same vulgarization as those who think magic is capable of deterministically controlling (and hence predicting) the course of events. Motivational explanation is inherently post hoc. It does not follow that psychoanalytic therapy cannot be effective; rather that its effectiveness cannot be causal in the sense in which the term applies to physical causation.

The similarities between magico-religious and psychoanalytic practice are particularly striking in the case of shamanistic curing, as a number of observers, including Lévi-Strauss (1949) and Turner (1964) have pointed out. Shamanism combines activities that are nowadays usually separated. In contemporary terms, a shaman is a physician, psychiatrist, social worker, spiritual adviser, holy man, and chiropractor. The establishment of these as separate fields has enabled a far-going rationalization of each, at the cost, however, of the frequent failure to realize how closely interconnected are the various spheres addressed by these disciplines. In contrast, the shaman does not normally distinguish between physical and psychological disturbances, and the treatment often combines elements that we would consider medical and psychotherapeutic. It is the latter element, however, which usually predominates, as befits the essentially interpretive nature of the enterprise.

By all accounts, shamanistic curing has a relatively high rate of success, comparing favorably, for example, with Western medicine before the introduction of antibiotics. Some of this curing occurs through means that we would call medical, for example the use of herbal remedies. More commonly, the means employed are what we think of as psychological in nature. Here the power of suggestion appears to be of great importance. Such 'faith healing' (or its opposite, injury via sorcery), Lévi-Strauss points out, derives from three components: "first, the sorcerer's belief in the effectiveness of his techniques; second, the patient's or victim's belief in the sorcerer's power; and, finally, the faith and expectations of the group, which constantly acts as a sort of gravitational field within which the relationship between sorcerer and bewitched is located and defined" (1949, 162). This 'gravitational field' is of course the mythically established lifeworld.

The power of such sorcery is illustrated by numerous accounts of the infliction of death by exorcism or the casting of spells. Lévi-Strauss describes one such case in which a person apparently dying from sorcery was brought into a hospital, placed in an oxygen tent, and fed intravenously. "He gradually recovered, convinced that the white man's magic was the stronger" (1949, 179). One wonders if the cure might also have been mainly due to the power of suggestion.

While suggestion is clearly of great importance in shamanistic practice, according to Lévi-Strauss and Turner there are cases that go beyond suggestion, and effect a cure by means of genuine interpretation and often some elements of 'working through' in the psychoanalytic sense.

Shamanistic curing can take a wide variety of forms, but as a rule the crucial phase is explanatory and takes the form of an interpretation that is intended to reveal the roots of the malady. There typically follows a 'working through' phase, in which the cure is achieved by activity based on the insights of the interpretation. The first phase generally consists of a ceremonial divination in the process of which the shaman will often enter a trancelike state in which he visits the other world. The result is a diagnosis in the form of a story in which the shaman describes the otherworldly events that have led to the illness. Perhaps, for example, a part of the soul of the victim has been abducted by a hostile spirit. The next phase is a ritual in which the whole community often participates, and in which the shaman may, for example, enter into battle with the hostile spirit, rescue the abducted part of the soul and reunite it with the rest, thus effecting the cure. As always, of course, failure is attributed to the superior powers of the adverse spirits.

Lévi-Strauss describes the process as follows:

The shaman provides the sick woman with a *language*, by means of which the unexpressed and inexpressible, psychic states can be immediately expressed. And it is the transition to this verbal expression – at the same time making it possible to undergo in an ordered and intelligible form a real experience that would otherwise be chaotic and inexpressible – which induces the release of physiological process, that is, the reorganization, in a favorable direction, of the process to which the sick woman is subjected. . . .

In both cases [psychoanalysis and shamanistic curing] the purpose is to bring to a conscious level conflicts and resistances which have remained unconscious, owing either to their repression by other psychological forces [or to nonpsychic sources]. In both cases also, the conflicts and resistances are resolved, not because of knowledge, real or alleged, which the sick woman progressively acquires of them, but because this knowledge makes possible a specific experience, in the course of which conflicts materialize in an order and on a level permitting their free development and leading to their resolution. This vital experience is called *abreaction* in psychoanalysis. (1949, 193–94, italics in original)

Both the psychoanalytic and the shamanistic interpretations bring to conscious awareness psychic activity that has heretofore been unconscious because it has been repressed or else because the sufferer has been unable unaided to give such activity conscious verbal expression. It is a mistake to draw a contrast between the psychoanalytic interpretation as a literal description of the unconscious as against the symbolical or metaphorical account of the shaman. Any attempt to give linguistic expression to unconscious intentionality involves a selective, filtering, altering process which is the more profound because we are translating something not from one language to another, but from one world to another. The psychoanalytic interpretation is in principle no closer to and no farther from the literal truth than the shamanistic.

The contrast is on more solid ground when we note that the psychoanalytic interpretation describes the thoughts, wishes, fantasies, and beliefs of the *patient*, whereas the shamanistic interpretation speaks of the activities of otherworldly powers that are foreign to the sufferer's selfhood. The shamanistic interpretation *externalizes* the intentional activity of the victim, whereas in the psychoanalytic interpretation this activity is *internalized*, i.e., treated as an inner psychic process. The two methods are equally artificial, but in opposite directions. As we have seen, the inner-outer distinction is entirely absent in the topographic unconscious, where intentional states are characteristically fused with their objects.

The inner-outer distinction is by no means foreign to pre-Modern cultures, as might be expected from the fact that it springs, as we have seen, from the very nature of language. The division of the human self into body and soul or spirit, for example, seems to be universal. What is salient here about the shamanistic interpretation is that unconscious intentionality is presented as alien to both aspects of the victim's self, inner and outer, body and soul. In this the shaman remains true to the magico-religious stance, in which the sacred is experienced as 'wholly other'. The psychoanalyst, in contrast, interprets the unconscious thought as the patient's own.

A second difference concerns the private character of psychoanalytic treatment as against the thoroughly social nature of the shamanistic cure. Here, as with the previous point, we must guard against too superficial a contrast. Psychoanalysis, at least in its classic form, is a very private interaction between two persons which is carefully shielded from public view. This seems to differ sharply from the shamanistic cure as a public ceremony in which the whole community typically participates. Yet both are embedded in and derive their meaning from their lifeworld context, and in that sense they are both public or communal activities. In this one respect, if in no other, the psychoanalytic session is similar to the confessional of the Catholic Church, in that they share the property of being strictly private and confidential sessions which nevertheless derive their meaning from the surrounding lifeworld.

The significant contrast lies elsewhere, in the specific character of the otherworldly powers of which the shaman speaks. These powers are a part of the lifeworld; their existence is recognized by all and their activities, in general, can be carried out with respect to anyone, or at least anyone within a specified group. It is true that one occasionally finds spirits whose powers are specific to only one person. They are, so to speak, personal daemons, comparable to the individual neurosis that afflicts the psychoanalytic patient. For the most part, however, daemons and other supernatural beings operate within the public domain, in the community at large, or at least a portion of it.

This point holds even more strongly for the myths and symbols that form the basic fabric of lifeworld reality. The fact that these have an unconscious origin is by now widely recognized. But we are dealing here not with the individual unconscious but with the collective unconscious of the community. These myths and symbols are group products; they are by and large the same for all, and they spring from unconscious motives and ideas common to all.

The Concept of the Collective Unconscious

I need at the outset to differentiate the idea of the collective unconscious from the usage of its best-known exponent, Karl Jung. For Jung, (1936–54) the collective unconscious takes the form, at its most basic level, of certain universal archetypes genetically embedded in the human psyche. In other words, they constitute inborn ideas, imprinted by many generations of human experience. In contrast, the position taken here is that what is inborn is, on the motivational side, a set of instinctual drives and, on the cognitive and emotional side, a set of capacities and ways of dealing with the world. These are far more structured in their activity than Freud thought, but are nevertheless totally devoid of any specific predetermined content or object. The contents and objects of intentionality arise instead from experience, i.e., from the confrontation of our innate capacities and proclivities with the world.

Jung's argument rests mainly on the fact that there are certain mythic symbols, ideas, and themes which appear to be universal. Assuming the unconscious origin of these, Jung concluded that there must be basic unconscious contents, or at least the basis for these, which are the same everywhere, and which therefore must be innately given. But the notion of specific innate ideas seems farfetched, and in any event is not required to explain such uniformities. It is enough to hold that the basic *character* (as distinct from the contents) of the unconscious is the same everywhere, along the lines presented in earlier chapters here.

The salient point is that there are certain foundational facts of the human condition that are the same everywhere. We are born of woman, we grow up and then we grow old, we make a living or fail to do so; we suffer, we enjoy, we wonder, and we die. These facts are as true of princes as of paupers, of aborigines as of nuclear physicists. It is therefore hardly surprising that there are widespread and sometimes striking similarities in mythic ideas and symbols throughout the kaleidoscope of the lifeworlds, and reasonable to suppose that these reflect much the same unconscious content – without the need to conclude that we are dealing with innate ideas.

Jung's use of the term 'collective' in 'collective unconscious' is also rather loose. Strictly speaking the term refers to something that is characteristic of a social or organizational totality, as in a 'collective' farm or 'collective' security. The term 'universal unconscious' is more appropriate for Jung's use of the term, and 'collective unconscious' is better used in a narrower sense, as applicable to specific lifeworlds, and especially to specific communities. As such it pairs well with Durkheim's 'collective consciousness'.

An example of the influence in conscious life of what Jung would call the 'collective' but which I will instead call the 'universal' unconscious is the theme in fiction, folklore, and fantasy, of the splitting of the human person or personality into two persons, who are in some respects the same (e.g., in appearance) and in others radically different (e.g., in personality). The theme, in a host of variations (*dopplegangers*, identical twins with opposite characters, werewolves, etc.), is truly universal, and endlessly strange (uncanny) and fascinating to all ages and ranks of society. The unconscious basis on which this rests, I suggest, is the splitting that occurs everywhere in infancy between the 'good' and 'bad' self, 'good' and 'bad' mother, 'good' and 'bad' father.

When it comes to specific communities, the unconscious lives of the members take on a special character and form unique to the group. Here we have the true collective unconscious, in which the similarities of unconscious content and objects among the members of the collectivity pertain to a wider area of content, and are closer, than is found in the universal unconscious. Especially in small, close-knit groups, the collective unconscious can be treated as a single idea or complex of ideas, shared among the members in much the same sense that the meaning of the word 'cat' can be understood as a single collective idea, instead of a set of similar ideas in the minds of the individual members of the group.

The universal unconscious consists of a set of basic themes or concepts which manifest themselves in a myriad of different ways. The concept focuses on what humans have in common across this range of variation. The collective unconscious is something that pertains to one collectivity, as distinct from others. Its explanatory force is to account for differences between cultures, not similarities among individuals.

The collective unconscious is created by the impact of the lifeworld on the underworld. Just as the unconscious shapes the lifeworld, so the lifeworld shapes the unconscious, on both the individual and the social level. Not only the collective consciousness, but also the collective unconscious emerges from the interaction of the conscious and unconscious levels of experience within a social collectivity. Both are group, not individual, phenomena. On the level of the individual, we can examine how life experience shapes the unconscious of this particular person. On the level of the social whole, we can examine how the lifeworld has shaped the unconscious of the members of a community into a common pattern and common content, shared, within a certain range of individual variation, by all or virtually all of the group members.

The Nature and Genesis of the Collective Unconscious

For my description of the nature of the collective unconscious, and the way in which it arises from the interaction of lifeworld and underworld, I will draw on a long tradition, stretching from Plato to Habermas, by developing a 'just so' story, an imaginary history designed to reveal the logic of the case, without pretending to be an accurate factual account.

Let us imagine an archaic or early traditional society, perhaps a tribe, living in relative isolation from other lifeworlds. Since I am assuming an already existing social organization, we must suppose that the ties of identification basic to any social organization have already been formed, as described in the previous chapter. Moreover, there must be a system of social authority. Let us assume that there is a relatively equal division between the sexes, with men having authority in some areas, and women in others. Since the life-world always feeds back and shapes the underworld, of course, it must also be the case that the unconscious lives of the members take a form distinctive to the group, but since this is precisely the process I am trying to account for, I must, in a counterfactual way, ignore this and assume that on this level the group members have no more in common than what is found universally. Hence, while their superegos will combine male and female elements, as in all societies, it is assumed that the specific formations are diverse, with no one pattern predominating.

Now let us suppose that a long dormant nearby volcano suddenly becomes active, erupting with some frequency, but at irregular intervals. Naturally the members of the tribe will seek an interpretive explanation for this uncanny and awesome activity. If they do so individually, we can expect a wide variety of answers, depending on the personality of the interpreter. The pictures drawn will all have strong projective elements, but will vary among the individuals, depending on their different conscious and unconscious orientations. But the projections will not be thrown onto a blank screen; rather, the nature of the event will encourage certain kinds of interpretations and discourage others. A volcanic eruption strongly suggests a powerful emotional outburst, either sexual or aggressive in nature, perhaps a combination of both, while the periodic nature of the eruptions suggest a personality that is steady or contained most of the time, but given to occasional fits of passion. It is not necessary for the onlookers themselves to share these traits to any great extent, consciously or unconsciously. All that is needed to see the volcano, for example, as angry is at least a modicum of rage buried somewhere, to form the basis for the projective interpretation. In short, the various individuals will have different interpretations, reflecting their own conscious and unconscious characters, but these differences will be mitigated by common factors springing from the inherent suggestiveness of the event.

However, we are dealing here with the origins of a myth, which is a social, not an individual product. While we might expect varying interpretations at the start, in time they will coalesce into a single interpretation accepted by all. We should expect the lateral identifications among the group members, and the concomitant pressures toward uniformity and conformity to play a large role here. The views of the more influential members of the group, especially those in authority or thought to possess sacred powers, would of course have the greatest weight in this process. The emergent mythic interpretation would have a variable basis in the individual personalities of the members. At one extreme some individuals might form a strong projective identification, based on their own unconscious character. At the other extreme others might accept the myth almost entirely out of conformity to the group view, with little or no projective backing from their own personalities.

To continue the hypothetical example, let us suppose that the mythic interpretation that emerges sees the volcano as a male deity, who requires sacrifice and other observances by tribe members, and is pacific and beneficent if they behave as required, but becomes explosively angry if his wishes are disobeyed. The point I wish to emphasize is that this mythic interpretation need not be the product of any strong and relatively uniform unconscious formations among the group members. The nature of the volcanic activity would suggest a god of this kind to people of widely different personalities.

Once the volcano god is established as an objectively given part of the lifeworld, however, he is bound to have a significant psychological effect, both conscious and unconscious, on the group members. On the conscious level, we can expect males in a position of authority to look up to the god as a kind of role model, worthy of imitation. Correspondingly, since they are surrogates and spokesmen of the god, their authority will increase, both absolutely and in relation to female authority. Both the nature and distribution of authority within society will be tilted toward what is suggested by the character of the god.

Those growing up in this society will now encounter a changed pattern of authority, influenced by the powerful figure of the volcano god. As a result, the introjects forming the core of their superegos will become much more similar than formerly, more heavily weighted on the male side, and assuming much of the specific character exhibited by male authority figures, and especially their divine prototype. The unconscious superegos of the members will begin to assume a pattern common to and specific to the members of the group. The result will be a powerful further reinforcement of the uncanny sacred character of the volcano and the authority patterns that have been shaped in his image, which will further shape and unify the unconscious patterns that they reflect. I propose that the collective unconscious emerges out of such a spiral.

It is a commonplace to say that a myth such as that of the volcano god anthropomorphizes nature, but here we may note two correlative facts. First, the frightful, uncanny activity of the volcano has been incorporated into the lifeworld, as something which has meaning, is explicable, and therefore can be dealt with. In this respect the volcano has been not so much anthropomorphized as socialized. Second, the unconscious intentionality of the members of the group has been crystallized into a collective formation, of which the myth is the conscious lifeworld expression. The salient point is not that the mountain has been anthropomorphized, but that *the unconscious has been naturalized* (read into external nature) *and then socialized* (brought into the conscious lifeworld).

In discussing the mythic significance of the cycle of the phases of the moon, Eliade has written, "It might be said that the moon shows man his true human condition; that in a sense man looks at himself, and finds himself anew in the life of the moon" (1963a, 184). This expresses an important truth: such externalizations of the unconscious provide an avenue for self-awareness and self-understanding. The other side of this truth is that we have here a two-way street, via which, in the same process, the unconscious is itself reshaped in the image of the world. Through the activity of magico-religious thought a part of the underworld has been externalized into the lifeworld and a part of the lifeworld has been internalized into the underworld. A myth is an interpretation which involves, in Gadamer's (1965) terms, a "fusion of horizons" between conscious and unconscious in which the chasm between the two worlds has in some respects been bridged.

Eliade is correct when he insists on the original meaning of myth as a true story, for myth tells the truth about the unconscious. It may be objected that such truth is purely metaphorical in nature. Indeed, Lévi-Strauss has asserted that every myth is a metaphor. In the light of my earlier discussion of Lacan, the use of the term 'metaphor' is here itself rather metaphorical; often what is involved is a psychic mechanism such as displacement, but with that proviso Lévi-Strauss's point is well taken. The same, however, can be said for every conscious expression of the unconscious, which is, as Freud put it, both a translation and a transformation. The important difference is that in the one case we have an individual phenomenon: the expression of a particular person's unconscious in the lifeworld, while in the other case we have a group phenomenon, the lifeworld expression of the collective unconscious.

There are thus two avenues by which the unconscious enters the lifeworld. First, once language is learned, we are able to translate some of our unconscious intentionality into conscious lifeworld terms (and in doing so transform it). In the life of the individual, conscious and unconscious now enter into a mutually shaping interaction. In this process the lifeworld is something objectively given, it is the shaper, not the shaped: it may be utilized and related to in various ways, but except in the case of very rare individuals, the lifeworld itself remains unaffected by the individual's activity. When individual consciousness is born, the lifeworld is already there, and when consciousness ceases, the lifeworld remains in being.

Second, by the process I have outlined, the unconscious intentionality of the several members of the group can enter consciousness via mythic thinking, and in doing so coalesce into a collective consciousness, which builds the lifeworld, and which in turn feeds back and produces a collective unconscious. On the collective level, consciousness and unconsciousness, lifeworld and underworld now enter into a mutually shaping interaction. Here the lifeworld is not a 'given': it is formed and reformed by the ongoing interaction. To understand the deepest kind of historical change, the evolution of the lifeworld, we must take into account the role played by the unconscious.

—— Sources

Freud and Weber continue to be the most important debts. Obviously, Durkheim 1912; Otto 1917; and Eliade 1957, 1963a, 1963b, and 1968, have been heavily drawn on. Ricoeur 1967 and 1984, and Geertz 1973, have also been influential. Hart 1975 treats myth from a Husserlian perspective. In addition to the anthropological works cited in the text, see Tambiah 1968. I have gone along with the frequent equation of 'shamanism' with magical curing by sorcery, despite the narrower definition in Eliade 1951. I suspect that Turner's 1964 account of shamanistic curing, where it emerges as something quite akin to group therapy by a Freudian oriented psychiatric social worker, is closer to the mark than the comparison with classical psychoanalysis of Lévi-Strauss 1949, but I have followed the latter account because it afforded me a better opportunity to make the comparison/contrast between magical and psychoanalytic interpretation. For shamanistic curing as psychotherapy, see also Peters 1978.

Beginning with such works as Radin 1927 and Evans-Pritchard 1937, anthropologists have been taking magical thought and practice more and more seriously, and by now the traditional cultural chauvinism toward non-Western societies has largely vanished (e.g., Horton 1967, Campbell 1989). With a few exceptions (e.g., Winch 1964) the philosophers have moved much more slowly.

The most sophisticated recent attempt to argue the superiority of Modern (Occidental) culture is that of Habermas (1981a, 43–74). Habermas still operates with the outmoded Enlightenment classification of worldviews into mythic, religious-metaphysical, and Modern. He accepts Weber's thesis of the *Entzauberung* (Habermas's term is 'demythologization') of Modernity. In contrast to all other cultures, he argues, Modernity has freed itself of the fetters of the mythic orientation, and so is able to arrive at a stance which can claim universal validity, characterized by a "readiness to learn" (62) and a "cognitive adequacy" (60) which enables "the coherence and the truth of . . . statements . . . as well as the effectiveness of the plans of action dependent on them" (60).

Habermas's argument falls through once it is recognized that a mythic worldview is foundational for *all* cultures, including Modernity. What is special about the Modern mythic understructure is its secular disguise, which cuts it off from the process of rationalization that other cultures are able to undertake. As a consequence, it retains a primitive closeness to the unconscious which enables the kind of savage breakthroughs that have characterized this century.

In particular, Habermas holds that Western scientific rationality is universally valid in principle, but has been hypostatized by "a pattern of cultural and societal rationalization that helps cognitive-instrumental rationality to achieve a one-sided dominance not only in our dealings with external nature, but also in our understanding of the world and in the communicative practice of everyday life" (66). But this hypostatization is *intrinsic* to Modernity, because it expresses a mythic view already evident in the Book of Genesis, and which is also, it may be added, the underlying basis of Habermas's division between nature and humanity.

The self-understanding of Modernity needs to be extended to an examination of its mythic roots, a project which is not furthered by denying their existence.

While the bulk of this chapter is an attempt to integrate work drawn from a variety of sources, the final section, on the collective unconscious, is as far as I am aware original, and entirely specula-tive in nature. I have developed this idea for three reasons.

First, it carries through the central theme of the book, the inter-play of conscious and unconscious. Durkheim's idea of the collec-tive consciousness has become foundational for much contemporary sociology. Such a fundamental idea as a social norm, for example, is unintelligible unless one posits something of the kind. From a Freudian perspective, all conscious thought has an unconscious basis. But it seems impossible to account for a *collective* conscious-ness as based on an aggregate of the unconscious processes of sepa-rate individuals. It would seem necessary to assume the existence of a *collective* unconscious basis.

Second, given the argument that the basic character and mode of operation of unconscious intentionality is the same everywhere, and on the further supposition that conscious thought always derives from and (in one way or another) expresses unconscious thought and motivation, how is one to account for the enormous diversity among (and for that matter within) past and present lifeworlds? It would seem necessary to posit distinctive unconscious uniformities beneath the distinctive features of each lifeworld.

Third, we have the problem of the explanation of large-scale his-torical change. The question of the origins of Modernity is a case in point. Beginning with Marx and Weber, there has been a huge amount of study and an enormous literature on the topic. But, in my view at least, the answers remain as elusive as ever. Perhaps this is because unconscious forces play a crucial role in such change. But, here again, the notion of the unconscious playing a role in history would seem to require that such unconscious intentionality be collective in nature.

8

THE
UNCONSCIOUS
IN HUMAN LIFE

In previous chapters the approach has been broadly developmental and historical. In the evolution of both individual and social life, when a new stage or phase is reached, as a general rule it does not replace what is already there, but adds to it. The development is cumulative, and the past remains active in the present, not always as strongly as originally, but often to an important extent. In this final chapter, I will switch to a synchronic approach in which the past is treated as contained in the present, and materials spread out sequentially in the previous chapters are considered as a contemporaneous whole. I shall also take up more fully two issues touched on only briefly earlier: the nature of authenticity and the relativity of lifeworlds.

The Unconscious in the Conscious Life of the Individual

Unconscious intentionality not only lies underneath, but also, contrary to what is often supposed, suffuses and pervades the entire conscious life of the person. Like the air we breathe, it is invisible and unnoticed, but continuously enters into and sustains our conscious lives. It does so in a wide variety of ways, sometimes relatively directly and sometimes highly indirectly, and with an equally wide range of intensity, sometimes a shout, sometimes a whisper. The route by which repressed intentionality finds its way to conscious awareness is usually especially indirect and disguised. I will begin, however, with material that is not repressed.

Let us take sexual desire as an example. On the unconscious level, the desire will, in part, take the form of awareness of the intensely radiating presence of the other person, in perception or imagination. If the other is present, his or her demeanor and comportment will be a part of what is perceived, and if the attraction is mutual, this will undoubtedly be noted, via the often subtle clues to which unconscious awareness is so sensitive, and contribute its quality and intensity to the total global perception.

This perceptual, emotional, and desireful experience will be accompanied by an entourage of fantasies – i.e., imagined events – of sexual interaction with the other, ranging from playful flirtations to a variety of full-scale sexual encounters, plus, very possibly, a range of speculative fantasies about the consequences of these imagined events.

More than this, the other person will inevitably be unconsciously identified with important figures from the past, including most likely one or both parents. Here the fantasies will take on an incestuous tone, and the imagined consequences will proliferate darkly.

Freud once likened the unconscious id to a seething cauldron, a comparison which underestimates the structured character of even the most primitive mental activity, but which aptly points to the hugely exfoliated and turbulent character of intensely felt and motivated unconscious experience. Only a fraction of such intentionality ever enters consciousness, and it does so in a strongly altered form. Naturally the incestuous and other forbidden components will be repressed, but I am leaving them aside for the time being. Even with respect to unconscious materials which are not repressed, processes of selection, modification, and transformation are at work. First, the inner and outer aspects of the experience are separated, at least to a degree. The desire for the other is distinguished from the other who is desired. Second, the modalities of awareness – perception, desire, emotion, cognition, memory, fantasy – are more or less separated. Third, the ontological modes in which the objects of awareness can occur are separated out, into real, pretend, imaginary, fictional, and so on. Fourth, objects and events (perceived, imagined, or remembered) are conceptualized in linguistic as against prelinguistic terms. Fifth, cognitive capacities, such as categorical organization, reality assessment and testing, and ability to foresee the probable outcome of alternative actions, are greatly enhanced. It has been traditional in the psychoanalytic literature to see such cognitive processes of reality assessment as an ego function – i.e., as confined to the system conscious-preconscious – but this is in error. Rather, the advent of conscious-preconscious thought greatly enhances the substantial previously established cognitive capacities of unconscious thought already in effect.

To continue the example, even leaving aside what is repressed, not all the unconscious contents of the sexually charged awareness of the other will be translated/transformed into consciousness. As we have seen, the very categorical structure of conscious-preconscious thought plays a filtering role. Furthermore, at any given moment much of what comes through will not attain full consciousness. For example, in the absence of the other, full play may be given to sexual fantasies, while realistic factors are relegated to the preconscious. On the other hand, where the other is present, say at a social or occupational occasion, the fantasies will be confined to the preconscious, awaiting a more appropriate moment for their conscious expression.

Despite all these processes of alteration and filtration, however, it remains the case that much conscious awareness consists of the unconscious made conscious, and to that extent the unconscious is not underneath, but *in* the lifeworld, brought there via a direct though transformative and selective route. This point holds, in fact, for the full range of conscious-preconscious thought. To a very substantial extent, the unconscious is not a separate realm, but is an integral and vital part of the conscious, verbally articulated lifeworld.

To a lesser and more qualified degree, the same point holds for repressed intentionality, which rarely if ever remains wholly unconscious. The path to consciousness, however, is usually indirect, often very much so. What becomes conscious serves not only to express, but also to conceal, what is unconscious. Sometimes the unconscious thought and its conscious expression are opposites: via reaction formation, what is unconsciously loved and desired may be consciously hated and abhorred. Moreover, much of the intensity of the unconscious motivation is often lost in transit. My treatment has departed from Freud's in a number of respects, but, as is so often the case, he is right about the central point. The main structural line within the psyche is created not by the topographic division between unconscious and conscious-preconscious awareness, but by repression, which serves to cut lifeworld off from underworld – not completely, but to a significant degree.

Earlier, I discussed the impoverishment of the self which repression can create. Such impoverishment can extend to the entire personality. In connection with this theme, I would like to take up the topic of the nature of personal 'authenticity'.

Authenticity

In Modern philosophy the notion of authenticity was given its first important treatment by Heidegger (1927). In his hands, as well as those of others – e.g., Habermas (1981b) – the idea seems rather formalistic and empty, with the result that there are no criteria to determine what authenticity consists of concretely, either in general or in the particular case.

Under Heidegger's influence, the theme of authenticity was taken up by the existentialists, most notably Sartre (1943), for whom the creation of an authentic identity or selfhood is a central element of the existentialist project. As with Heidegger, there are no clear philosophical or psychological guidelines as to the actual content of such authenticity; so from the existentialist perspective the choice of what kind of person one is to become is purely arbitrary. What is required is that the decision be made as to who one is to be, and then resolutely put into action in one's life. The authentic person is self-created.

The paradoxical nature of the idea of self-creation was noted already by Plato, and if the arguments in the previous chapters are given weight, the extent to which we can deliberately shape our own personalities on a preconceived plan is quite limited. What normally occurs is at best a surface transformation which leaves the basic personality untouched. It is no accident that Sartre was led at one point to deny the existence of the unconscious, for the idea decisively undermines the existentialist project.

Despite the difficulties in the notion of authenticity in the hands of such figures as Heidegger and Sartre, their treatments seem to me nevertheless to contain an insight, which I will attempt to retain in my own reformulation of the concept.

The position taken here is that authenticity is a way of being in the lifeworld, such that the personality, and especially the unconscious personality, is able to achieve there a relatively full expression in action and identity. As such, authenticity applies primarily to the personality and only secondarily to the self. I shall develop this view via an example.

Suppose we have someone who is a medical doctor, a practicing physician. To be a doctor, or course, is to occupy a socially (and legally) defined role. Doctors are supposed to act in certain ways, and to have certain attitudes and motivations, as expressed, for example, by the Hippocratic oath. I shall begin by considering the relation of this role to the doctor's self, and then broaden the canvass to treat the whole personality. A doctor's role can relate to her self in a variety of ways. At one extreme, she could regard the role as something wholly exterior to her 'I', like a part in a play, which she performs for one reason or another – perhaps financial gain, perhaps a desire for respect and deference, perhaps to fulfill a promise to a dying parent – but which she does not regard as an expression of her selfhood. This is a case of insincerity, not inauthenticity: the role is not an expression of her self, and the attitudes and motivations out of which her behavior springs are not what they appear to be.

On the other hand, the doctor might accept her role more fully, to the extent that being a doctor becomes a part of her identity. Here, the role has been internalized, the appropriate motives and attitudes are adopted as her own, and she acts the part out of conviction, quite aside from questions of expediency or other motivations external to the role. In this case, the role performance is sincere, but not yet necessarily authentic. To decide the issue, it is necessary to examine the motivational springs of the role performance more closely.

To continue the example, suppose further that in childhood the doctor had always been a 'good girl', who lived up relatively well to the standards and expectations of her parents. With the formation of her 'I' her identity became established along those lines. When she grew up, she transferred her desire to live up to the expectations of her parents to a desire to live up to the expectations of social authority at large. The identity of a good girl grew into the identity of a good doctor. She not only plays the part, but she sees herself as having the appropriate motivations, and indeed she does, at least on the conscious level. In that sense the selfhood is quite genuine.

But, in this example, the basis of her identity as a doctor in her personality as a whole is quite narrow. It rests mainly, perhaps entirely, on her desire to be the adult equivalent of a good girl. The role requirements could be just anything at all, and she would live up to them with equal sincerity. Her goal of helping patients get well rests entirely on her desire to do her job, not on any genuine caring for them. Had chance placed her in charge of the torture chamber in the Inquisition, she would have performed this job with equal diligence, without the need for any substantive change in her personality. Her identity as a doctor is inauthentic, because while the *fact* that she performs her task is grounded in and expresses her personality, *what* she does is not. What has happened is that the socially defined role has been internalized but not integrated with the rest of the personality, probably because the original 'Me' of a 'good girl' was never so integrated.

The pattern I am describing is a common one. Many people live decent, law-abiding lives for no other reason than that is what is expected of them. As the experiments of Milgram (1975) have shown, such people will not hesitate to act in a cruel or destructive way if told to do so by someone in authority. Here we have the explanation of what is otherwise inexplicable, how the most 'civilized' nation in Europe could be the site of the horror of the holocaust. There were of course some authentically evil people among both leaders and followers, but, as the detailed study of Katz (1993) has shown, the majority of Germans who participated in the genocidal program were 'ordinary people', lost, as Heidegger would say, in the world of Nazism.

If the human personality and self were wholly products of the life-world, *everybody* would be like this, and there would be no good or bad, authenticity or inauthenticity, but only many conformists and a few deviants, who, as Nietzsche bitingly put it, would go voluntarily to the lunatic asylum. But this is not the case. As I have argued, the basic character of the person is not produced by society, but only influenced by it. The relation of the personality, especially the unconscious personality, to society is as a consequence highly variable and frequently quite complex. What I am pointing to here is the variability of the degree to which the personality can express itself in – in Freudian terms, be discharged into – conscious life-world activity. This is not primarily a matter of the integration of the conscious and unconscious components of the self into what Kohut (1971) has called a 'cohesive self'. Authenticity is instead measured by the degree to which the person as a whole is able to *find* herself in the world.

Two of the most dramatic examples of such authenticity may be mentioned briefly. The first is to be found in charismatic leadership, where the unconscious life of the leader shines through into the life-world so strongly that the unconscious resources of the followers are powerfully awakened and mobilized. The second is artistic production, in which the inner vision of the artist is concretized, expressed, and fulfilled. Art that does not succeed in expressing the personality of the artist is inauthentic, at best mere decoration.

Authenticity does not require that the unconscious motivation of behavior be conscious. Suppose, for example, that a prosecuting attorney's vigorous pursuit of justice in the courtroom has its unconscious roots in a sense of guilt and need for punishment, which finds its expression, via displacement, in securing the conviction of lawbreakers. In that case, nevertheless, the pursuit of justice is an authentic expression of the prosecutor's own personality. Such unconscious roots, of course, create the danger that the prosecutor may become overzealous, and succeed in obtaining the conviction of innocent people. One should not confuse authenticity with responsibility, much less morality. Much but not all ethnic and racial prejudice is authentic in the sense developed here, because it constitutes an expression of unconscious forces strongly embedded in the overall personality. One needs to distinguish between an authentic anti-Semite and one whose prejudice is simply a matter of going along with the crowd.

It is true that what is unconscious usually manages to find its way into consciousness in any case, but for the inauthentic person what is a shout on the unconscious level emerges into consciousness as a whisper, audible only to those with trained ears. In contrast, even highly indirect expressions of the unconscious can carry much of the original motivation with them, and these must be regarded as authentic, for the remoteness of the connection is overcome by the immediacy of the emotional intensity. To repeat, this is not to be confused with morality or integrity. The hatred that obsesses the bigot, for example, is often an authentic shining through of unconscious rage and loathing toward the self, the unconscious as actively present in the lifeworld.

So far, authenticity has been treated as something that pertains to the individual, but the term can be used in a collective sense as well. In the previous chapter I developed the idea of the basic myths of a religion as an expression of the collective unconscious of the group. As long as this is the case, a religion can be said to be authentic. However, if the rituals that reenact the mythic stories fail to evoke such a collective unconscious and bring it to presence in the lifeworld, the religion has become inauthentic, and having lost its unconscious roots, will be forced to rely more and more on its ideological superstructure, the nexus of worldly interests and powers in which it is embedded, and the inertia of tradition and empty ritual. Deprived of the life of its unconscious roots, the tree will stand, now shorn of its leaves and flowers, perhaps for a long time, but eventually it will fall to the ground, all at once or piece by piece. An inauthentic individual can survive and prosper; not so an inauthentic religion.

The Conscious in the Unconscious Life of the Individual

In contrast to the material just discussed, the reverse process, when consciousness reaches down and effects changes in unconscious thought, is relatively neglected in the psychoanalytic literature. There are some exceptions. Freud's view of the origin of 'fixed', as against 'mobile' investments (cathexes) is an example. As described earlier, already at the one-word (lexical) stage, language acts to enhance the presence of absent objects, and hence to stabilize both the awareness of objects and the intensity of the unconscious attachments to them. This helps explain the durability of primitive fantasies and object attachments which are formed after the lexical stage has been reached, in the second year.

More generally, as conscious awareness carries along with it the unconscious intentionality of which it is the translation, at the same time it reaches down to stabilize and reshape that intentionality. Meanwhile those elements which have not been so translated and transformed remain actively in place, as a part of the total (conscious and unconscious) experience.

Not only conscious awareness, but also the lifeworld in which this consciousness is embedded, has a shaping and structuring effect on the unconscious. The lifeworld always opens up a range of possibilities for the conscious expression of unconscious intentionality, and closes off another range of possibilities. Those motivations which are able to find expression are thereby shaped and strengthened, and those which cannot will be partly diverted, so that the original motive will be weakened. In this way the unconscious personality will be structured and altered.

Perhaps an example will make this clear. Suppose that there are two boys with initially identical personalities, and who in particular have an ambivalent attitude toward those in authority. On the one hand, they are motivated to comply with the commands and expectations of authority figures, such as teachers, policemen, community leaders, and so on; on the other hand they both also have a rebellious streak, and wish to act against and in defiance of such people. Naturally, we should expect such ambivalence to have its unconscious roots in the original Oedipal conflicts, as well as in pre-Oedipal formations.

Now let us place the two boys in radically different environments, the one in a well to do family living in the suburbs, the other a member of the urban underclass living in the slums. Obviously, the life chances of the two are quite different. If the rich boy plays his cards with reasonable prudence, his chances of winding up in a remunerative and prestigious career are excellent, while for the poor boy to get ahead in similar terms, he needs to be exceptionally bright, diligent, and lucky. For most in his position, such an outcome is not a reasonable hope.

While it is hazardous to generalize to the individual case, we should expect that in most instances, by the time they reach adolescence, the two will have sharply different personalities, extending well into the unconscious level. Take the suburban youth first. For him, playing by the rules will pay big dividends. We should expect him to develop a conscience, in which these rules are internalized. He belongs to the world of the wealthy and the powerful and he will identify with them. These identifications will in turn feed back and strengthen the underlying superego identifications, and so strengthen his conscience. His rebelliousness will be confined to minor incidents, unlikely to get him into serious trouble. The bulk of the hostility to authority will be repressed, taking its place beside the underlying Oedipal rage. Lacking suitable opportunities for behavioral expression, much of this anger will be displaced into distant and socially acceptable channels. By the time he reaches adulthood, the balance of forces between the two sides of the original ambivalence will have been changed not only on the conscious level, but unconsciously as well, and a partial solution to the original Oedipal dilemma will have been worked out.

For the other youth, in contrast, the grapes of unattainable conventional success will appear sour, and the negative side of the ambivalence toward those in authority will have free rein. This will weaken his identifications with such persons and undermine the underlying Oedipal identifications, at least on the positive side. The strongest identifications will be formed with the members of a peer group, very possibly a street gang whose values and behavior are, from the point of view of the official values, more or less deviant.

The youth may well form a strong conscience, but what is internalized will be the normative rules of this group. The original Oedipal ambivalence will be reversed, or at least a very different side of it will be strengthened. The anger will be directed toward the official hierarchy, surrogates of the 'bad' Oedipal parents, and the desire to conform focused on the peer group, and its subculture values. We now have two people who differ sharply, both in conscious personality and the unconscious formations which this personality expresses. The lifeworld has reached out and shaped the unconscious life of the two strongly but differently, because of their different life situations and life chances.

The above hypothetical example has ignored what is usually a decisive shaping factor, family life. If the lower-class boy were a member of a close-knit family, where his parents were strongly ambitious that he move up in the world, and hence expected and demanded much of him, while at the same time the upper-class boy had the kind of permissive and uncaring family life depicted by Lasch in *The Culture of Narcissism* (1978), the two outcomes might have been reversed.

As the above examples suggest, the familiar tenet of psychoanalytic theory that a person's basic character, especially the unconscious character, is more or less permanently established by the age of six or eight, needs to be qualified. In the first place, adolescence is also an important formative period, especially for women, and indeed, as Erikson has argued, to some extent, one's character continues to evolve throughout life. The general point is that personality is always shaped in part by the lifeworld and the particular position of the individual within the lifeworld, and this shaping process extends to the unconscious.

A brief discussion of Freud's essay "Character and Anal Eroticism" (1908) will perhaps serve to clarify this point further. Here Freud described a certain type of person as "noteworthy for a regular combination of the three following characteristics. They are especially *orderly, parsimonious* and *obstinate*. Each of these words actually covers a small group or series of interrelated character-traits" (169). Obviously, these character traits manifest themselves in the context of conscious lifeworld activity. Freud goes on to assert that these traits are displacements of, and receive their motivational impetus from, an anal-erotic sexual orientation which is unacceptable in our society and which has therefore been repressed. The consciously evident character traits are expressions of this unconscious sexual orientation. He concludes as follows:

> We can at any rate lay down a formula for the way in which character in its final shape is formed out of the constituent instincts: the permanent character-traits are either unchanged prolongations of the original instincts, or sublimations of those instincts, or reaction-formations against them. (1908, 175)

Here Freud is stressing, as usual, the degree to which consciously manifested character is an expression of the person's basic instinctual orientation. In arguing that there is also a current in the opposite direction, I would like to make three points.

First, Freud states that it is the social prohibitions of our civilization that are responsible for the repressions and subsequent displacements of the anal-erotic desires which result in this particular character type. In another civilization, more permissive towards anal eroticism, the results might have been different. Furthermore, as I have just argued, one can expect different results for different positions *within* a given lifeworld. To put the matter more accurately, the aggregate results can be expected to be different for populations occupying different positions within the lifeworld. So, both for groups and in the individual case one cannot reason from basic instinctual orientation to consciously manifested personality unless one also takes into account lifeworld and position within lifeworld. Since Freud was dealing almost exclusively with upper-middle-class Europeans with a relatively uniform lifeworld situation, in his discussions this factor receded into the background as occasionally mentioned context.

Second, an orientation at a given developmental stage, such as anal eroticism, is never the *only* way in which the sexual drive manifests itself in the unconscious. As has been stressed, the earlier stages of a person's developmental history always remain active, and even a powerful fixation cannot be expected to rule out at least a modicum of subsequent development. Moreover, a fixation at a given level is generally the result of a regression from a later stage, which will remain at least residually active. The human unconscious is a very complex affair, and to say that a person's basic sexual orientation is anal erotic in character, can mean only that this is the most heavily invested aspect of a complex sexual orientation, and the one which is most strongly expressed in conscious activity.

Third, the evolution of the unconscious character of the individual slows drastically after adolescence, but change can still occur, especially in response to important life changes, such as marriage, divorce, the death of someone close, or a loss or drastic change of job. Not all of the multiplicity of unconscious motivations and formations that are present can find significant expression at the same time, even given the wide variety of possible condensations and compromise formations at the disposal of the individual. Important events, or even the passage of time, can result in an alteration in the balance of forces in the unconscious, bringing previously dormant tendencies into greater activity and thence into conscious expression, while mitigating the effect of heretofore dominant formations.

To summarize: (1) Unconscious and conscious thought and experience interact pervasively. Unconscious intentionality is continuously finding its way into consciousness, where it is expressed in the modes of conscious thought. Conversely, conscious intentionality feeds back into the unconscious, where it is expressed in the modes of unconscious thought. Much of the unconscious, however, remains unaffected. (2) The development of the unconscious character of the individual is strongly affected by conscious lifeworld experience, and even in maturity the lifeworld can continue to exercise a shaping influence on this character.

The Interplay of Conscious and Unconscious on the Level of Society

In treating the interplay of conscious and unconscious factors on the level of society, I will be running repeatedly into the issue of relativity. Here two themes will come to the fore: the question of the extent to which reality, and especially social reality, is socially constructed, and the question of the relativity of lifeworld perspectives and divergent perspectives within lifeworlds. I have already had something to say on these questions; in the remainder of this concluding chapter they will be explored further. In doing so, it will be necessary to be more explicit about the use of the two perspectives from which the analysis has proceeded: the intentional stance in the natural and the phenomenological attitudes. Heretofore I have often shifted from one attitude to the other without notice; now I must serve notice when doing so.

In chapter 6, I described at some length how all social organization is sustained by and takes its basic character from identifications which are, or have their roots in, the unconscious. In the following chapter, a crucial part of the lifeworld was examined, the world of the sacred. What distinguishes a sacred act or thing is its possession of magical power, which was identified as something quite real, the motivational power of the unconscious shining through into the lifeworld. At the heart of every religion is a system of myth, a story or stories which recount the origins of both the sacred and profane worlds and their inhabitants, and define the basic relations among these. Such myths also represent the unconscious shining through into the world, but this time we have, I speculated, a genuine collective unconscious. I would like here to explain somewhat further the rationale for this theoretical idea.

One of the traditional problems of political and social theory is the question of what makes possible and sustains social orders. Given the inequities, inequalities, and afflictions found in every society, even the most beneficent, why do people support them, or at least put up with them? Already this was a central issue in Plato's *Republic* and the problem has been of major concern to social and political theorists ever since.

The most important part of the answer, I believe, lies in an idea which was already adumbrated by Plato, and which has received its classic statements in the Modern era in the writings of Rousseau, Hegel, and Durkheim. Rousseau drew the distinction between the general will and the will of all. This distinction is closely similar to the one found in linguistics between 'language' (*la langue*) and 'speech' (*la parole*), between the rules that govern the use of language and the actual speech acts of the users. Although a language is a group product, those who speak it experience its rules as given objectively, independently of the wills of the speakers. In practice the individual using the language will depart from its rules from time to time, and indeed may not even be aware of some of them.

If a given departure of the practice of a language from its rules becomes widespread enough, it will eventually become incorporated in the language. There is thus an ongoing interplay between language and speech. In the short run, language governs speech, but not completely. In the long run, speech governs language.

Language is a part of the normative system of a social order, and the relation between language and speech is a special case of the relation between the normative system and the actual conduct of social action. The individual experiences the normative rule as objectively given, binding, and often divinely sanctioned. One of the main aspects of Durkheim's "collective consciousness" is the system of normative rules as reflected in the awareness of the group members. Actual practice will often depart to some extent from these norms, but if the departure is significant and frequent, the normative system will either change or break down. Just as speech is impossible without language, stable organized social action requires a system of social norms which the members of the collectivity are aware of as given objectively (i.e., independently of their particular wills) and binding. Durkheim's notion of the collective consciousness thus supplies an answer to the question of the nature of the cognitive and motivational foundations of social order: the cognitive foundation is the awareness of the norm as laid down independently of one's will, and the motivational foundation is the desire to obey it because it is experienced as authoritative.

These cognitive and motivational foundations in turn rest on unconscious subfoundations. In chapter 6, I described how the motivational springs of the binding force of a norm lie in the largely unconscious superego. In the following chapter, I introduced the idea of the collective unconscious as the counterpart of the collective consciousness.

From the phenomenological attitude, for the members of a collectivity, a social norm is experienced as objectively given: as existing independently of their awareness, like the tree in the field. There will be individual variations in the precise details as to how each individual understands the rule, but each collectivity has its own procedures whereby such variations can be dealt with and corrected should they be of any consequence. It is to be noted that the same point holds for the tree in the field. It may not appear to be exactly the same for all, but socially defined processes of reality testing are available for the reconciliation of differences. So we are justified in treating both the social norm and the tree as products and objects of a collective consciousness, experienced in the same way by the group members, testable and correctable as to content, and so quite rightly regarded by them as objectively 'there'.

All this is in accordance with the central phenomenological principle that all reality is socially constructed. But what are we to make of the ontological standing of the tree and the social norm when we move from the phenomenological to the natural attitude? I will take the tree first. Following Husserl, I have grounded the existence of the tree in the lifeworld. But there is more than one lifeworld, each of which sees the tree differently and, moreover, may have its own way of testing reality. Furthermore, there are wide variations in perspective within some lifeworlds. As I pointed out in the first chapter, this raises the question of relativity anew, on a deeper plane. We are now in a position to meet this problem. It has turned out that the lifeworld is not the ultimate, but only the penultimate perspective. Beneath the lifeworld lies the underworld open to unconscious awareness, and while lifeworlds vary, the basic character of the underworld is the same for everyone. For infants, prior to language, the tree is the same everywhere, because the perceptual processes employed are innate. With the advent of the linguistically constituted lifeworld, this initial conceptualization of the tree is revised according to the categorical modes peculiar to the lifeworld, and we now have not one tree but many: one for each lifeworld. But the original tree remains in unconscious awareness, and is swept up and included in the background of the conscious experience. The contents and objects of conscious experience are relative to lifeworld, but the underworld is universal, and provides the origin and ground of the lifeworld, both motivationally and cognitively. Here is where the relativity of the lifeworlds comes to an end.

I shall have more to say about trees later. Meanwhile I will switch ontological gears by moving from things which have a purely physical existence, like trees and thunderstorms, to events which have an intentional character, specifically actions. It will be recalled that an action has been defined as voluntary behavior that has a meaning for the actor, including a motive. Whereas trees and thunderstorms, when experienced or imagined, become the *objects* of intentional states, an action *contains* intentional states as components. On the unconscious level, in performing an action, or becoming aware of the act of another, the intentionality of the action is experienced as fused with its physical performance. In this respect the experience of the act does not differ from the experience of the tree. It is only with the advent of consciousness that we are able to differentiate the two aspects: the physical performance and its motivation.

Now, still in the natural attitude, let us move to a third category, that of a social norm. In contrast to a tree, a social norm is not something physical, nor, in contrast to an act, does it have a physical side or dimension. The latter point follows from the distinction between the system of norms and the system of social action, allied to the distinction between language and speech. Furthermore, a social norm is not something psychological. As Durkheim insisted, a social norm is a *social* not a psychological fact. It has an intentional character, in that it is about something, but it is not an intentional 'state' in the sense of being a mental act. Its ontological standing is the same as that of language: it has a propositional character which takes the form of a rule, and it is an emergent product of the interactions of the members of a collectivity over time. As in the case of a linguistic rule, a social norm is something objectively there, like a tree, and a belief in or perception of its existence and character is just as open to empirical verification as it is for a tree. Among sociologists, the point that a social norm is a social not a psychological entity is familiar and generally recognized by all except hard-core behaviorists, but is often difficult to accept by those whose primary orientation is psychological. I urge that such readers think the point through in terms of the distinction between language and speech, discussed briefly above.

While both the tree and the social norm are objectively there, independently of the awareness of any particular person, they otherwise have a quite different ontological standing. From the phenomenological perspective, of course, *everything* in the lifeworld is socially constructed, and this is quite correct as long as we stay on the conscious level. Matters are different, however, in the natural attitude, where, in the present case, social norms are socially constructed and trees are not. Social norms arise from the interaction of the members of a collectivity in a process that is much the same from both perspectives. From the natural attitude, however, the tree is not socially but *biologically* constructed. The seed germinates, takes root in the soil. If there is a forest fire, the tree, as Husserl said, burns. It is an important insight that when we suspend onto-logical judgments everything in the world emerges as a product of human intentionality, but this should not be allowed to obscure the fact that when we go back to the natural attitude, as we must if we want our inquiry to have any empirical bite, the tree and the social norm have a very different ontological standing.

The situation changes drastically when we move to the level of unconscious awareness. Here, from the phenomenological perspec-tive, the tree is constructed not by society but by the individual, in a process which is not social but psychological. The tree is con-structed independently by every person who sees or thinks about it. The reason why a tree turns out to be the same for everybody is that on the unconscious level the processes by which we become aware of the world, and the categories by which we conceptualize the world, are the same for everybody, a fact which requires the supposition that these processes and ways of categorization are innate. In the natural attitude, and from a lifeworld perspective which is able to take the unconscious into account, consciously apprehended trees differ from one lifeworld to another, but they all derive from the unconsciously apprehended tree, which is the ground and common denominator of them all.

The unconscious basis of social norms is more complex and in-direct than is the case with trees. I have already described the pro-cess whereby social norms grow out of the interaction of the members of social organizations, and how these organizations, in turn, are built out of lateral and vertical (superego) identifications. Children initially become aware of social norms by noting the consequences of observing or not observing them. Just as touching a hot stove has unpleasant consequences, so does (for example) hitting a younger sibling. Not long after the advent of language and consciousness, children begin to become aware of social norms as rules that they and others are expected to observe, on pain of sanctions. They are now aware of the rule *as a rule*, and while their compliance continues in part to be motivated by fear of sanctions and hope of reward, very possibly there is an additional motive to obey. It may be that the rule is obeyed in part because, as with the rules of grammar or eating with a spoon, it is simply the way things are done. Whether or not this factor is operative, children become able to recognize and observe social norms on this level during about the four- to six-year-old period.

So far, I have been treating social norms as comparable to language, where the distinction between the objective, externally given norms, and the performance of the members of the group in relation to them, corresponds to the distinction between language and speech. The comparison, however, has its limits. First, in contrast to linguistic rules, social norms are often perceived not as a part of the nature of things, but rather as the commandments of authoritative beings, divine or human. Second, in contrast to linguistic rules, as we have seen, the binding power of social norms has important unconscious roots, even where the norms have not been internalized. Third, internalization adds a whole new dimension. I will take up internalization a little later, after considering an aspect of the interplay between conscious and unconscious in the case where the norm is not internalized.

A social norm has a dual character. First, there is the naming or description of an act (e.g., breaking a promise); second, there is the statement or judgment that such an act is wrongful. This duality requires that awareness of the norm be on the conscious-preconscious level, because of the propositional character of the second element. On the unconscious level an act, or the idea of an act (e.g., patricide), can be experienced as horrible or dangerous, but the idea that the act is wrongful is inherently linguistic.

Now let us take as an example an act that would not ordinarily be experienced as horrible or dangerous, except for the fact that it is a grave normative offense, for example, for a Christian, spitting on a cross. For someone ignorant of Christianity, such an act would not seem very special. The gravity of the offense springs from its relation to Christian beliefs and symbols. For the believer, however, the act is not only judged to be a grave offense, it is *experienced* as a terrible act. The psychological origins of the prohibition against spitting on the cross are clear enough. Basically, it is an offense against God the father and therefore a violation of the Oedipal prohibition. The original unconscious Oedipal hatred, as well as the reaction against this hatred, are mobilized and shine through into consciousness as horror at the sight or even thought of the deed.

The unconscious thought is not the expression of a social norm, because it does not have a propositional character. Unconsciously, the observed or imagined deed is not wrongful; it is horrible. Here the conscious prohibition is the vehicle whereby the connection is made between the Oedipal feelings and the act of spitting on the cross. This connection would never occur purely on the unconscious level. It is necessary for the unconscious formation to be externalized into a system of consciously held religious beliefs, including the beliefs clustered around the symbol of the cross. Only then can the act take on its powerful unconscious meaning. In this instance, as is often the case, first the unconscious shapes the conscious lifeworld, then the lifeworld evolves in partial independence of its unconscious sources, and then it feeds back to the unconscious, bringing something new with it.

I have argued that a social norm which is experienced as something external, either the command of an authoritative leader or an objectively valid rule, is not something psychological. The *awareness* of the norm is of course a mental act, as is, for example, the awareness of a tree. But the social norm is no more inside the mind than the tree. Even an *internalized* norm is not necessarily something psychological. Schematically, such a norm consists in an awareness of the norm, a belief in its rightness, and a desire to conform that is motivated more or less independently of the influence of accompanying external sanctions. As we have seen, in common with externalized norms, but via an additional psychic action, these motivations derive their force from the largely unconscious superego. On the conscious level, which, as I have argued, is the only level on which a norm can be experienced *as a norm*, there are two ways in which an internalized norm can be conceptualized. On the one hand, it can be seen as binding because it is inherently right or authoritatively given, independently of one's will. In this case, the norm remains external. On the other hand, it can be integrated into the 'I' and experienced as the dictate of one's own conscience, grounded not in the objective nature of reality but the subjective character of one's identity. Here, on the level of the individual, the norm assumes a psychological existence as an inner mirror of the external social rule.

Conclusion

In this final section, I will summarize the conclusions on questions of relativity which have emerged from my analysis of the nature and influence of unconscious thought in human life. It will be recalled that I distinguished two broad aspects of this theme: the implications raised first by the thesis of the social construction of reality, and second by the different perspectives found among and within lifeworlds. These two aspects are interconnected.

From a phenomenological perspective all reality is socially constructed. This is a valuable insight. But it must be recalled that this perspective requires a deliberate 'bracketing' of all ontological judgments from the course of inquiry. Once this stance is taken, the term 'reality' can only mean 'what those whose intentional life is being described *take* reality to be.' Hence, from this perspective the thesis of the social construction of reality simply states that the members of every lifeworld construct a picture of the nature of reality, and that this picture varies widely from one lifeworld to another.

What makes this conclusion so disturbing is the critique of the metaphysical tradition of Modern philosophy opened up by Husserl and carried through by Heidegger and his followers. The conclusion that emerged from this critique is that it is futile to attempt to discover any grounding for human knowledge more basic than the lifeworld perspective, and consequently there is nothing to go by other than what people take reality to be.

If all lifeworlds had essentially the same perspective, this conclusion would not be very unsettling, but since lifeworld perspectives can differ markedly, we are faced with the situation of an indefinite number of different and incommensurate pictures of reality, all equally valid, with no rational basis for choice among them.

For example, earlier I wrote that while a tree is socially constructed from a phenomenological perspective, from the natural attitude it is biologically constructed. By 'natural attitude', of course, I meant the natural attitude of my own lifeworld, more specifically, the sector of this lifeworld in which I live. The biologically constructed tree is what I *take* it to be, from that perspective. From the natural attitude of another lifeworld, the tree may be something quite different. Of course, I have available methods for testing the adequacy of my understanding of what the tree is, and the scientific method of the botanist is a refinement of these methods. As long as I stay within the perspective of my lifeworld, this handles the question of objectivity. But other lifeworlds may have different methods of testing the adequacy of their vision, and they may be equally effective, within that framework.

If the tenet is granted that the lifeworld is the ultimate ground on which our understanding of the world rests and from which it proceeds, it seems to me that there is no escaping the radical relativism that is so widespread in contemporary thought. It is precisely this tenet that I have challenged in this work, not on philosophical but on empirical grounds. The ultimate basis for human understanding is not the lifeworld, but the world which opens up to unconscious awareness, a world which lies both beneath and, as I have argued, *within* the lifeworld. And this world is the same for everyone, regardless of lifeworld differences. This conclusion is of course open to challenge, as is any conclusion which rests on empirical grounds, and it cannot be denied that much more is needed by way of cross-cultural study. The evidence is nevertheless formidable, and the conclusions drawn from this evidence seem to me justified, at least on a provisional basis.

The distinctive features of unconscious intentionality and its objects have been summarized above, and need not be repeated here. Suffice it to say that despite the fact that unconscious awareness fuses perception, cognition, feeling, and desire into a global whole, it builds a fully developed *world*, complex, well articulated, and strongly invested. This world is the foundation of the conscious lifeworld, and it remains pervasively present within the lifeworld, sometimes shaping it unobtrusively and indirectly, sometimes shining through in a relatively direct fashion. It is true that the lifeworld in its own turn feeds back and in some respects exercises a strong influence over unconscious thought. I have even suggested the existence of a collective unconscious which, in contrast to Jung's conception, is not universal but specific to particular collectivities. But these additions to the contents and objects of unconscious awareness do not erase what is already there; they overlay it. They add new content without modifying what is already there to a significant degree. At bottom the unconscious is the same everywhere, the very heartbeat of the common humanity of homo sapiens.

This common basis renders the relativity of lifeworlds and lifeworld sectors only relative. Relative to each other, lifeworlds can differ profoundly, and a far greater variety is possible than has yet occurred, as science fiction authors and other thinkers of a speculative bent have suggested. One should not underestimate the importance of these differences, and the difficulties that they pose to communication and comity. But relative to the unconscious all of these variations have the same grounding and origin. It is this relation that establishes what lifeworlds have in common, and creates the possibility of the achievement of common understandings and perhaps even common action across the cultural divides.

Sources

Authenticity. There is a substantial literature on this subject. Heidegger 1927 and Sartre 1943 are foundational. For a critique of Heidegger's position, see Guignon 1984. A well-known work, which treats the relation between sincerity and authenticity, is Trilling 1972 (see especially chapter 6, "The Authentic Unconscious"). More recent discussions of authenticity are to be found in Habermas 1981b, Tugendhat 1986, and C. Taylor 1991. For analyses of Sartre's rejection of the Freudian unconscious, see Soll 1981 and Neu 1988.

The classic discussion of the evolution of self and personality in adolescence and beyond is Erikson 1950. Plaut and Hutchinson (1986) emphasize the importance of puberty in the psychic development of women.

The discussion of the foundation of social order draws on my 1969 treatment. This work, however, was written before I had begun my study of Husserl, and my restudy of Freud and Weber, and does not represent my current position on a number of issues. I remain comfortable, nevertheless, with the treatments in that work of the distinction between power and authority, and their institutionalization into the political and economic subsystems of society, which is one reason why these topics have not been addressed in this book.

The treatment of social norms caps off my attempt to synthesize the insights of Durkheim, Freud, and Husserl, and is intended to replace my 1969 formulations.

On relativity, see Wilson 1970, Hollis and Lukes 1982, Bernstein 1983 and 1988, and Guignon 1990. Bernstein's view that "the truth of hermeneutics is pluralism, not relativism," seems to apply to Gadamer. As Warnke has put it,

> For Gadamer, the point of hermeneutics is to overcome distances between cultures and historical epochs. . . . Historical and cultural perspectives are not conceived of as systems of ideas closed off from one another, but as vantage points for reciprocal evaluation and thus for a continuing convergence of views. (1985, 356)

That is undoubtedly Gadamer's intention. The problem is that such a "fusion of horizons" requires a preexisting common ground from which to proceed, and the extreme form of the linguistic turn taken by him and others would seem to preclude such a common ground except *within* a given tradition.

Habermas's project to overcome the relativity of lifeworlds via a universally valid process of rational communication is itself culture bound, because it rests on the tenet of the intrinsic superiority of Modernity, and is unrealistic as well, because it requires the abandonment of a mythic orientation to the world, which, as I have argued, is basic to all social orders.

WORKS CITED

Anderson, Benedict. 1983. *Imagined Communities: Reflections on the Origin and Spread of Nationalism*. London: Verso.

Armstrong, D. M. 1981. *The Nature of Mind and Other Essays*. Ithaca: Cornell University Press.

Astington, Janet W., Paul L. Harris, and David R. Olson. 1988. *Developing Theories of Mind*. New York: Cambridge University Press.

Baillargeon, Renee, Elisabeth Spelke, and Stanley Wasserman. 1985. "Object Permanence in Five-Month-Old Infants." *Cognition* 20:191–208.

Bernstein, Richard J. 1983. *Beyond Objectivism and Relativism*. Philadelphia: University of Pennsylvania Press.

————. 1988. "Metaphysics, Critique, and Utopia." *Review of Metaphysics* 42:255–73.

Bisiach, Edoardo, and Anthony J. Marcel, eds. 1988. *Consciousness in Contemporary Science*. New York: Oxford University Press.

Blos, Peter. 1974. "The Genealogy of the Ego Ideal." *The Psychoanalytic Study of the Child* 29:43–88.

Brenner, Charles. 1982. "The Concept of the Superego: A Reformulation." *Psychoanalytic Quarterly* 51:501–25.

Brentano, Franz. 1874. "The Distinction between Mental and Physical Phenomena." In *Realism and the Background of Phenomenology*, ed. R. M. Chisholm. Glencoe, Ill.: Free Press, 1960.

Bretherton, Inge, and Marjorie Beeghly. 1982. "Talking about Internal States: The Acquisition of an Explicit Theory of Mind." *Developmental Psychology* 18:906–21.

Broughton, J. 1978. "Development of Concepts of Self, Mind, Reality, and Knowledge." *New Directions for Child Development* 1:75–100.

Bullock, Merry, Rachel Gelman, and Renee Baillargeon. 1982. "The Development of Causal Reasoning." In *The Developmental Psychology of Time*, ed. W. J. Friedman. New York: Academic Press.

Cairns, Dorion. 1972. "The Many Senses and Denotations of the Word *Bewusstsein* ('Consciousness') in Edmund Husserl's Writings." In *Life-world and Consciousness: Essays for Aron Gurwitsch*, ed. Lester O. Embree. Evanston: Northwestern University Press.

Call, Justin D. 1980. "Some Prelinguistic Aspects of Language Development." *Journal of the American Psychoanalytic Association* 28:259–89.

Campbell, Alan Tormaid. 1989. *To Square with Genesis: Causal Statements and Shamanic Ideas in Waypâpí*. Edinburgh: Edinburgh University Press.

Carey, Susan. 1985. *Conceptual Change in Childhood*. Cambridge: MIT Press.

Carr, David. 1987. *Interpreting Husserl: Critical and Comparative Studies*. Dordrecht: Martinus Nijhoff.

Carruthers, Peter. 1989. "Brute Experience." *Journal of Philosophy* 86:258–69.

Chisholm, Roderick M. 1981. *The First Person: An Essay on Reference and Intentionality*. Minneapolis: University of Minnesota Press.

Damon, William, and Daniel Hart. 1982. "The Development of Self-understanding from Infancy through Adolescence." *Child Development* 53:841–64.

———. 1988. *Self-understanding in Childhood and Adolescence.* Cambridge: Cambridge University Press.

Darwin, Charles. 1872. *The Expression of the Emotions in Man and Animals.* Chicago: University of Chicago Press, 1965.

Davidson, Donald. 1980. *Essays on Actions and Events.* New York: Oxford University Press.

Demopoulis, William, and Ausonio Marras, eds. 1986. *Language Learning and Concept Acquisition: Foundational Issues.* Norwood, N.J.: Ablex.

Dennett, Daniel C. 1987. *The Intentional Stance.* Cambridge: MIT Press.

———. 1988. "Why Everyone is a Novelist." *Times Literary Supplement* No. 4, 459:1016, 1028–29.

Descartes, René. 1642. *Meditations on First Philosophy,* trans. Donald A. Cress. Indianapolis: Hackett, 1979.

Dixon, Keith. 1977. "Is Cultural Relativity Self-Refuting?" *British Journal of Sociology* 28:75–100.

Douglas, Mary. 1969. *Purity and Danger: An Analysis of the Concepts of Pollution and Taboo.* London: Routledge and Kegan Paul.

Drummond, John J. 1988. "Modernism and Postmodernism: Bernstein or Husserl?" *Review of Metaphysics* 42:275–300.

Durkheim, Emile. 1893. *The Division of Labor in Society,* trans. George Simpson. New York: Free Press, 1964.

———. 1912. *The Elementary Forms of Religious Life,* trans. Joseph Ward Swain. New York: The Free Press, 1965.

Eliade, Mircea. 1951. *Shamanism: Archaic Techniques of Ecstasy,* trans. Willard R. Trask. Princeton: Princeton University Press, 1964.

———. 1957. *Myths, Dreams, and Mysteries,* trans. Philip Mairet. New York: Harper and Row, 1975.

———. 1963a. *Myth and Reality,* trans. Willard R. Trask. New York: Harper and Row.

———. 1963b. *Patterns in Comparative Religion,* trans. Rosemary Sheed. New York: Meridian (New American Library).

———. 1968. *The Sacred and the Profane.* New York: Harcourt Brace.

Emde, Robert N. 1988. "Development, Terminable and Interminable: 1.

Innate and Motivational Factors from Infancy." *International Journal of Psychoanalysis* 69:23–42.

Erikson, Erik H. 1950. *Childhood and Society.* New York: W. W. Norton.

———. 1958. *Young Man Luther.* New York: W. W. Norton.

———. 1968. *Identity, Youth and Crisis.* New York: W. W. Norton.

Evans-Pritchard, E. E. 1937. *Witchcraft, Oracles and Magic among the Azande.* London: Oxford University Press, 1968.

Fagan, Joseph F., III. 1976. "Infants' Recognition of Invariant Features of Faces." *Child Development* 47:627–38.

Fairbairn, W. Donald. 1941. "A Revised Psychopathology of the Psychoses and Psychoneuroses." *International Journal of Psychoanalysis* 22:250–79.

Feldman, Carol Fleisher. 1988. "Early Forms of Thought about Thoughts: Some Simple Linguistic Expressions of Mental States." In *Developing Theories of Mind*, ed. Astington, Harris, and Olson.

Feldman, H., S. Goldin-Meadow, and L. Gleitman. 1978. "Beyond Herodotus: The Creation of Language by Linguistically Deprived Deaf Children." In *Action, Symbol, and Gesture: The Emergence of Language*, ed. A. Locke. New York: Academic Press.

Field, Tiffany M., Robert Woodson, Reena Greenberg, and Debra Cohen. 1982. "Discrimination and Imitation of Facial Expressions by Neonates." *Science* 218:179–81.

Fivush, Robyn. 1987. "Scripts and Categories: Interrelationships in Development." In *Concepts and Conceptual Development*, ed. Neisser.

Flavell, John H. 1988. "The Development of Children's Knowledge about the Mind: From Cognitive Connections to Mental Representations." In *Developing Theories of Mind*, ed. Astington, Harris, and Olson.

Flavell, John H., Eleanor R. Flavell, and Frances L. Green. 1983. "Development of the Appearance-Reality Distinction." *Cognitive Psychology* 15:95–120.

Føllesdal, Dagfinn. "Noema and Meaning in Husserl." *Philosophy and Phenomenological Research* 50:263–71.

Foucault, Michel. 1986. *The Care of the Self*, trans. Robert Hurley. New York: Random House.

Freud, Anna. 1936. *The Ego and the Mechanisms of Defense.* New York: International Universities Press, 1946.

Freud, Sigmund. *The Standard Edition of the Complete Psychological*

Works of Sigmund Freud, 24 vols., ed. James Strachey. London: Hogarth Press, 1953–66.

————. 1894. "The Neuro-psychoses of Defence." In *Standard Edition*, vol. 3.

————. 1895. *Project for a Scientific Psychology.* In *Standard Edition*, vol. 1.

————. 1900. *The Interpretation of Dreams.* In *Standard Edition*, vols. 4 and 5.

————. 1905. *Jokes and Their Relation to the Unconscious.* In *Standard Edition*, vol. 8.

————. 1908. "Character and Anal Eroticism." In *Standard Edition*, vol. 9.

————. 1913. *Totem and Taboo.* In *Standard Edition*, vol. 13.

————. 1914. "On Narcissism: An Introduction." In *Standard Edition*, vol. 14.

————. 1915a. "The Unconscious." In *Standard Edition*, vol. 14.

————. 1915b. "Instincts and Their Vicissitudes." In *Standard Edition*, vol. 14.

————. 1915c. "Thoughts for the Times on War and Death." In *Standard Edition*, vol. 14.

————. 1917. "Mourning and Melancholia." In *Standard Edition*, vol. 14.

————. 1919. "The Uncanny." In *Standard Edition*, vol. 17.

————. 1920. *Beyond the Pleasure Principle.* In *Standard Edition*, vol. 18.

————. 1920a. "The Psychogenesis of a Case of Homosexuality in a Woman." In *Standard Edition*, vol. 18.

————. 1921. *Group Psychology and the Analysis of the Ego.* In *Standard Edition*, vol. 18.

————. 1923. *The Ego and the Id.* In *Standard Edition*, vol 19.

————. 1925. "Some Additional Notes on Dream Interpretation as a Whole." In *Standard Edition*, vol. 19.

————. 1927. *The Future of an Illusion.* In *Standard Edition*, vol. 21.

————. 1930. *Civilization and Its Discontents.* In *Standard Edition*, vol. 21.

Gadamer, Hans-Georg. 1960. *Truth and Method.* New York: Crossroads Publishing, 1975.

————. 1976. *Philosophical Hermeneutics*, ed. and trans. D. E. Linge. Berkeley: University of California Press.

Gallup, Gordon G., Jr., and Susan D. Suarez. 1986. "Self-awareness and the Emergence of Mind in Humans and Other Primates." In *Psychological Perspectives on the Self*, vol. 3, ed. Suls and Greenwald.

Garfield, Jay L. 1989. "The Myth of Jones and the Mirror of Nature: Reflections on Introspection." *Philosophy and Phenomenological Research* 50:1–26.

Geertz, Clifford. 1973. *The Interpretation of Cultures*. New York: Basic Books.

Gelman, Susan A. 1988. "The Development of Induction within Natural Kind and Artifact Categories." *Cognitive Psychology* 20:65–95.

Gelman, Susan A., Pamela Collman, and Eleanor E. Maccoby. 1986. "Inferring Properties from Categories versus Inferring Categories from Properties: The Case of Gender." *Child Development* 57:396–404.

Gelman, Susan A., and Anne Watson O'Reilly. 1988. "Children's Inductive Inferences within Superordinate Categories: The Role of Language and Category Structure." *Child Development* 59:876–87.

Gleitman, Lila. 1986. "Biological Dispositions to Learn Language." In *Language Learning and Concept Acquisition*, ed. Demopoulis and Marras.

Golding, Robert. 1982. "Freud, Psychoanalysis, and Sociology: Some Observations on the Sociological Analysis of the Individual." *British Journal of Sociology* 33:545–62.

Golinkhoff, Roberta, Carol G. Harding, Vicki Carlson, and Miriam E. Sexon. 1984. "The Infant's Perception of Causal Events: The Distinction between Animate and Inanimate Objects." In *Advances in Infancy Research*, vol. 3, ed. L. P. Lipsitt and C. Rovee-Collier. Norwood, N.J.: Ablex.

Gould, James L., and Peter Marler. 1987. "Learning by Instinct." *Scientific American* 256:74–85.

Griffin, Donald. 1984. *Animal Thinking*. Cambridge: Harvard University Press.

Guignon, Charles B. 1984. "Heidegger's 'Authenticity' Revisited." *Review of Metaphysics* 38:321–39.

————. 1990. "Philosophy after Wittgenstein and Heidegger." *Philosophy and Phenomenological Research* 50:649–72.

Habermas, Jürgen. 1967. *On the Logic of the Social Sciences*, trans.

Sherry Weber Nicholson and Jerry A. Stark. Cambridge: MIT Press, 1988.

―――. 1981a. *The Theory of Communicative Action*. Vol. 1, *Reason and the Rationalization of Society*, trans. Thomas McCarthy. Boston: Beacon Press, 1984.

―――. 1981b. *The Theory of Communicative Action*. Vol. 2, *Lifeworld and System: A Critique of Functionalist Reason*, trans. Thomas McCarthy. Boston: Beacon Press, 1987.

Haldane, John. 1988. "Psychoanalysis, Cognitive Psychology, and Self-Consciousness." In *Mind, Psychoanalysis and Science*, ed. Peter Clark and Crispin Wright. Oxford: Basil Blackwell.

Hanna, Robert. 1993. "Logical Cognition: Husserl's *Prolegomena* and the Truth in Psychologism." *Philosophy and Phenomenological Research* 53:251–76.

Harris, Paul, and Paul Heelas. 1979. "Cognitive Processes and Collective Representations." *European Journal of Sociology* 20:211–41.

Hart, James G. 1975. "Mythic World as World." *International Philosophical Quarterly* 15:51–69.

Harter, Susan. 1983. "Developmental Perspectives on the Self-System." In *Handbook of Child Psychology*. Vol. 4, *Socialization, Personality, and Social Development*, ed. E. M. Hetherton. New York: Wiley.

―――. 1986. "Cognitive-Developmental Processes in the Integration of Concepts about Emotions and the Self." *Social Cognition* 4:119–51.

Heibeck, Tracey H., and Ellen M. Markman. 1987. "Word Learning in Children: An Examination of Fast Mapping." *Child Development* 58:1021–34.

Heidegger, Martin. 1927. *Being and Time*, trans. John Macquarrie and Edward Robinson. New York: Harper and Row, 1962.

Hobsbawm, Eric J. 1990. *Nations and Nationalism Since 1780: Program, Myth, Reality*. Cambridge: Cambridge University Press.

Hoffman, M. L. 1977. "Empathy, Its Development and Pre-Social Implications." *Nebraska Symposium on Motivation* 25:169–217.

Holland, Ray. 1978. *Self and Social Context*. New York: St. Martins Press.

Hollis, Martin, and Steven Lukes, eds. 1982. *Rationality and Relativism*. Cambridge: MIT Press.

Horton, R. 1967. "African Traditional Thought and Western Science." *Africa* 37:50–71.

Hume, David. 1748. *A Treatise of Human Nature.* In *Hume's Moral and Political Philosophy,* ed. Henry D. Aiken. New York: Haffner, 1948.

Husserl, Edmund. 1910–11. *Philosophy as a Rigorous Science,* trans. Quentin Lauer. In *Phenomenology and the Crisis of Philosophy.* New York: Harper and Row, 1965.

———. 1913. *Ideas Pertaining to a Pure Phenomenology and to a Phenomenological Philosophy. First Book: General Introduction to a Pure Phenomenology,* trans. F. Kersten. The Hague: Martinus Nijhoff, 1982.

———. 1925. *Phenomenological Psychology,* trans. J. Scanlon. The Hague: Martinus Nijhoff, 1977.

———. 1929. *Cartesian Meditations,* trans. Dorian Cairns. Boston: Martinus Nijhoff, 1970.

———. 1954. *The Crisis of European Sciences and Transcendental Philosophy,* trans. David Carr. Evanston: Northwestern University Press, 1970.

Jacobson, Edith. 1964. *The Self and the Object World.* New York: International Universities Press.

Johnson, Carl Nils. 1988. "Theory of Mind and the Structure of Conscious Experience." In *Developing Theories of Mind,* ed. Astington, Harris, and Olson.

Johnson-Laird, Phillip N. 1988. "A Computational Analysis of Consciousness." In *Consciousness in Contemporary Science,* ed. Bisiach and Marcel.

Jung, C. G. 1936–1954. *The Archetypes and the Collective Unconscious,* trans. R. F. C. Hull (*Collected Works.* Vol. 9, part I: Bollingen Series #20). New York: Pantheon Books, 1959.

———. 1954. *Answer to Job,* trans. R. F. C. Hull. London: Routledge and Kegan Paul.

Kagan, Jerome. 1989. *Unstable Ideas: Temperament, Cognition, and Self.* Cambridge: Harvard University Press.

Kakar, Sudhir. 1978. *The Inner World: A Psychoanalytic Study of Childhood and Society in India.* Delhi: Oxford University Press.

Katz, Fred C. 1993. *Ordinary People and Extraordinary Evil: A Report on the Beguilings of Evil.* Albany: State University of New York Press.

Keil, Frank C. 1986. "The Acquisition of Natural Kinds and Artifact Terms." In *Language Learning and Concept Acquisition,* ed. Demopoulis and Marras.

————. 1987. "Conceptual Development and Category Structure." In *Concepts and Conceptual Development*, ed. Neisser.

————. 1989. *Concepts, Kinds, and Cognitive Development*. Cambridge: MIT Press.

Keil, Frank C., and N. Bateman. 1984. "A Characteristic to Defining Shift in the Development of Word Meaning." *Journal of Verbal Meaning and Verbal Behavior* 23:221–36.

Kellman, Philip J., and Elizabeth S. Spelke. 1983. "Perception of Partly Occluded Objects in Infancy." *Cognitive Psychology* 15:483–524.

Kelly, I. W. 1981. "Logical Consistency and the Child: A Critical Examination of Piaget's View." *Philosophy of the Social Sciences* 11:15–18.

Kernberg, Otto. 1975. *Borderline Conditions and Pathological Narcissism*. New York: Jacob Aronson.

————. 1976. *Object Relations Theory and Clinical Psychoanalysis*. New York: Jacob Aronson.

————. 1982. "Self, Ego, Affects, and Drives." *Journal of the American Psychoanalytic Association* 30:893–918.

Kohut, Heinz. 1971. *The Analysis of the Self*. New York: International Universities Press.

————. 1977. *The Restoration of the Self*. New York: International Universities Press.

Kurtz, Stanley N. 1992. *All the Mothers are One: Hindu India and the Cultural Reshaping of Psychoanalysis*. New York: Columbia University Press.

Lacan, Jacques. 1949. "The Mirror Stage as Formative of the Function of the I." In *Ecrits*.

————. 1966. *Ecrits*, trans. Alan Sheridan. New York: W. W. Norton, 1977.

Lakoff, George. 1987. "Cognitive Models and Prototype Theory." In *Concepts and Conceptual Development*, ed. Neisser.

Lasch, Christopher. 1978. *The Culture of Narcissism*. New York: W. W. Norton.

Lavine, T. Z. 1981. "Internalization, Socialization, and Dialectic." *Philosophy and Phenomenological Research* 42:91–110.

Leahy, Robert L., and Stephen R. Shirk. 1985. "Social Cognition and the Development of the Self." In *The Development of the Self*, ed. Robert L. Leahy. New York: Academic Press, 1985.

Lee, David. 1986. *Language, Children, and Society: An Introduction to Linguistics and Language Development.* New York: New York University Press.

Leslie, Alan M. 1987. "Pretense and Representation: The Origins of 'Theory of Mind.'" *Psychological Review* 94:412–26.

———. 1988. *The Necessity of Illusion: Perception and Thought in infancy.* In *Thought without Language*, ed. Weiskrantz.

Leslie, Alan M., and Stephanie Keeble. 1987. "Do Six-Month-Old Infants Perceive Causality?" *Cognition* 25:265–88.

Lévi-Strauss, Claude. 1949. "The Sorcerer and His Magic." In *Structural Anthropology*, trans. Claire Jacobson and Brooke Grundfest Schoepf. Boston: Basic Books, 1963.

Lewicki, Pawel. 1986. *Nonconscious Social Information Processing.* New York: Academic Press.

Lewis, Michael. 1986. "Origins of Self-knowledge and Individual Differences in Early Self-Recognition." In *Psychological Perspectives on the Self*, vol. 3, ed. Suls and Greenwald.

Lewis, Michael, and J. Brooks-Gunn. 1979. *Social Cognition and the Acquisition of Self.* New York: Plenum.

Lewis, Michael, and L. Michalson. 1983. *Children's Emotions and Moods: Developmental Theory and Measurement.* New York: Plenum.

Lichtenberg, Joseph D. 1981. "Implications for Psychoanalytic Theory of Research on the Neonate." *International Review of Psychoanalysis* 8:35–52.

———. 1983. *Psychoanalysis and Infant Research.* Hillsdale, N.J.: Analytic Press.

Livesley, W. J., and D. B. Bromley. 1973. *Person Perception in Childhood and Adolescence.* New York: Wiley.

Loewald, Hans W. 1962. "Internalization, Separation, Mourning, and the Superego." *Psychoanalytic Quarterly* 31:483–504.

Lyotard, Jean Francois. 1974. "The Dream Work Does Not Think," trans. Mary Lyden. In *The Lyotard Reader*, ed. Andrew Benjamin. Oxford: Basil Blackwood, 1989.

Mahler, Margaret S., F. Pine, and A. Bergman. 1975. *The Psychological Birth of the Human Infant.* New York: Basic Books.

Marcel, Anthony J. 1983a. "Conscious and Unconscious Perception: Experiments on Visual Masking and Word Recognition." *Cognitive Psychology* 15:197–237.

————. 1983b. "Conscious and Unconscious Perception: An Approach to the Relations between Phenomenal Experience and Perceptual Processes." *Cognitive Psychology* 15:238–300.

————. 1988. "Phenomenal Experience and Functionalism." In *Consciousness in Contemporary Science*, ed. Bisiach and Marcel.

Markman, Ellen M. 1987. "How Children Constrain the Possible Meaning of Words." In *Concepts and Conceptual Development*, ed. Neisser.

————. 1989. *Categorization and Naming in Children: Problems of Induction.* Cambridge: MIT Press (Bradford).

Markman, Ellen M., and Gwyn F. Wachtel. 1988. "Children's Use of Mutual Exclusivity to Constrain the Meaning of Words." *Cognitive Psychology* 20:121–57.

Marshack, Alexander. 1971. *The Roots of Civilization: The Cognitive Beginnings of Man's First Art, Symbol and Notation.* New York: McGraw Hill.

McDevitt, John B., and Margaret S. Mahler. 1986. "Object Constancy, Individuality, and Internalization." In *Self and Object Constancy: Clinical and Theoretical Perspectives*, ed. Ruth F. Lax, Sheldon Bach, and J. Alexis Burland. New York: Guilford Press, 1986.

McIntosh, Donald. 1969. The *Foundations of Human Society.* Chicago: University of Chicago Press.

————. 1970. "Weber and Freud: On the Nature and Sources of Authority." *American Sociological Review* 35:901–11.

————. 1979. "The Empirical Bearing of Psychoanalytic Theory." *International Journal of Psychoanalysis* 60:405–31.

————. 1977a. "Habermas on Freud." *Social Research* 44:652–98.

————. 1977b. "The Objective Bases of Max Weber's Ideal Types." *History and Theory* 16:265–69.

————. 1983. "Max Weber as a Critical Theorist." *Theory and Society* 12:69–109.

————. 1986a. "The Economy of Desire: Psychic Energy as a Purely Psychological Concept." *Psychoanalysis and Contemporary Thought* 9:405–35.

————. 1986b. "The Ego and the Self in the Thought of Sigmund Freud." *International Journal of Psychoanalysis* 67:429–48.

————. 1993. "Cathexes and Their Objects in the Thought of Sigmund

Freud." *Journal of the American Psychoanalytic Association* 41:679–709.

———. 1994. "Language, Self, and Lifeworld in Habermas's *Theory of Communicative Action*." *Theory and Society* 23:1–33.

———. 1994. "Husserl, Freud, Weber, and the Method of the Human Sciences" (unpublished manuscript).

Mead, George Herbert. 1934. *Mind, Self, and Society,* ed. Charles W. Morris. Chicago: University of Chicago Press.

Medin, Douglas L., and William D. Wattenmaker. 1987. "Category Cohesiveness, Theories, and Cognitive Archeology." In *Concepts and Conceptual Development*, ed. Neisser.

Meissner, W. W. 1970–72. "Notes on Identification." *Psychoanalytic Quarterly* (three parts) 39:563–89; 40:277–302; 41:224–60.

———. 1980. "The Problem of Internalization and Structure Formation." *International Journal of Psychoanalysis* 61: 237–48.

Merleau-Ponty, Maurice. 1945. *Phenomenology of Perception*, trans. Colin Smith. London: Routledge and Kegan Paul, 1962.

Mervis, Carolyn B. 1985. "On the Existence of Prelinguistic Categories: A Case Study." *Infant Behavior and Development* 8:293–300.

———. 1987. "Child-basic Object Categories and Early Lexical Development." In *Concepts and Conceptual Development*, ed. Neisser.

Michalson, Linda, and Michael Lewis. 1985. "What Do Children know about Their Emotions and When Do They Know It?" In *The Socialization of Emotions*, ed. Michael Lewis and Carolyn Saarni. New York: Plenum, 1985.

Michaud, Thomas A. 1987–88. "Schutz's Theory of Constitution: An Idealism of Meaning." *Philosophy Research Archives* 13:63–71.

Milgram, Stanley. 1975. *Obedience to Authority: An Experimental View*. New York: Harper and Row.

Natanson, Maurice. 1963. "A Study in Philosophy and the Social Sciences." In *Philosophy of the Social Sciences, A Reader*, ed. Maurice Natanson. New York: Random House.

Natterson, Joseph. 1991. *Beyond Countertransference: The Therapist's Subjectivity in the Therapeutic Process*. Northvale, N.J.: Jason Aronson.

Neisser, Ulrich, ed. 1987. *Concepts and Conceptual Development: Ecological and Intellectual Factors in Categorization*. Cambridge: Cambridge University Press.

Neu, Jerome. 1988. "Divided Minds: Sartre's 'Bad Faith' Critique of
Freud." *Review of Metaphysics* 42:79–101.

Nietzsche, Friedrich. 1886. *Beyond Good and Evil*, trans. Helen
Zimmern. In *The Philosophy of Nietzsche*. New York: Random
House, 1940.

Olson, David R., and Janet W. Astington. 1986. "Children's Acquisition
of Metalinguistic and Metacognitive Verbs." In *Language Learning and
Concept Acquisition*, ed. Demopoulis and Marras.

Otto, Rudolph. 1917. *The Idea of the Holy*, trans. John W. Harvey.
London: Oxford University Press, 1950.

Parfit, Derek. 1986. *Reasons and Persons*. New York: Oxford
University Press.

Parsons, Talcott. 1952. "The Superego and the Theory of Social
Systems." In *Social Structure and Personality*. London: Free
Press, 1964.

Pearson, Roger. 1985. *Anthropological glossary*. Malaram, Fla.: Roger E.
Krieger Publishing.

Peters, Larry. 1978. "Psychotherapy in Tamang Shamanism." *Ethos*
6:63–91.

Plaut, Eric A. 1979. "Play and Adaptation." *Psychoanalytic Study of the
Child* 34:217–32.

———. 1984. "Ego Instincts: A Concept Whose Time Has Come."
Psychoanalytic Study of the Child 39:235–58.

Plaut, Eric A., and Foster L. Hutchinson. 1986. "The Role of Puberty in
Female Psychosexual Development." *International Review of
Psychoanalysis* 13:417–32.

Poulin-Dubois, Diane, and Thomas R. Shultz. 1988. "The Development
of the Understanding of Human Behavior: From Agency to
Intentionality." In *Developing Theories of Mind*, ed. Astington, Harris,
and Olson.

Radin, Paul. 1927. *Primitive Man as Philosopher*. New York: Dover
Publications, 1957.

Reeder, Harry P. 1984. "Public and Private Aspects of Language in
Husserl." In *Language and Experience: Descriptions of Living
Language in Husserl and Wittgenstein*. Washington: Center for
Advanced Research in Phenomenology and Unversity Press of
America.

Ricoeur, Paul. 1967. *The Symbolism of Evil*, trans. E. Buchanan. New York: Harper and Row.

————. 1970. *Freud and Philosophy: An Essay on Interpretation*, trans. Denis Savage. New Haven: Yale University Press.

————. 1984. "Myth As the Bearer of Possible Worlds." In *A Ricoeur Reader: Reflection and Imagination*. Toronto: University of Toronto Press, 1991.

————. 1992. *Oneself as Another*, trans. Kathleen Blamey. Chicago: University of Chicago Press.

Roitblat, H. L., T. G. Bever, and H. S. Terrace, eds. 1984. *Animal Cognition*. Hillsdale, N.J.: Lawrence Erlbaum Associates.

Roland, Alan. 1988. *In Search of Self in India and Japan*. Princeton: Princeton University Press.

Rorty, Richard. 1979. *Philosophy and the Mirror of Nature*. Princeton: Princeton University Press.

Rosenberg, Jay F. 1986. *The Thinking Self*. Philadelphia: Temple University Press.

Sandler, Joseph. 1960. "On the Concept of the Superego." *Psychoanalytic Study of the Child* 15:128–62.

Sartre, Jean-Paul. 1943. *Being and Nothingness*, trans. Hazel E. Barnes. New York: Philosophical Library, 1956.

Saussure, Ferdinand de. 1922. *Course in General Linguistics*, trans. Wade Baskin. New York: McGraw Hill, 1966.

Schafer, Roy. 1968. *Aspects of Internalization*. New York: International Universities Press.

————. 1974. "Problems in Freud's Psychology of Women." *Journal of the American Psychoanalytic Association* 22:459–85.

Schluchter, Wolfgang. 1981. *The Rise of Western Rationalism: Max Weber's Developmental History*. Berkeley: University of California Press.

Schreifers, H. 1990. "Lexical and Conceptual Factors in the Naming of Relations." *Cognitive Psychology* 22:111–42.

Schutz, Alfred, and Thomas Luckmann. 1973. *The Structures of the Lifeworld*. Evanston: Northwestern University Press.

Searle, John R. 1983. *Intentionality: An Essay in the Philosophy of Mind*. Cambridge: Cambridge University Press.

Seidenberg, Mark S. 1986. "Evidence from Great Apes Concerning the Biological Bases of Language." In *Language Learning and Concept Acquisition*, ed. Demopoulis and Marras.

Selman, Robert L. 1980. *The Growth of Interpersonal Understanding.* New York: Academic Press.

Shatz, Marilyn, Henry M. Wellman, and Sharon Silber. 1983. "The Acquisition of Mental Verbs: A Systematic Investigation of the First Reference to Mental States." *Cognition* 14:301–21.

Snodgrass, J. G. 1984. "Concepts and Their Surface Representation." *Journal of Verbal Learning and Verbal Behavior* 23:3–22.

Sofer, Gail. 1990. "Phenomenology and Scientific Realism: Husserl's Critique of Galileo." *Review of Metaphysics* 44:67–94.

Sokolowski, Robert. 1984. "Intentional Analysis and the Noema." *Dialectica* 38:113–29.

Soll, Ivan. 1981. "Sartre's Rejection of the Freudian Unconscious." In *The Philosophy of Jean-Paul Sartre*, ed. P. A. Schlidd. LaSalle, Ill.: Open Court Press.

Spelke, Elisabeth. 1987. "Where Perceiving Ends and Thinking Begins: The Apprehension of Objects in Infancy." In *Perceptual Development in Infancy*, ed. Albert Yonas. Hillsdale, N.J.: Lawrence Erlbaum Associates.

———. 1988. "The Origins of Physical Knowledge." In *Thought without Language*, ed. Weiskrantz.

Stern, Daniel N. 1985. *The Interpersonal World of the Infant.* New York: Basic Books.

Strachey, James. 1934. "The Nature of the Therapeutic Action of Psychoanalysis." *International Journal of Psychoanalysis* 50:275–92.

Strauss, Mark S. 1979. "Abstractions of Prototypical Information by Adults and Ten-Month-Old Infants." *Journal of Experimental Psychology: Human Learning and Memory* 5:618–32.

Streri, Arlette, and Elizabeth S. Spelke. 1988. "Haptic Perception of Objects in Infancy." *Cognitive Psychology* 20:1–23.

Sullins, Ellen S. 1991. "Emotional Contagion Revisited: Effects of Social Comparison and Expressive Style on Mood Convergence." *Personality and Social Psychology Bulletin* 17:166–74.

Suls, Jerry, and Anthony G. Greenwald, eds. 1986. *Psychological Perspectives on the Self*, vol. 3. Hillsdale, N.J.: Lawrence Erlbaum Associates.

Tambiah, S. 1968. "The Magical Power of Words." *Man* 3:175–206.

Taylor, Charles. 1964. *The Explanation of Behaviour.* New York: Humanities Press.

————. 1971. "Interpretation and the Sciences of Man." *Review of Metaphysics* 25:3–51.

————. 1980. "Understanding in Human Science." *Review of Metaphysics* 34:3–23.

————. 1991. *The Ethics of Authenticity*. Cambridge: Harvard University Press.

Taylor, Marjorie. 1988. "The Development of Children's Understanding of the Seeing-Knowing Distinction." In *Developing Theories of Mind*, ed. Astington, Harris, and Olson.

Taylor, S., and S. Fiske. 1975. "Point of View and Perceptions of Causality." *Journal of Personality and Social Psychology* 32:439–45.

Tenbruck, Fredrich H. 1980. "The Problem of Thematic Unity in the Works of Max Weber." *British Journal of Sociology* 31:316–51.

Terrace, H. S. 1985. "Animal Cognition: Thought without Language." In *Animal Intelligence*, ed. Weiskrantz.

Trilling, Lionel. 1972. *Sincerity and Authenticity*. Cambridge: Harvard University Press.

Tugendhat, Ernst. 1986. *Self-consciousness and Self-determination*. Cambridge: MIT Press.

Turner, Victor W. 1964. "A Ndembu Doctor in Practice." In *The Forest of Symbols*. Ithaca: Cornell University Press, 1967.

Walker, Stephen. 1983. *Animal Thought*. London: Routledge.

Wanner, Eric, and Lila Gleitman, eds. 1982. *Language Acquisition: The State of the Art*. Cambridge: MIT Press.

Watson, Stephen. 1988. "Heidegger, Rationality, and the Critique of Judgement." *Review of Metaphysics* 41:461–99.

Weber, Max. 1922. *The Sociology of Religion*, trans. Ephraim Fischoff. Boston: Beacon Press, 1963.

————. 1923. *Economy and Society*, ed. Guenther Roth and Claus Wittich. New York: Bedminster Press, 1968.

————. 1923a. *The Theory of Social and Economic Organization*, trans. A. M. Henderson and Talcott Parsons. New York: Oxford University Press, 1947.

————. 1946. *From Max Weber: Essays in Sociology*, trans. H. H. Gerth and C. Wright Mills. New York: Oxford University Press.

————. 1903–11. *The Methodology of the Social Sciences*. New York: Free Press, 1949.

———. 1923. *Max Weber on Law in Economy and Society.* Cambridge: Harvard University Press, 1954.

Weiskrantz, Lawrence, ed. 1985. *Animal Intelligence: Proceedings of a Royal Society Discussion Meeting Held on 6 and 7 June 1984.* Oxford Psychology Series No. 7. Oxford: Clarendon Press.

———. 1988. *Thought without Language.* Oxford: Clarendon Press.

Wellman, Henry. 1988. "First Steps in the Child's Theorizing about the Mind." In *Developing Theories of Mind*, ed. Astington, Harris, and Olson.

Welton, Donn. 1973. "Intentionality and Language in Husserl's Phenomenology." *Review of Metaphysics* 27:260–97.

Wilson, Bryan, ed. 1970. *Rationality.* Evanston: Harper and Row.

Wimmer, Heinz, Jürgen Hogrefe, and Beate Sodain. 1988. "A Second Stage in Children's Conception of Mental Life: Understanding Informational Accesses as Origins of Knowledge and Belief." In *Developing Theories of Mind*, ed. Astington, Harris, and Olson.

Winch, Peter. 1958. *The Idea of a Social Science and its Relation to Philosophy.* London: Routledge & Kegan Paul.

———. 1964. "Understanding a Primitive Society." *American Philosophical Quarterly* 1:307–24.

Winson, Jonathan. 1985. *Brain and Psyche: The Biology of the Unconscious.* New York: Anchor Press, Doubleday.

Wittgenstein, Ludwig. 1933–35. *The Blue and Brown Books.* New York: Harper and Row, 1960.

Wright, G. H. von. 1971. *Explanation and Understanding.* Ithaca: Cornell University Press.

INDEX